Planners and Politicians
Liberal Politics and Social Policy, 1957–1968

Canada's national social-security system is a valued and integral part of our national character. Recent government cutbacks, however, have put the future of the welfare state in jeopardy. Focusing on the development of the Canada Pension Plan and medicare – the cornerstones of Canada's social net – *Planners and Politicians* is a timely examination of the Liberal Party's role in the development of national social policies.

P.E. Bryden reveals that Liberal politicians were largely responsible not only for designing the social security legislation but also for creating its justification. She points out that not only did party organization, the structure of Canadian federalism, and internal party power shifts influence the development and implementation of social programs, but the opposite proved also to be true: the commitment to social security imperatives changed the shape of both the Liberal Party and federalism.

Planners and Politicians explores the interrelationship among social programs, federal-provincial relations, the role of the bureaucracy in devising and legitimizing policy, and the nature of political power in the modern Canadian state. By considering social policy as part of national policy and recognizing that the federal government was shaped by the imperatives of the programs it was designing, this book offers a new perspective on Canadian social policy and the evolution of the state.

P.E. BRYDEN is assistant professor of history, Mount Allison University.

Planners and Politicians

Liberal Politics and Social Policy, 1957–1968

P.E. BRYDEN

McGill-Queen's University Press
Montreal & Kingston • London • Buffalo

© McGill-Queen's University Press 1997
ISBN 0-7735-1650-6

Legal deposit fourth quarter 1997
Bibliothèque nationale du Québec

Printed in Canada on acid-free paper

This book has been published with the help of
a grant from the Humanities and Social Sciences
Federation of Canada, using funds provided by
the Social Sciences and Humanities Research Council
of Canada.

McGill-Queen's University Press acknowledges the
support received for its publishing program from
the Canada Council's Block Grants program.

Canadian Cataloguing in Publication Data

Bryden, Penny
    Planners and politicians : Liberal politics and social
    policy, 1957–1968
    Includes bibliographical references and index.
    ISBN 0-7735-1650-6

    1. Canada – Politics and government – 1957–1963.
    2. Canada – Politics and government – 1963–1968.
    3. Canada – Social policy. 4. Liberal Party of
    Canada – History. I. Title.
    FC608.S6B79 1997   971.064 C97-900425-X
    F1029.9.B79 1997

Typeset in Sabon 10/12
by Caractéra inc., Quebec City

In memory of my father, M. Philip Bryden

Contents

Acknowledgments ix

Introduction xi

1 The St Laurent Approach to Social Policy, 1955–57 3

2 Conflicting Solutions to Liberal Party Problems, 1957–60 27

3 The Planning and Preparation of a Social-Policy Agenda, 1960–63 54

4 Early Obstacles to Pension Reform, 1963 78

5 Changing Liberal Tactics and the Completion of Pension Negotiations, 1963–66 100

6 Federal-Provincial Negotiations over Health Insurance, 1964–65 124

7 Liberal Party Dynamics and the Achievement of Medicare, 1965–68 145

Epilogue 164

Notes 171

Bibliography 215

Index 229

Acknowledgments

The genesis of this book occurred at York University where, as a graduate student, I had the opportunity to study in a superb intellectual environment and was introduced to a vast range of ideas and methodologies that have shaped, both directly and indirectly, the structure and content of this volume. In its first incarnation, this was a doctoral dissertation written under the supervision of J.L. Granatstein. He taught me, through his own example, the importance of primary-source research and the pleasures of finding "good stuff." Christopher Armstrong and John Saywell were the other members of my supervisory committee. They read through innumerable drafts and made incisive comments about structure, style, and argument both at the dissertation stage and with respect to the revised manuscript. That I have not always taken their advice, or have done so only slowly, does not diminish the respect with which I hold them as critics or the value I place on their friendship. I met James Struthers at my dissertation defence in his role as external examiner. At the time, he gave me sound advice that was important in this work's transition from thesis to book, and he has offered enthusiastic encouragement ever since.

The staffs of the National Archives in Ottawa, the Ontario Archives in Toronto, and the Queen's University Archives in Kingston have been unfailingly helpful – retrieving copious numbers of boxes quickly, photocopying too many pieces of paper, and pointing me in the direction of new or little-known material that I might find interesting. I am particularly grateful to Loretta Barber in Ottawa for her ongoing interest in this project, and to Jim Suderman in Toronto for facilitating my examination of the John Robarts Papers.

Numerous people agreed to grant me access to private or restricted manuscript collections in their possession. It would have been impossible to write this book without the permission of Robert Bryce, Paul Hellyer, the late Paul Martin, Geoffrey Pearson, and John Gordon. All of the people who agreed to discuss with me their own recollections of this period did so with good humour. I am particularly indebted to Tom Kent and Al Johnson, who not only gave generously of their time but also were supportive of the project from the outset.

In writing the original dissertation, I was financially assisted by the Ontario government and the Walter Gordon Foundation. The final chapters of the thesis, and its subsequent rewriting into book form, were completed in the agreeable atmosphere of Mount Allison University, where I was supported by the McCain Fellowship in the Arts. The book has been published with the assistance of a grant from the Aid to Scholarly Publications Programme of the Social Science Federation of Canada.

At McGill-Queen's University Press, I have met with encouragement and speedy work from the outset. Philip Cercone and Peter Blaney have been consistently supportive, and Curtis Fahey has been an author's dream of a manuscript editor. Their work has probably spoiled me.

Throughout my undergraduate and graduate studies my mother and father were generously supportive, even if at times they thought my ambition would exceed my grasp. I received news of my father's death just hours before I expected to complete this manuscript, and in the days that followed I was comforted in the knowledge that he knew it had been accepted for publication. What he perhaps did not know was that his example of rigorous scholarship and sheer love of learning helped to shape me as a scholar, and thus this book is not only for him but because of him.

Introduction

The United States has always cast a long northerly shadow on Canada, but with the arrival of the North American Free Trade Agreement Canadians have asked themselves even more frequently than usual what makes us unique. The additional concerns imposed by domestic constitutional dilemmas have increased the intensity with which we search for those common characteristics, institutions, and principles that, in spite of divisions between regions and races, mark us as members of a national community. Overwhelmingly, we point to our national social security system, which is at once common to all provinces and markedly more advanced than our neighbours' to the south. It has become one of the most integral manifestations of our national character.

This was not always the case. The Canadian social-security net, or welfare state – that complex array of legislation that includes both means-tested programs and services designed to meet a more universal need – has developed slowly and amidst profound and sometimes bitter political debate. Its completion has been a relatively recent phenomenon: Canadians had to wait until the 1960s before securing contributory old age pensions and a national health-insurance scheme. Still, despite the difficulties inherent in expanding the welfare state, the national Liberal Party was ultimately successful in identifying public needs, designing solutions to national social problems, and finally implementing programs that were both universal in coverage and national in scope. These final and most significant features of the Canadian social-security system were fashioned and put in place as part of a coherent national policy of social betterment. By expanding federal activity into fields that had previously been considered provincial, Ottawa was able to define a new and important area of responsibility for itself, and its actions in creating a strong federal presence in the social-security field were in marked contrast to its more traditional preoccupation with national economic management.[1] The achievement of new policy goals thus benefited both the public and the national government – the former because health insurance and contributory pensions were important social protections; the latter because, in defining a new role for the national government, Ottawa became identified with significant social advances. The process has come full circle: it is now the Canadian public that identifies with and holds dear the original national purpose of the social policies of the 1960s while the state threatens to retreat.

The scholarly community has responded to the increasing public interest in understanding the nature and future of the welfare state by producing a vast library of both general studies and those devoted to an understanding of specific measures. While this is particularly true in the United States, the Canadian welfare state has not gone unnoticed. The theoretical and conceptual frameworks used to explain the welfare state offer some interesting insights into the impetus behind the legislative provision of social services and the various rents in the mesh of the social-safety net, but none are completely satisfactory. Ultimately, all leave unanswered certain questions about social-security development that this study hopes to address.

Those people who have worked on the origins of the American welfare state have produced the clearest theoretical models for understanding the phenomenon.[2] Their contributions embrace a variety of different explanations for the timing of different social-security initiatives and, more recently, have begun to examine the extent of legislative inclusiveness from the perspective of race, class, and gender. The question of timing, and most particularly the apparent reluctance of the American state to introduce policies like those of its European counterparts, has variously been explained by pointing to the need of industrial societies to protect the population from unnecessary social and economic dislocation;[3] the effect of elusive "national values" on forcing or preventing the government from acting to protect its citizens;[4] the pressure from business to introduce legislation that will help it maintain a compliant workforce;[5] and the reverse, the pressure from business to avoid social-security legislation, which is seen as anathema to the fluid functioning of capitalist society.[6] Clearly, some of these perspectives are at odds with each other, but each suggests important avenues of investigation into the role of industrial development, political culture, and employer-employee relations in explaining the nature of the development of the welfare state in the United States. The relative absence of a focus on the role of government actors has been redressed with the emergence of the "new institutionalism" or the structured-polity approach, which views the state as an independent, not a dependent, variable in explaining the genesis of legislation.[7] Other recent work on social policies aimed specifically at women seeks to elucidate the role of voluntary organizations in achieving legislative victories, and a frequent conclusion is that women have been marginalized by the policies themselves.[8]

While students of the welfare state in Canada have not produced the same quantity of studies as their Americanist colleagues, they have nevertheless shown an increasing interest in the origins of social security north of the border. Interestingly, the Canadian-based studies tend to focus on somewhat different questions and are also more likely to fall outside the ambit of the theoretical perspectives identified above. Though the Marxist interpretation stressing class conflict has found fertile ground in Canada, and recent work has emphasized the gendered dimension of social-policy developments, few recognizable "schools" have developed in the field of Canadian welfare-state history.[9] The present study will not change that situation.

My analysis of this subject did not find its original impetus in any particular theory. Rather, I began by examining the origins of the package of social legislation enacted in the 1960s in an attempt to understand why this period produced such a flurry of national social-security measures, most notably the Canada Pension Plan and medicare, while previous decades had seen only piecemeal programs aimed at providing a few strands in the social-welfare net. To solve this puzzle, I consulted the government records and private manuscript collections of all the likely actors – voluntary associations, labour groups, the civil service, and the politicians. Most significantly, it appeared that the social-policy legislation of the Pearson government went beyond the often inchoate demands emanating from the private sector. What emerged was a sense that the political actors, both in Parliament and in the backrooms, were largely responsible not only for designing the social-security legislation but also for creating its justification. Thus, this has become a study of the politics of the period between 1957 and 1968 examined through the window of social policy. Its interpretation of the politics of social policy in these years, which finds its genesis in the records of the past and not the theories of the present, differs considerably from those commonly offered by students of social welfare, public policy, and politics.

By beginning with the disorder of past events and moving slowly towards creating some semblance of order, I believe that I have brought to light a number of important patterns. Somewhat surprisingly, not all of them have to do with social policy but deal rather with the nature of power in the Canadian political state. First, the Liberal Party had to undergo significant trauma, laying bare the weaknesses of the internal structure it developed through the 1940s and 1950s, before it could begin to address the question of the federal government's role in the provision of social services. Secondly, the appearance of a new generation of politicians and bureaucrats provided the necessary catalyst to preparing a social-policy agenda. Thirdly, the realities of governing and the growing schism between Liberals firmly and not-so-firmly committed to implementing national-social programs forced legislators and their advisors to adopt a variety of strategies not anticipated while in opposition. Finally, earlier achievements in social-policy legislation had an important impact on the shape of subsequent efforts in the field.

The particular slice of the past that is examined here is also in contrast to the work of previous historians and political scientists, because the emphasis is on one political party and its particular social-policy initiatives. The social programs implemented during the Pearson era are examined as distinct developments in the post-war world. This study recognizes the social program of the Liberal Party as a new approach to national policy, and it therefore examines social-security developments in a much broader political context than is common. Not only did party organization, the structure of Canadian federalism, and power shifts within the Liberal Party have an influence on the development and implementation of social programs, but the opposite proved also to be true: the commitment to social-security imperatives changed the shape of both the Liberal Party and federalism. By focusing on the social policies advanced within a discrete time period and under the leadership of one political party, this book hopes to underline the full impact of the social-security legislation of the Pearson era. It also aims to redress the weaknesses of some earlier studies.

Most treatments of the rise of the modern welfare state have offered useful glimpses into some aspect of social-security development but fall somewhat short of placing social policy within the framework of political activity. The results of these different approaches have thus informed my study but have not shaped it. Recognizing the fact that Canadian developments in the field of social policy occurred at roughly the same time as similar developments in other countries, many scholars have adopted the comparative approach. Their comparisons of Canadian social security to that introduced abroad focus on the context of federalism, examining how the federal structure affected the policy development.[10] Those scholars who have focused on Canada have tended to narrow their research even further and single out one particular social policy for study.[11] In following this approach, they tend to utilize public-policy models, thus again revealing the parallels between their work and that being done in the United States. The current emphasis is on society- versus state-centred explanations for social-policy development, the former emphasizing the effects of class cleavages and the latter stressing the significance of the bureaucracy on the development of particular social-security programs.[12] Most historians have ignored these methodological paradigms and have tended to examine social policy within the context of a broader study either of key political figures or of the post-war period more generally.[13]

Each of these approaches has its weaknesses. First, portrayals of the two and a half decades after the war as a monolithic period of social-policy advances obscure the differences between the programs implemented under Louis St Laurent and those designed during Lester Pearson's administration. The National Health Grants, the 1951 expansion of the old-age-pension program, and the introduction of hospital insurance in 1957 can best be understood as the first stage in welfare-state development in Canada, tentative early steps taken by a federal government more concerned with the old imperatives of coordinating an economic infrastructure. In contrast, the Canada Pension Plan and the comprehensive health insurance implemented under Pearson represent a much more complete appreciation of the national responsibility for social welfare and a more dramatic move into provincial jurisdiction. Only when viewed as two discrete episodes of policy development can the innovations of the Pearson government be truly understood.

Secondly, the tradition of examining the development and implementation of each of the social programs independently encourages confusion about the significance of social policy in general and again obscures the uniqueness of the programs implemented in the 1960s. While the St Laurent initiatives in pensions and health were conceived largely independently, the same cannot be said of the Pearson programs. During its period in opposition in the Diefenbaker years, the Liberal party designed programs that would alleviate the insecurity of old age and ill health, and it designed these social-welfare measures with a recognition of their interdependence and of their importance to the completion of a comprehensive social-security net. In studying the negotiations surrounding each of the policies separately, scholars have not only failed to note that during the Pearson administration social programs were devised as part of a broad policy of social betterment, but they have also been blind to the implications each program had for subsequent developments in the field.

Thirdly, the question of whether social-policy development has been most affected by institutional factors or by societal pressure or cleavages has had the unfortunate effect of redirecting scholarly attention away from the possibility of multiple influences. Most society-centred approaches, which assess the effect of specific interest groups on the achievement of legislative action, have tended to focus on those policies that were intended to affect one particular group. These include welfare programs, unemployment insurance, and mothers' assistance. The policies examined in this study are unique in that they are universal programs and do not therefore necessitate an explanation of the exclusion of particular social or racial groups. More important, while institutional variables such as the federal structure and bureaucratic demands are emphasized here, so too are the effects of policy on political structures. One of the conclusions offered is that the social-security objectives of the Pearson era were influenced by institutional imperatives but at the same time these same objectives had an enormous impact on the shape of institutions. This is especially true in terms of changes to the political party and federalism, institutions that are too often regarded as relatively static.

Finally, because Pearsonian social policy has been viewed within the general context of post-war developments, historians and political scientists have awarded the story of the implementation of such programs as the Canada Pension Plan and medicare only a small place in the history of the period.[14] Moreover, in attempting to distinguish the Pearson administration from the earlier Liberal government of St Laurent, they have tended to focus on other examples of the unique nature of government in the 1960s. They have not avoided the question of social policy, but instead they have emphasized the federal-provincial negotiations necessary to achieve social-policy legislation on the national level. In examining one aspect of social-policy development to the exclusion of other important factors, scholars have attributed too much importance to the decentralizing tendencies of the Pearson government. While it is true that on one level the 1960s saw a loosening of central controls over the administration of programs at the provincial level, these concessions to provincial autonomy, when viewed within the context of social policy more generally, served to enhance the role of the national government and strengthen Canadian unity. Only by accepting a degree of provincial variation was the federal government able to ensure that its legislation in areas traditionally reserved for the provinces would be accepted. Too often scholars have looked for the seeds of our current constitutional disunity in the politics of the 1960s and have pointed to social-policy arrangements as indicative of the beginning of serious constitutional battles.[15] In reality, the Liberal government of the 1960s defined a new method of negotiating with the provinces and, in the process, carved out a new national function.

By regarding social policy as part of national policy, and by recognizing that the federal government was shaped by the imperatives of the programs it was designing, this book offers a new perspective both on Canadian social policy in general and on the politics of the 1960s. It does not embark on completely uncharted water, however. To the extent that this study does not find much evidence that either political pressure from the right or the left, voluntary organizations, or class-based interest groups had much influence on the shape of social-policy initiatives, it falls under the category of a state-centred explanation. While previous experiments in the provision of social services – both at the provincial level and in the private sector – can be regarded as an important backdrop to the advances of the 1960s, they did not significantly alter the shape of national pension or health policies. In the case of the national social-security achievements of the Pearson period, the general popularity of the proposals was a pre-condition of their being pursued, but the genesis, formulation, justification, and, of course, implementation all occurred within the state and as a result were the handiwork of key policy actors. The definition of the national "state" that is used here, however, is broader than that conceived by others. It includes not just the bureaucracy but also political parties and the institutions of government, thus finding the primary centre of action within the polity itself.

Moreover, because this study offers not only a better understanding of the development of social policies in the 1960s but also an assessment of the structure of politics in the period, it goes beyond being merely a state-centred interpretation of policy developments. By using the window of two important legislative achievements to understand better the Liberals in opposition and as the government during the years between 1963 and 1968, this book can also be regarded as a policy-centred interpretation of the evolution of the state. The necessary party restructuring that occurred following the Liberal loss of power in 1957 provided new opportunities for policy development; the return to power in 1963 produced constraints on policy implementation; and the social programs themselves, once in place, transformed the political environment, simultaneously impeding and facilitating further social-policy development.

Planners and Politicians

1 The St Laurent Approach to Social Policy, 1955–57

Senator Charles "Chubby" Power, a stalwart of Liberal cabinets since the time of Mackenzie King, had surprisingly bad timing around elections. He was present when both Wilfrid Laurier and Mackenzie King learned of their electoral defeats, and he met Prime Minister Louis St Laurent a few hours after the results of the election of 10 June 1957 became clear. In the latter contest, the Liberals had been defeated by John Diefenbaker's Conservative Party, to the surprise of journalists, bureaucrats, and politicians alike.[1] In Power's opinion, St Laurent's mood "matched up to any of his predecessors, no tears, no recriminations, no bittness [sic]." But there was no avoiding the fact that "he was surprised, terribly so" by Diefenbaker's minority victory, particularly since it was at the expense of nine of his most respected cabinet colleagues.[2] In fact, election outcomes have rarely surprised the participants to the degree that the 1957 election shocked the ruling Liberals; that it did suggests that the government had been grossly unaware of the mood of the country and had been guided, or misguided, by some internal logic that failed to appear logical to the voters. Policies in the field of social security were particularly poorly designed to attract voters to the Liberal Party, but it was one area in which it was almost impossible for the St Laurent government to detect any problems since the programs were generally successful in the context of the goals the politicians had set. Yet, when the situation is viewed from the outside, it seems clear that the federal government failed to take the initiative in establishing national social programs, failed to respond to the public demand for benefits that reflected changes in the cost of living, and failed to campaign on a platform that suggested any change from the policies of the past. The electorate responded by voting for the Conservatives; the ousted government members responded with surprise, completely baffled about what they could have done so wrong. Long after 1957, many were still baffled.

Social policy had an ambiguous place in the rhetoric and policy of the mid-twentieth-century Liberal Party. Though members of the King and St Laurent administrations viewed their commitment to social-welfare programs as one of the jewels in the Liberal policy crown, their rather incomplete record of achievement in the area suggests that there was more talk than action. Some policy initiatives came at the urgings of other parties, most importantly the implementation of a basic old-age-pension scheme in 1927. Afterwards, the experience of the Depression and of the Second World War encouraged the national Liberals to confront the issue of social security more directly. By 1940 it had become apparent that the provinces did not have the financial ability to fulfil their constitutional duties in the social-security field, and the growing centralization of government activity occasioned by the war increased the feasibility of activity at the national level. The final report of the Rowell-Sirois commission on federal-provincial relations in 1940 recommended a national unemployment-insurance plan and noted that in the future the federal government might be called upon to administer the more expensive social programs such as health insurance. Although most of the provinces rejected the recommendations of the report, the civil service remained committed to national responsibility for social security.[3] George Davidson, deputy minister of health, was characteristic of the progressive bureaucrats in arguing that "we can only attain a well-rounded system of social security in Canada if the federal government ... is prepared ... to accept the responsibility of giving leadership, guidance and assistance to the provinces in the development of provincial services."[4] Ottawa thus pushed ahead on a variety of specific social-security programs.

Encouraged by Ian Mackenzie, minister of pensions and national health, the cabinet agreed in February 1942 to the formation of the advisory committee on health insurance, naming physician and federal director of public health services J.J. Heagerty as chairman. Written with considerable input from the medical community, the Heagerty report incorporated all of the principles outlined in a statement of principles on health insurance issued by the Canadian Medical Association (CMA) in 1937. These included the stipulation that the government cover the premiums of the indigent at full value, that the administration be under an independent health insurance commission, that the plan be compulsory only for people below a set income level, and that people earning more than that level were eligible only for voluntary enrolment in a hospital-insurance scheme.[5] However, as the Heagerty report moved to the special committee on social security, which had been set up to examine the proposals and draft legislation, labour and agricultural associations voiced their opposition to the heavy influence of the medical community in the administration of the plan and their representations effectively suspended the implementation of national health insurance.[6] Instead, the government's attention turned rather quickly to family allowances, a program that, though lacking a long history of political discussion, had three advantages over health insurance: it promised to help stabilize post-war economic conditions, appease Quebec, and woo Saskatchewan before it turned to the Co-operative Commonwealth Federation (CCF).[7] Although the family-allowance program was introduced not as a component of a broader security net but with an eye to wage control and income maintenance, and although health insurance had failed, the federal Liberals still managed to demonstrate some commitment to social security during the wartime period and after 1945 they continued to govern as if they had already established their position in the field. The provinces, meanwhile, proved to be increasingly intractable about relinquishing their jurisdiction. More important, many provincial governments were investigating the possibility of offering their own social-security schemes, and this, too, made them less willing to assent to the federal government's proposals.

The federal government provided its most complete statement of both health insurance and old age pensions in a Green Book presented at the 1945 federal-provincial conference, but, because the package tied social-security measures to the acceptance by the provinces of distasteful fiscal arrangements, little came of the discussions. Five years later, the two levels of government met at another conference. Although the topics of discussion were again fiscal arrangements and social security, this time the acceptance of one did not hinge on the acceptance of the other. Paul Martin, minister of national health and welfare, believed that old age pensions were the most pressing problem and that health insurance should be dealt with secondarily. Careful to appear firm in his commitment to social programs, but also not wanting to repeat the inconclusiveness of the 1945 conference, Martin emphasized that "these reiterations of our continued adherence to the objectives of social security policy set forth in the 1945 Proposals form now a highly important part of the framework within which we approach our discussions with the provinces in December [1950]."[8] The conference reached a landmark agreement on old age pensions (now officially renamed Old Age Security) and the necessary constitutional amendment to permit the implementation of a universal scheme, but again the politicians failed to make any decisions on health insurance.

What the St Laurent government lacked, and what had been missing from the previous King administration, was a coherent, systematic approach to social security. While the Liberals could make statements suggesting the importance of viewing social policies as interconnected, like those contained in the Green Book proposals, they seemed overly willing to approach the field in a piecemeal fashion, introducing legislation only when it was relatively simple to achieve and the effect at the polls would be the greatest. Not only did the federal government appear hesitant to conceptualize social security, it demonstrated remarkable acquiescence to the provinces. Its reluctance to initiate national social programs is nowhere more apparent than in the negotiations over hospital insurance in 1955 and 1956, by which time both the provincial governments and private organizations had strengthened their resolve to follow their own social agendas.

By 1955 the Liberals had discovered the difficulties of securing social-policy agreements with the provinces and had gone a long way to abandoning their earlier commitments to further national social-security measures. Indeed, the negotiations between Ottawa and the provinces over hospital insurance, which began in earnest that year, demonstrated that the federal government was ill-prepared to play anything other than a reactive role. Unable to articulate a comprehensive approach to social policy, the St Laurent Liberals essentially waited until the provincial pressure for action reached the boiling point and then responded in such a manner as to appear to have been in favour of a national program all along. Once Ottawa began negotiating seriously, its vision of the final program became apparent, but absent from the discussions was any real initiative on the part of the federal government. In a time when it was becoming increasingly obvious that the provinces were prepared to accept national leadership in the provision of social services, the federal government failed to provide anything other than a knee-jerk response to provincial demands.

The genesis of discussions on hospital insurance provides a clear indication that Ottawa had given little thought to providing comprehensive public protection against the expense of health-care treatment. Despite the inclusion of a general commitment to hospital insurance in the Liberal platform of 1953, the federal-provincial conference called for October 1955 was primarily to discuss the tax-rental agreements, with social-policy negotiations playing only a minor role. Meeting with representatives of the provincial governments in April to discuss possible items for inclusion on the agenda, Prime Minister St Laurent confined his interest in social-security measures to those designed to combat unemployment. He was nearing the end of his public career and "fatigue and age had pretty well extinguished his reform zeal."[9] Unemployment was a pressing problem but other social concerns could easily wait for a more activist government. In particular, hospital insurance could wait until there was sufficient evidence of provincial support to ensure the program's viability. No one in St Laurent's government seemed aware that that time had already come.

Ontario premier Leslie Frost, Conservative by party affiliation but red Tory by action, was left to offer the most comprehensive argument in favour of including health insurance as a topic of discussion in October. He reasoned that "the study of health insurance [at the conference] would help to clarify the thinking of all in a field in which there unquestionably is a great deal of misunderstanding and confusion."[10] Premier Tommy Douglas of Saskatchewan, whose successful provincial hospital-insurance program was one of the greatest achievements of his administration, W.A.C. Bennett from British Columbia, who had led the Social Credit Party to electoral victory in part because of the administrative chaos of the provincial hospital-insurance program, and Premier Douglas Campbell of Manitoba, where there was no provincial scheme, all agreed with Frost's sentiment.[11] Significantly, the premiers also expressed the need for a greater sense of national purpose in planning social programs. "Too often," Douglas argued, "we have been preoccupied with fragments of a National program when we ought to have been concentrating on an over-all comprehensive plan for the well-being and security of the Canadian people."[12] St Laurent did not go as far as the premiers, but he did overcome his reluctance and eventually agreed to place health insurance on the agenda.

In reality, Premier Frost of Ontario had been forced into a leadership role on the issue of health insurance by St Laurent's inactivity and refusal to initiate proceedings. Although Ontario was prepared to consider national health insurance, Frost's advisers clearly envisaged using existing private-insurance companies for the administration of the plan as opposed to some form of public administration. Ontario's commitment to health insurance was thus based on the development of a scheme designed along free-enterprise lines. Moreover, in discussions with federal Deputy Minister of Health George Davidson, Frost's principal economic adviser, George Gathercole, "conveyed the general impression that basically Frost would sooner leave things as they are and do nothing about health insurance, but felt that this was an untenable position and that something probably had to be done about it."[13]

Interestingly, it was initially this "untenable" position that Prime Minister St Laurent took.

The original reluctance of the government to place health insurance on the agenda put the federal civil service in the difficult position of having quickly to prepare the federal proposals. The bureaucrats believed that the introduction of diagnostic services should be undertaken as the first step towards more comprehensive coverage. They thought that a hospital-care program, either implemented concurrently with diagnostic services or after, was the obvious next step, if only because a number of provinces had already implemented government-sponsored hospital insurance. While the officials agreed on the importance of universality, they could not reach agreement on the formula for dividing the costs between the federal and provincial governments or on the tactics the federal government should use either at the upcoming conference or during the implementation stage.[14] The positions of the Ontario and federal governments thus differed considerably, but Ottawa was less well prepared and was also in a position of having to respond to provincial initiatives.

When the premiers and the prime minister met again in October 1955, St Laurent faced two quite opposite problems. Health insurance was unquestionably within provincial jurisdiction, and the reigning Liberals did not "wish to be a party to a plan for health insurance which would require a constitutional change or federal interference in matters which are essentially of provincial concern."[15] The second problem, as Finance Minister Walter Harris put it, was to "ensure the retention of the initiative by the federal government" and "create the impression in the public mind that the federal government had made a more or less definite proposal, and that if action failed to result, it was not because of lack of initiative and interest on the part of the federal government."[16] The incompatibility of these two positions – on the one hand not wanting to interfere, on the other hand wanting to appear to have initiated – did not occur to either the officials or the politicians in Ottawa. The federal tactic of suggesting that some moneys would be available to provinces which provided first diagnostic services, followed later by the implementation of hospital insurance, was designed as a solution to the twin concerns but in reality solved neither.[17]

Despite the federal intentions, it was again Frost who offered the most comprehensive statement at the conference on the implementation of a program of health-services insurance. Although he was a reluctant initiator, at least according to his economic adviser, Frost's aides had ensured that their leader was well versed on the issue of health insurance. The government had sponsored a study of the issue prior to the federal-provincial conference; the resulting report submitted by health-services researcher Malcolm Taylor was a thorough analysis of the political and economic environment in Ontario in the mid-1950s as well as a convincing argument in favour of full hospital insurance. The Ontario premier was thus much better prepared than his federal counterparts to set national health insurance on its course. He outlined five alternative insurance schemes, including diagnostic services, a home-care program, assistance in covering extraordinary hospital expenses, maternal and infant hospital care, and, finally, a comprehensive hospital-services plan. The Ontario government preferred the all-inclusive alternative, but in order to accommodate the possibility of different provincial agendas and budgets, Premier Frost had carefully outlined various less expensive steps towards the final goal of full hospital coverage. As one of the participants at the conference, and the primary drafter of the alternatives, has noted, "the Frost statement, with its specific alternative proposals, had an almost electrifying effect on the conference ... Never before had there been such a specific health proposal from the largest province, with alternatives designed to elicit maximum support from the other provinces."[18]

Saskatchewan and British Columbia again supported the Ontario position, not surprisingly since both provinces had begun to implement their own hospital-insurance schemes, but the conference as a whole failed to reach any conclusions on implementation. Instead, the participants agreed to strike a committee of health and finance ministers to consider the issue in more detail.[19] Although Ontario ministers would participate, a separate group of Ontario officials continued to work towards the implementation of a provincial hospital-insurance system. They did so despite Frost's fears that the "Federal government and the ten provinces will continue to move in different directions, creating a hodge-podge that no one will be able to disentangle."[20] The federal government's failure to provide the necessary leadership and direction for a truly national hospital insurance program was a key factor in Ontario's decision: had Ottawa started the process with a viable plan of its own, provincial initiatives might have been stymied.

In January 1956 the federal-provincial health insurance committee presented its findings, as did Ontario's hospital-insurance inquiry. The two reports were similar, but not identical. The Ontario position was that the federal government would be responsible for approximately 60 per cent of all costs while the provincial contribution would be raised through premiums and co-insurance and mental hospitals and tuberculosis sanatoria would be covered in addition to diagnostic services, hospital care, and home care. The federal offer was more restrictive. The health insurance committee proposed a scheme that did not include asylums, sanatoria, or home care and required a majority of the provinces to agree before there would be any federal contributions. It further stipulated that the federal contribution would be 25 per cent of the average per-capita costs for hospital care across the country, plus 25 per cent of the average per-capita cost for the province times the number of insured people in that province. The final variable should be high, since the federal government also demanded that coverage be universally available.[21] The Ontario delegation worried that the federal share of the costs was significantly lower than expected, and that each province would have to commit itself to the establishment of a plan prior to knowing for sure whether there would be any contribution from Ottawa at all. Negotiations continued, however, between a newly struck Ontario hospital-insurance committee and the federal representatives, with early agreements on cost estimates boding well for future discussions.

Subsequent meetings were not so productive as it became obvious that the two governments were working from somewhat different agendas. As far as the federal officials were concerned, they had "put forward a definite proposal: it remains now for the provinces to consider carefully this proposal and indicate their willingness to proceed," and the issue was no longer one for serious negotiation.[22] It is clear that, having failed to see that the provinces were ready for some form of national health insurance, the federal government attempted to usurp the initiative from the provinces and proceed according to its own hastily devised plan. Without Ontario, however, a national hospital-insurance scheme would be difficult either to justify or to implement, and so both intra- and inter-governmental discussion continued. Meanwhile, outside organizations that had been interested in the question of health insurance prior to the federal-provincial negotiations increased their activity in the field. Hospital insurance was looming larger than had been anticipated even a year earlier.

The CMA greeted the results of the 1955 and 1956 discussions between the two levels of government with mild enthusiasm because it looked as if massive changes to the existing health system would be averted. Some well-placed individuals, such as J.A. Hannah, the managing director of a physician-organized medical-insurance consortium, argued that "no real advantage will be gained by the government 'picking up the chips' of the present inefficient system, consolidating bad practices under a deluge of money, or trying to preserve the status quo,"[23] but theirs were voices in the wilderness. The CMA hierarchy expressed some reservations about the escalating costs to taxpayers inherent in a shared-cost program and about the profession's ability to ensure high-quality medical training in the face of increased pressure to staff hospitals. This last issue could cause serious problems within the medical community, considering that the diagnostic aspect of the proposed scheme would substantially increase the use of radiology and laboratory medicine, fields that were not sufficiently well developed to be able to adapt rapidly to the new demands. Ultimately, however, the CMA believed that "we may console ourselves with the hope that the economists of government know what they are doing, and that in the universal application of hospital care insurance the benefits to our patients will outweigh the difficulties which we perceive."[24] The fact that governments at both levels were conscious of the need to structure a health-insurance system which would be acceptable to the medical community, and constantly solicited its input, served to make the CMA much less intransigent than other interest groups. Moreover, hospital insurance was considerably less intrusive vis-à-vis physicians' independence than full health insurance.

In contrast, the insurance industry in Canada felt seriously threatened by the federal government's proposals. The provision of insurance against ill health did not have a long history in Canada, but it had quickly become an important aspect of the business of insurance companies. Life-insurance representatives had informed the wartime Heagerty commission that they were in favour of government-sponsored health insurance, but the hearing had been held when health coverage was in its infancy and most insurance agencies had not realized the lucrative nature of the business. By 1954, ten years after the hearings, "all persons in the life insurance business who endorsed the ... views as then expressed" had "recanted."[25] In the wake of the federal-provincial conference, most members of the insurance industry wanted a system that would ensure the continuation of their monopoly over the provision of insurance against illness and hospitalization. Lobbying the Ontario government seemed the more effective route than devoting much attention to the federal level, since the Ontario proposal at the federal-provincial conference had articulated the importance of maintaining principles of free enterprise. Noting that 70 per cent of the Ontario population was already covered by the existing private-insurance schemes available, the Canadian Life Insurance Officers Association (CLIOA) submission to Ontario's health committee argued against replacing a system that worked well. Not only were most of the people already covered, but "from a cost point of view alone, governments should not supplant private insurance."[26] The CLIOA also foresaw considerable administrative and ideological difficulties in enforcing a compulsory system, as demanded by the federal requirements, and argued that private, voluntary plans were better equipped to cover their subscribers and more comprehensive in their coverage.

Privately, insurance officers also knew that the onset of state health insurance would put an end to a lucrative component of their own business.

The federal government was certainly aware of the rhetoric of the insurance companies, but it was not alarmed. In fact, George Davidson was able to write to his minister that he found it "very reassuring that the only voices raised to date in criticism of the hospital insurance program are the commercial insurance companies ... In fact, I'd be a bit puzzled," he allowed, "and a little bit worried if the insurance boys ... were to express themselves as being in favour of the plan."[27] The CLIOA's pressure on the Ontario government allowed Ottawa to recapture some of the momentum in the health-insurance debate. The federal government's proposals required public administration of a hospital-insurance program, and so it could be argued that, in advocating the use of existing insurance carriers, the Ontario government was being manipulated by the insurance industry. If forced to choose between the federal scheme and that of the insurance companies, the public would unquestionably side with the government.

While the initiative had come from Ontario, the balance had begun to shift. Organized labour fully supported government efforts to introduce national hospital insurance, largely because labour itself had achieved "a considerable measure of social security on its own through collective bargaining and the establishment of welfare plans affecting those working in large numbers for particular employers."[28] Because employers had already succumbed to worker demands for adequate and compulsory union-sponsored health coverage, it seemed odd to George Davidson that they would condemn a similar government-sponsored plan for others. Furthermore, Davidson thought the suggestion that increasing welfare costs were harming Canadian competitiveness was "bunk" considering that virtually every other country had already instituted a system of health insurance. "If the only way we can maintain a competitive position with the rest of the world is by depriving our people of a national system for financing our medical and hospital expenses," he cautioned, "it is long since time we stopped bragging about our great productive system of free enterprise."[29]

The absense of any other, more broadly based opposition to the government's position forced the insurance companies to change their tactics. Instead of focusing solely on their own industry's ability to cover the health-insurance needs of the majority of the population and the dangers of state action, the CLIOA began to emphasize a specific division of responsibility. The most appropriate manner for the government to subsidize health costs would be to cover non-active-treatment hospitals (such as convalescent hospitals and tuberculosis sanatoria), the needs of the indigent, the elderly, and others unable to obtain insurance, and all hospital stays in excess of a year. The private insurance companies proposed to do the rest.[30] Yet, notwithstanding this concrete proposal, the federal government continued to view the insurance companies with suspicion, unable to discard the perception that their views represented nothing more than the self-serving opinion of a threatened industry. The industry's relatively recent interest in hospital and health insurance increased the sense that the issue was money and not services.

Despite the fact that numerous outside organizations had opinions on the proposed hospital-insurance and the expected medical-insurance schemes, they were all forced to play a waiting game while the federal and provincial governments perfected their draft legislation. The medical profession, insurance industry, and business groups were able to express reservations about the government's preliminary deliberations and present their own proposals for methods of containing skyrocketing health-care costs, but none had yet received a tangible government draft on which to base its concerns. The two levels of government were entangled in negotiations, almost, but not quite, oblivious to the views of extra-parliamentary associations.

In early December 1956 Premier Frost proudly presented St Laurent with the Ontario proposal, reached "within the context of the Federal proposals." The premier was particularly pleased that "we have considered it desirable to obtain a coverage from 85 to 90 per cent of our people as soon as possible. At the same time, the method and the introduction of this plan will provide for maximum efficiency of administration, which is essential if costs are to be kept down and within control." Frost's immediate concern was when the federal government would let Ontario know whether "the way is clear for us to proceed" given the estimated two years to bring the plan into operation.[31] Ontario also needed assurances that the rest of the country would agree to Ottawa's health-insurance policy, for without such agreement the province could not receive a significant federal contribution to its own plan.

After its initial reservations about interfering with provincial jurisdiction over health insurance, the federal government was intent on dictating the terms of a hospital-insurance plan and was less than impressed with Ontario's scheme. Having discussed the matter with the appropriate authorities, St Laurent replied to Frost that the Ontario proposal might be sufficient to receive federal funding but only if Ottawa was "guaranteed" that 85 to 90 per cent of the Ontario population would be covered.[32] Frost took this as "a rejection of our proposal which has been discussed over several months."[33]

Despite the prime minister's clarification that "the eighty-five to ninety per cent coverage which we mentioned and about which you express concern was the figure which you yourself had mentioned in a context which we thought indicated that you expected to achieve this when your plan was established," the issue was to remain a sticking point for the two governments. Ottawa was convinced that if it was going to contribute to a plan, and "justify the very substantial contribution from our general tax revenue," it was absolutely essential that "the plan must not only be available to all but in fact be generally utilized."[34] Frost was loathe to be tied to an estimated degree of coverage and argued that "an interpretation of the term 'universally available' should not be imposed which in fact is not justified and could make the administration of the hospital insurance plan difficult and expensive, and perhaps altogether impossible."[35] Since the Ontario plan would be offered on a voluntary basis, with compulsory coverage applying only to indigents, it was important for the federal government to ascertain whether the terms of the program were sufficiently attractive to entice the majority of the population to enrol voluntarily. George Davidson felt that one method of ensuring a high degree of participation was for all employee groups of ten or more to be compulsorily included, a step that would probably guarantee that the federal requirements were met.[36]

Despite what seemed like an imminent breakdown of negotiations, by the beginning of March 1957 the two levels of government had reached an agreement on hospital insurance. Ontario accepted the stipulation that coverage be available to all residents of the province and would use "every possible means" to bring as many people into the scheme as it could. This was not a mandatory scheme, which Ottawa had not demanded, but instead a program that would combine both voluntary and compulsory aspects.[37] Ontario's one remaining concern was whether it would be able to count on federal participation – which was not guaranteed until seven of the provinces accepted the terms laid out by Ottawa. By the spring of 1957, only British Columbia, Alberta, Saskatchewan, and Manitoba had agreed in principle, all provinces that had already implemented some form of hospital insurance. Nevertheless, the federal government proceeded "towards the development of a reasonably uniform agreement covering arrangements with all the provinces which intend to participate," assuming that ultimately a majority of the provinces would join the national program.[38]

On 10 April 1957 the House of Commons unanimously passed the Hospital Insurance and Diagnostic Services Act. The four western provinces were the first to join the program on 1 July 1958. Ontario and Nova Scotia followed on 1 January 1959, after the new Diefenbaker administration removed the seven-province stipulation for federal funds. Once the federal Liberal government had acted, however, the way was clear for the provinces to implement hospital insurance, despite the seemingly long time some of them took to put their final agreements together.[39] The federal government had been a somewhat reluctant participant in the hospital-insurance debate, preferring to dictate terms and react to provincial initiatives than to conceptualize social security as a national responsibility, but a plan had ultimately been achieved. The implementation of the program obscured the reality of the genesis of the idea.

On other issues of social security the federal government was not so lucky. When relying on national initiatives, as was the case in the preparation of the 1957 budget, the Liberal Party again demonstrated its profound inability to understand public opinion on social-security benefits. This time, its shortcomings could not be concealed since the opposition parties were only too eager to cite such failures as evidence of a government grown increasingly out of touch with the needs of Canadians.

With the implementation of a national hospital-insurance program, one commentator has noted that there was "a growing acceptance of public responsibility for assuring a more planned and orderly development of hospital and related services and facilities."[40] The public interest in pensions was especially keen and further demonstrated that there was an increasingly widely held sentiment in favour of national responsibility for the well-being of the population. The national Liberals, however, did not sense the winds of change. In 1957 they still focused their attention on the responsibility of government to provide sound economic management for the country as a whole rather than to ensure the social welfare of the individual. The very fact that they had governed Canada for twenty-two years on the basis of this principle led them to believe that they could and would continue to do so. Over the course of the last generation, the Liberals had successfully cultivated the myth, both within their own ranks and among the public at large, that they "are responsible for prosperity – by their wise and businesslike management of our affairs – [and] that the cabinet is composed of supermen who could not be duplicated by another party."[41] By 1957 the myth had begun to wear a bit thin, and the perpetrators of it had begun to tire.

There was ample evidence in St Laurent's final year as prime minister that the Liberals were governing the country as if by divine right, the most obvious example being their manipulation of Parliament during the infamous pipeline debate in May and early June 1956. Those were the antics of a governing party which thought itself invincible, not merely because of its size or longevity but because of its inherent superiority. Another indication that there was much wrong with the Liberal Party had been provided a couple of months earlier. With Finance Minister Walter Harris's budget of March 1957, it became clear not only that the Liberals' economic policy lacked public support but also that the party had fundamentally misunderstood what the public thought was the responsibility of a national government.

By the late 1950s, the bureaucrats in the Department of Finance were firmly committed to the principles of Keynesianism and were experiencing considerable success in convincing the politicians of its value in economic planning. In theory, Keynes's proposition that governments can create a stable economy through the manipulation of demand made sense. Using fiscal and monetary tools, and encouraging countercyclical spending during periods of recession and countercyclical saving during relatively buoyant economic periods, the government could lessen the fluctuations of the natural business cycle. In practice, however, Keynesianism demanded an ability to forecast accurately the economic climate and quickly respond to the anticipated fluctuations. This proved difficult for mere mortals, and downright impossible for a group of men with conflicting hypotheses about the future economic situation. From a purely political point of view, only one side of Keynes's general theory was popular with the electorate. While encouraging spending during periods of recession by lowering taxation levels and interest rates was greeted enthusiastically, the necessary corollary, encouraging savings in prosperous times by raising taxes and reducing government subsidies and expenditures, was bound to receive a much more negative reaction.

During the preparation of the 1957 budget, advisers in the departments of finance and trade and commerce differed on what was likely to happen to the Canadian economy in the coming year. In retrospect, their failure to agree was understandable. Since the end of the Second World War, Canada had experienced relatively consistent growth in the gross national product and unemployment figures that hovered around 3 per cent throughout most of the period. The year 1957 marked a turning point as the Canadian economy entered a period of recession characterized by low levels of consumption spending, weak investment, and diminishing export levels, all of which produced unheard-of unemployment levels of over 7 per cent. Attempting to design policy on the bridge of this economic transition proved both difficult and debatable.[42] Officials in the Department of Trade and

Commerce urged Harris to adopt an expansionist budget to stimulate the economy, while those within his own department wanted to continue the policy of restraint to prevent inflation. A decision on the increase, if any, to social benefits hinged on which of the conflicting views the minister adopted.

Robert Bryce, assistant deputy minister of finance, was a powerful bureaucrat, and his opinions were careful and considered. He was Harris's trusted adviser, but he also had the prime minister's ear. In the days before the budget, Bryce tried to press home his reasons for supporting only small increases to the old age pension. While he believed that "Canada can afford some modest increase in these benefits," he also warned that "the timing of the increases involves some risks, because there is still a chance that we shall have ... inflationary conditions this summer and fall even though most of us expect the upward movement to slacken by midyear." He encouraged a restrictive budget, arguing that if it proved to be an inappropriate response, "it would be better to make the [increases] next fall when the slackening of the inflationary pressures is apt to be more evident."[43] Both the politicians and officials expected the Liberals to be returned to power, and both were content to wait to make any significant budgetary changes. On the basis of such advice, Harris opted to increase the old age pensions by the relatively small amount of $6 a month and increase old age assistance, disabled and blind allowances, family allowances, and war veterans' allowances by equally paltry sums, despite Minister of Trade and Commerce C.D. Howe's warning that the boom was ending and the Bank of Canada's tight money policy would only encourage that downward trend.[44]

The budget turned out to be a grave mistake. Not only did it underline the fact that Keynesianism was not perfectly suited for Canadian realities, it also proved unpopular politically and revealed the Liberals' failure to consider the need for greater activity in the field of social security. Over the next few months, it became clear that the Liberals had introduced a restrictive budget just as the country entered a period of recession. In forecasting a $258-million surplus, the government was guilty of implementing measures aimed at economic conditions that had already passed. The Harris budget was a cautious one and anathema to the Keynesian design. The confident assumptions of the immediate post-war era that "a straightforward economic analysis could and would be followed by the automatic introduction of countercyclical measures" had proven false.[45]

The electorate did not care whether Keynesian policies were being followed or whether they were effective. Far more important was the fact that, despite widespread public expectations that the old-age pension increases would be significant, the finance minister had introduced what many considered a niggardly increase. Political commentators, however, did not immediately focus on the pensions as a source of concern. To the contrary, for a budget that was seen as having both to combat inflation and to prepare the path for an election, the result seemed a rather careful navigation between Scylla and Charybdis. Even the Conservatives seemed "to fear that the budget may not be particularly unpopular."[46] A public-opinion survey published on 27 April indicated that Liberal support had dropped only 1 point to 47 per cent since February while the Conservatives remained steady at 32 per cent.[47] Nevertheless, the parliamentary debate foreshadowed the position opposition parties would take in their attacks on the pension increase. Stanley Knowles, speaking for the CCF, believed that there was a twofold problem with the pension increase. Because the Liberals had granted an increase on the eve of an election without having conducted the necessary preliminary study of national needs, Knowles accused them of pandering to voters. More important, however, was his contention that since 1949 the gross national product had climbed from $16 billion a year to $30 billion, an increase of over 80 per cent. Instead of government assistance reflecting the national wealth, Knowles proclaimed, "the government asks our older people ... to settle for an increase, in what we pay them out of our great national wealth, of only 15 per cent or $6 a month."[48]

John Diefenbaker, the recently elected leader of the national Progressive Conservative Party, agreed that the increase was insufficient and that "it cannot be justified and this government must be held accountable. An additional amount is necessarily required in order to permit our old age pensioners a reasonable opportunity."[49] And outside the House, Diefenbaker, mustering all of the outrage his years as a crusading prairie lawyer had instilled in him, turned pensions into a political weapon in a way no one had been able to predict. Always an effective stump-speaker, Diefenbaker used slogans and nicknames to get his message across to the voters, and whatever murky qualities the points might have, the monikers always stuck. As the election campaign heated up in the weeks before 10 June, calls of "six-buck Harris" echoed across the country. Armed with the information that "correspondence on the inadequacy of the Old Age Pension continues unabated" and that the reduction of the waiting period "is a very important topic in the minds of all ethnic groups," Diefenbaker decried the tiny increase as a feeble attempt to placate the aged voters, since it was too insignificant to address the problem of poverty.[50] While the Conservatives lagged behind the CCF in developing a comprehensive formula for determining old age pensions, they were more progressive than the Liberals in advocating a pension that would not just supplement the existing income of pensioners but represent something in the way of a share of the national wealth.

Both Harris and his advisers recognized the importance of the political effects of the budget and had been careful to weigh those considerations while the original drafting was being done. They had not anticipated the variety of directions from which the parliamentary opposition would aim their arrows. Instead of recognizing that the failure to produce the expected increase to the pensions would result in public outcry, the policy makers had worried that implementing significant increases "would help to set a pattern of important, permanent measures of this kind being taken immediately on the eve of elections without much advance notice or development of a case before public opinion on other than electoral grounds." In Bryce's mind, it was a practice that was to be especially avoided by "a government as responsible as this one" – a government renowned for its cautious management of the national economy.[51]

The debate over social-welfare policies that was waged in other forums across the country had not quite reached the ears of the federal Liberal politicians. As Winnipeg *Free Press* editor Tom Kent later suggested, "ideologically the 1950s were a conservative period in North America, and in its last few years of office the Liberal Government in most respects adjusted itself all too well to this philosophical mood – it fact, it stayed adjusted despite some rather odd discontents that about 1955 began to disturb segments of Canadian public opinion."[52] In announcing a monthly increase to the old-age pension of $6, the Liberals indicated their belief that the fundamental purpose of the benefit was to supplement the income of the aged, as opposed to providing for the income of the retired portion of the population. In this regard, the purpose of the pension had not changed substantially since the means-tested assistance to the aged poor was introduced in 1927. Yet the post-war period had seen a dramatic rise in earnings, highlighting the discrepancy between income while working and income after retirement.[53] By 1957 the provinces at least had noted an increasing public demand that some form of collective social security be pursued in lieu of the individual responsibility previously advocated. The federal Liberal government's policies had so far revealed at best a haphazard approach to social security.

In addition, the Liberal Party was slow to recognize that people were increasingly looking to the national government for direction in the field of social security. Shortly before the fall 1956 adjournment of the House of Commons, Paul Martin indicated that he expected that in the old age pension field "the provinces should pay any additional amount required" as they retained constitutional responsibility for the provision of pensions.[54] The federal government had adopted a similar approach to hospital-insurance negotiations, waiting for Ontario to take the initiative and set the time of the debate before dictating terms. It was a tactic that had served the federal government well in the past whenever an expensive demand was made but, with declining provincial revenues, was of decreasing utility. Martin was quick to point out in the debate over the budget that it is not "unfair to suggest that the provinces, having insisted on concurrent jurisdiction, should, in cases of need particularly, bear some of the responsibility for what is required by way of giving assistance to the aged of our country."[55] As far as the federal government was concerned, any criticism of the meagerness of the pension increase must also take into consideration the financial capacities of the provinces.

It was becoming all too apparent that the national politicians' view of their governmental responsibility was a barrier to the publicly held view of necessary social policy. In awarding such small increases in the old age pension and other benefits, Walter Harris and the Liberal administration were guilty not only of being stingy with the ample resources of government, as Diefenbaker accused, but also of failing to recognize the beginning of an important shift in public opinion regarding the responsibility of a national government to provide for both the economic and the social needs of the public. In order to catch up with public opinion, and also to combat the initiatives of provincial governments and other parties, the federal Liberals would have to make a fundamental change in their own view of individual versus government responsibilities. It was not a task that could be completed before the election of 10 June 1957.

The restrictive budget, combined with the antics of the pipeline debate and the declining energies of most of the important cabinet ministers, did not provide an effective take-off for the Liberal election campaign. As well, the party's top national policy-planning committee – the 236-member advisory council – had met only once between the 1953 and 1957 elections, indicating that the formulation of an election platform was left largely up to the individual ministers.[56] National Liberal Party policy, such as it was, was developed by a small group of cabinet ministers and "caucus meetings were used simply to inform members about government plans and to boost morale, rather than to work out agreements on what policies should be pursued."[57] Regional programs were devised by ministers most familiar with the concerns and demands of their area, with little attempt to coordinate the regional

with the national policy. At the outset of the campaign, however, none
of these weaknesses seemed to cast a shadow over the expectation that
twenty-two years of Liberal prosperity would continue into the 1960s.
Even on issues of social security, any negative effect the less-than-
generous $6-a-month increase might have had on the outcome was
expected to be offset by the Liberal legacy of sound government.

Since the Liberal Party was virtually devoid of any new ideas, the
main emphasis of the campaign was on the past. In his first national
address of the campaign, St Laurent reminded the public that "the
Liberal party, which has worked so successfully, for so many years for
our national development, has proved, by its record, that it has the
capacity to make constructive contributions to Canada's progress."[58]
Thus, by virtue of what had been accomplished in the past, the voters
were asked to assume that accomplishments would be made in the
future. This was a particularly important point to make in terms of
social policy, lest the public forget which party had been responsible
for the prosperity and security they now experienced. The Liberal
record in this area was one of which they were particularly proud and
in which "Paul Martin holds an honoured place. His name will forever
be linked with such major Liberal social measures as the National
Health Program, Old Age Security and now Hospital Insurance."[59]
Nevertheless, there was little evidence that the Liberals had any policies in mind that would perpetuate their "honoured" position in the
history of the development of social security.

The Liberal record, according to St Laurent, had illustrated that
they "have a national outlook rather than a regional outlook; and that
for Liberals there is one law for all Canadians – regardless of race or
creed or mother tongue – and a common concern for their welfare,
wherever they may live."[60] The redistributive aspect of social assistance was of particular importance to St Laurent's message, for it
underlined the Liberals' conviction that all should be able to share in
the national prosperity. Social-welfare policies had been implemented,
in part, he explained, so that "all the members of that large Canadian
family ... feel that they could all be equally proud of their Canadian
citizenship, and all happy that, as Canadian citizens, they were members of this prosperous Canadian family."[61] Regardless of the various
regional interests that might affect his audiences, St Laurent's message
rarely varied. The broad outlines for a speech delivered on his western
tour at the start of the campaign could easily have been the template
for speeches in the Maritimes. Each followed a three-fold strategy, first
stressing the Liberal goal of creating a climate for prosperity, followed
by the enunciation of the Liberal belief "in the family idea about
national and regional welfare – so that the whole nation helps those

regions that are not keeping up with the general prosperity," and concluding with an emphasis on the promotion of individual well-being through social programs.[62]

In addition to emphasizing the Liberal Party's largesse in terms of providing for the social welfare of the Canadian people, however, St Laurent had to be wary of going too far – both towards socialism and towards provincial jurisdiction. Every penny that came out of the public purse, he reminded Canadians, was spent wisely so as not to put undue strain on the economy. "There is no way by which government can create money out of thin air," he told his audiences, alluding to the extravagant promises of the CCF.[63] Similarly, St Laurent made clear that there was nothing about his government's measures that would in any way interfere with either the actions of provincial governments or individual incentive and responsibility. "Any idea of nonessential interference by the Government is repugnant to the Liberal Party," he clarified. "We believe that the private citizen must be left to his own initiative whenever possible and that if some help is required for the individual, that which is afforded by the national government must encourage rather than replace the help which the community or the province with its municipalities can give."[64]

While the prime minister travelled around the country delivering his message of Liberal achievements, unifying national social programs, and respect for financial conservatism and provincial and individual responsibilities in the delivery of assistance, his ministers were pursuing their own agendas on the regional level. Blessed, or perhaps cursed, with a cabinet composed of strong individuals, St Laurent, like King before him, allowed the ministers to reign over their province or region. Thus, the Liberal Party's assessment of the strength of its 1957 campaign could be centred solely on the relative merits of individual cabinet ministers and their provincial political machines – Jimmy Sinclair in British Columbia, Jimmy Gardiner on the prairies, an aging Stuart Garson in Manitoba, C.D. Howe with some regional help from Paul Martin and Walter Harris in Ontario, Uncle Louis himself in Quebec, and Jack Pickersgill in Newfoundland.[65] Each of these men had dispensed patronage and built up impressive networks of contacts and advisers, through which they were able to cultivate seemingly one-to-one relationships with their constituents and address those concerns that were essentially local in nature.[66] In this manner, the Liberal Party was seen to share the major interests of the provinces in the post-war period.[67] In short, the party utilized a two-level organizational structure, one that had served it well in other elections. The prime minister delivered messages that were "made as broad and as unspecific as possible," leaving "the mechanics of the sales campaign ... to the

constituent units of the party. An increasingly centralist party continued to draw electoral strength from a campaign organization which
was surprisingly decentralist, although the content of the message was
strongly national in scope."[68]

While the Liberals, using familiar tactics from their weather-beaten
bag of political tricks, were trying to convince the electorate that they
should be given a mandate for yet another term of office, Diefenbaker
and the Conservative Party were testing their new ideas on the Canadian voters. Although they were able to get great political mileage out
of the inadequacy of Harris's old-age-pension increase, they combined
their attacks with a measured consideration of alternative social-
security systems. Conservative member George Hees had already suggested in Parliament that there might be some utility in adopting the
American method of a contributory pension scheme. After a brief
examination of this possibility, Merril Menzies, one of Diefenbaker's
rare advisers from the academic community, noted that "from a theoretical and academic point of view, there is something to be said for
the American system. It is based largely on the insurance principle
with benefits being related to premiums ... made during working life.
Under that system the drone and the drudge would not get the same
benefit as they do under the Canadian scheme."[69] Despite the obvious
benefits of changing to a contributory system of pensions, Menzies
warned against making a policy statement during the election because
of the complicated logistics and the possible backlash against an attack
on Liberal social policy. Nevertheless, Diefenbaker announced that a
Conservative government would look into the possibility of restructuring the old age pension along contributory lines.[70]

The Tories approached the election with vigour, intent on convincing the public of the need for "a new unifying force, a new national
policy, a new national myth" in order to fill what they saw as the
Liberal policy vacuum.[71] Most of them agreed on the necessity of a
coherent social policy, although some Ontario and Quebec members
of the campaign committee felt that "the alternative [to the Liberal
plan] should be a national policy of provincial autonomy."[72] Ultimately, Menzies himself was largely responsible for articulating the
tenets of a new national policy, which was based on economic development. Reminiscent of John A. Macdonald's nation-building
National Policy, this approach was in response to the goal of successive Liberal governments to "maintain social policies and short-run
economic stability."[73] Since the "Liberals [had] parlayed the Rowell-
Sirois report into a quarter-century of Liberal rule," Menzies hoped
that the Conservatives would be able to do much the same with their
new national policy.[74] But, despite Menzies's claim that economic

development should be the major focus of the Conservative Party, Diefenbaker worked hard to cultivate his image as the champion of the underdog – which necessarily included a high level of social security. Most Conservatives accepted Diefenbaker's approach, if sometimes somewhat grudgingly. Deanne Finlayson, for example, argued that the Conservative Party would have to respond to "the whole trend of society, [which is,] unfortunately, directed to less self reliance and more dependence on government."[75] Menzies acknowledged this point but suggested that "the Conservative approach [should be] to show that welfare follows from production and if the real technical and human problems in production are met, welfare can be increased together with an increase in self-reliance."[76] In advertising their "resolute determination that the state shall be the servant of the people and that no government shall attempt to be their master,"[77] and in promising to investigate alternative social-security methods, the Conservatives gave the impression that they were more committed to action than the Liberals. While the Conservatives had not embraced the idea of completely restructuring the existing social-welfare system, on the hustings they demonstrated a clearer understanding of the political cachet of a well-knit social-security net than did their Liberal counterparts.

Of the three major national parties, the CCF had always been more devoted to principles than to the achievement of power and, perhaps as a result, it placed greater significance on social-security reforms. Although the Winnipeg Declaration of 1956 had toned down the socialism originally espoused in the Regina Manifesto of 1933, the CCF retained its strong commitment to social justice and security. The platform it carried into the 1957 campaign contained commitments to increase substantially the old age pension, the disability pensions, and family allowances and to establish a national health-insurance system with full medical, hospital, nursing, dental, and optical coverage.[78] The Liberals prided themselves on their own record in the field of social security and so were blind to the innovations that M.J. Coldwell and his followers were suggesting. They saw "nothing novel or dramatic" in the CCF program and believed that the only difference in terms of social security was "how far and how fast."[79] What the Liberals failed to realize was that the CCF was promoting an entirely different concept of social security. The measures that the CCF members advocated were not merely income supplements, as the Liberal assistance programs were; instead, the CCF's measures were based on the responsibility of government to provide social benefits as a universal right.

All three major parties issued statements on social security during the campaign of 1957. The Liberals chose to emphasize their record and remind the voters that there would be more of the same to come; both the Conservatives and the CCF promised to expand and in some ways change the existing structure but not remove any of the social programs already in existence. The one element that received the most attention was the increase to the old age pension, but except insofar as it held a certain emotional appeal to particular voters, social security was not the issue upon which the outcome of the election hinged.[80] Of much greater significance was the fact that the Conservatives, led by a charismatic man with powerful oratorical abilities, were seen to have a party with an agenda, a party committed to activist government, as opposed to the Liberal method of governing through the force of inertia. Election day, which saw the election of 112 Conservatives, 105 Liberals, 25 CCFers, 19 Social Crediters, and 4 independents, demonstrated that the Liberal Party had lost its ability to appeal to the voters.

Although hospital insurance had played only a minor role in the election, used by various Liberal campaigners as an example of their commitment to social welfare, the negotiations around it had been characteristic of the national Liberal Party's general approach to social security. The federal government did not introduce discussions about hospital insurance as part of a comprehensive program of social security. It was devoid of a coherent philosophy, and so the introduction of hospital insurance depended first on provincial initiatives and then on provincial concessions to a federal government intent on remaining identified with national social policies but reluctant to assume the necessary responsibility for them. The Liberals' half-hearted approach was even more evident on the old-age-pension issue, when an increase was offered for the purposes of political expediency and not out of a carefully defined approach to social security. The Conservatives and the CCF had both done their homework and on the campaign trail appealed to the voters with promises of a greater assumption of national responsibility and a more coherent approach to issues of pensions, health, and welfare. If the Liberals hoped to form the government again, they would first have to conduct a massive policy re-evaluation. This was the necessary first step towards better understanding the public perception of national government responsibility and ultimately formulating policies that would address those concerns and meet the demands for a viable system of social security. In opposition, the

Liberal Party could no longer demonstrate its commitment to social betterment merely by implementing discrete pieces of legislation: opposition demanded the fashioning of comprehensive alternatives to government programs. But a stint in opposition, without the responsibilities of governing, provided the opportunity for this necessary self-evaluation and restructuring. It also held out the possibility, as the Liberals were soon to discover, that backroom planning would overtake public opinion.

2 Conflicting Solutions to Liberal Party Problems, 1957–60

Although it was difficult for those associated with the Liberal Party to be sure of the extent of the damage in the immediate aftermath of the 1957 election, and even more difficult to accept responsibility for the destruction of the once great Liberal machine, many identified either party organization or party policy as areas in which some degree of reconstruction was necessary. Interestingly, those with the longest, most political, connection to the Liberal Party were apt to recommend merely superficial remedies to the party's woes. A few people, most notably those who had confined their interest in the Liberal Party to the backroom, the classroom, or the closet, suggested a much more thorough overhaul of the existing party policy and machinery. The opinions that were offered on social-security issues were especially revealing: the old guard persisted in believing that the Liberal social-policy record had been above criticism, while newcomers were prone to suggest a more comprehensive and expanded approach than had been pursued in the past. It would take years before the latter group achieved a dominant place in the party, but the mere existence of progressive thinkers in the first dark days of opposition served as something of a beacon for others.

While the results of the election of 10 June 1957 surprised professional political commentators and amateurs alike, it was the shape of the election results that were even more disturbing for the Liberals than the actual numbers. Regionally, they kept only their strongholds in Newfoundland and Quebec. Demographically, there was a sense that "the Liberal Party has failed to bring the young people along with [it and] ... labour has left."[1] But it was in terms of its pre-election organization that the results of 10 June threw the Liberal Party into chaos. Previously, it had been able to conduct relatively decentralized campaigns, confident that individual cabinet ministers would interpret both the national policies along regional lines and the regional sentiment for central-party consumption. The combination of the Liberals' loss of power and the electorate's rejection of most of the important regional bosses brought this form of ministerial organization to a standstill. It also encouraged criticism of the dangerous levels of power enjoyed by Liberal cabinet ministers. Political scientist David E. Smith would later claim that "everyone agreed that cabinet ministers had had too much power for too long," but it was obviously a dissatisfaction underestimated by the St Laurent Liberals.[2]

Loss of power inevitably results in changes to the relationships enjoyed by members of the ousted party. But for the Liberals, the effects of the 1957 election were more far-fetching than that. Because the electoral defeat had not been anticipated, it left the Liberals completely unprepared for a stint in opposition. And at the same time, the defeat suddenly turned on its ear the very manner in which policy was both conceived and disseminated.

Over the course of twenty-two consecutive years of Liberal government, a close relationship existed between the elite politicians and their bureaucratic advisers, to the extent that grass-roots input into policy matters was essentially non-existent. As early as 1955, J.E. Hodgetts had been able to say that cabinet ministers and civil servants were integrated into "a solid corps of senior officials which looks complacently into a common mirror and receives an acceptable answer to the collective question 'Who is now the fairest in the land?'"[3] With this elite-level cooperation, there was little need to engage in the process of policy evaluation, and the Liberal Party became increasingly unaware of what individual Canadians wanted from their national government. Following defeat, however, the Liberals lost access to the government bureaucracy and the party was forced to examine alternative methods of devising policy objectives.

Furthermore, the Liberals were also forced to rearrange their methods for publicizing their party platform. The party could no longer rely on the political prowess of such regional titans as Jimmy Gardiner and Stuart Garson, both ex-premiers, and their ability to define the national economic policies along provincial lines and to create a network of support through the judicious use of government patronage. Although this system of managing a political party had its weaknesses,

most particularly the possibility that "cabinet ministers might complicate political strategy [and] even distort national priorities," it had the
benefit of ensuring that regional demands were treated equitably by
the federal government.[4] The long period of power enjoyed by the
Liberal Party under King and St Laurent, however, served to enervate
the system of ministerial control. The locus of power was unquestionably Ottawa, and the longer the ministers and civil servants resided in
the capital, the more tenuous their hold on regional concerns became.[5]
Provincial elections during the 1950s had also not been kind to the
Liberal Party: by 1957 there were Liberal administrations in only
Newfoundland, Prince Edward Island, and Manitoba (which was soon
to go Conservative), a fact that negated the possibility of maintaining
decentralized regional party control through the aegis of the provincial
organization. The middlemen in the Liberal hierarchy – the civil servants, the cabinet ministers with strong provincial networks, and the
provincial premiers – had all evaporated in the aftermath of the first
Diefenbaker victory, leaving only a skeleton of central organizers and
politicians in Ottawa and the 40.5 per cent of the voting population
who had supported the Liberals.[6]

Suddenly without access to the patronage network, the bureaucratic
intelligentsia, or ministerial privilege, the Liberal Party was forced to
turn to its extra-parliamentary wing as a source of organizational
strength in the wake of electoral defeat. It was a logical step, and one
that had been taken, with varying degrees of success, by previous
opposition parties. Periods of opposition have traditionally provided
national parties in Canada the opportunity for introspection and
renewed attempts to attract support from different sectors of society,
a process usually resulting in a revivified central organization. During
the administration of R.B. Bennett from 1930 to 1935, the Liberals
had formed the National Liberal Federation to stimulate a rethinking
of policy and a rebuilding of popular supports and the Conservatives
had followed suit with a thinkers conference in Port Hope after their
own defeat in 1935.[7]

In the late 1950s, party rebuilding had to reconcile competing visions
of what the necessary internal evaluation would accomplish. Social
security proved to be the issue around which allegiances were formed.
Some commentators hoped that the revived party organization would
merely replicate the ministerialism of Liberal government, while others
envisioned a complete overhaul of the existing system. The former view
would facilitate the perpetuation of the Liberal Party as it had grown
under St Laurent – a party with strong ties to regional power bases
and structured to deal primarily with national economic development.
The latter view offered a more uncertain future but one that held out

the promise of confronting the growing demand for a national government willing to accept responsibility for increased social security. The prescriptions for change were widely divergent, and their respective proponents battled for supremacy between 1957 and 1960.

Explaining the electoral defeat was particularly difficult for those who had been most actively involved in the campaign, in a large part because it necessitated accepting a certain amount of responsibility. Even those who had not been seeking re-election in 1957 were somewhat reluctant to identify problems, since the cause of the defeat had obviously been a long time in gestation and a product of objectives pursued and strategies implemented over the course of the previous two decades. Yet virtually every Liberal in the country was implicated, however slightly, in the devastating loss to Diefenbaker's Conservatives. Veteran Liberal Brooke Claxton was one of the first to offer his official assessment of the Liberal weaknesses and his thoughts on how the party's position could be strengthened. Claxton had earned his political stripes under Mackenzie King and had retired to the board of directors of Metropolitan Life Insurance Company, but he continued to be held in high esteem by those of a younger political generation. He believed that the problem was essentially one of modifying policy objectives, going on the offensive against Diefenbaker, and in many ways returning to the formula that had been so effective in the late 1930s and 1940s. Although Claxton noted that one of the reasons for defeat in 1957 was that "the Conservatives have moved to the left of the Liberals, identifying themselves with small business and the little man," he did not seem to think that the Liberals should respond by clearly staking out their traditional middle ground and forcing the Conservatives to retreat to the right. Instead, he warned that "studies under way ... go a long way to show that the built-in increases in Canada's social security program have put the economy on a 'collision course' where so large a proportion of the national production will be spent on social services that not enough will be left to meet other costs ... What is needed is a fresh approach along traditionally Liberal lines and a fresh statement." To this end, he suggested that policy should be developed along the lines of "the place of the individual," with particular emphasis on "private enterprise and individual initiative."[8] His concern that successive Liberal governments had over-emphasized state responsibility in the social-security field was particularly telling for a man who had been minister of health and had been responsible for the wartime commitment to hospital and health insurance. Claxton's argument assumed that the Canadian electorate needed a right-of-centre political choice: if the Conservatives were not going to offer it, then the Liberals should.

Other politicians were less forthcoming, but as the wounds of the electoral defeat, both political and spiritual, began to heal, Senator J.J. Connolly started soliciting policy and organizational prescriptions from veteran Liberals. Connolly was regarded as quite conservative, at least in his approach to social-security spending,[9] and his own opinion of the place of the state in the private lives of the people shaped his choice of commentators in the aftermath of defeat. It was therefore not surprising that most of the responses to his request for input paralleled his own views. Connolly seemed to be most interested in Charles Dunning's perception of the present situation. A more consistently conservative Liberal than Dunning would have been difficult to find; since his days as premier of Saskatchewan and federal minister of finance, he had always been considered on the right-wing of the party. Dunning appreciated Connolly's interest in his opinions because he felt somewhat alone in his apprehension "with respect to the creeping Socialism which appears to be accepted as inevitable by all political parties, and which ... seriously threatens ... liberal philosophy." His main concern was that the contemporary Liberal government had failed to provide the necessary atmosphere for developing a national sense of individual responsibility. He argued that the ever increasing number of social services created "a tremendous and expensive machine to bring about redistribution of wealth by taxation, and lessening the sense of responsibility on the part of the individual citizen, and by so doing are decreasing both the dignity and the freedom of the individual person. I know it may not sound like practical politics to be flashing this kind of red light, but surely we Liberals must get back to fundamental thinking in terms of principles."[10] Connolly was intrigued by Dunning's suggestions and had them circulated at the National Liberal Federation.

There were others who expressed concern that the federal treasury was being rapidly depleted in the course of winning votes. Queen's University economist and former Ottawa mandarin W.A. Mackintosh urged caution in dealing with social security in the expectation that "events may make it possible to show that in regard to Dominion-provincial relations and social security, the present government is merely going a bit further than the previous government had hitherto been prepared to go, and has done so without presenting any accounting of the financial results."[11] Mackintosh thought that the generosity of the Diefenbaker government would sooner or later come back to haunt it and would be compared unfavourably to the fiscal restraint shown by the St Laurent Liberals. Stuart Garson, St Laurent's minister of justice, was essentially in agreement with the Mackintosh position. As far as he was concerned, the increases the Conservatives had already made to old age pensions would be virtually impossible for the Liberals to better. This being the case, he thought there was no profit in "discussing this subject at all, unless some presently unforeseen circumstance arises which makes it necessary for us to do so."[12]

All of these men were from an older generation of Liberals; they had been responsible for the direction of Liberal politics for the better part of three decades and had both created and benefited from the system which had let them run the country through the war and into the post-war period. They were thus particularly unsuited for the task of assessing the weaknesses that produced the surprising defeat of 1957. The problems they identified were ones of excess, and so they counselled retrenchment and a retreat to the traditional national responsibility of ensuring a sound economy. While some recognized the important role a cautious commitment to policies of social betterment had played in securing Liberal hegemony, these conservative commentators demanded closer attention to the "bottom line." Liberal journalist Bruce Hutchison, a man who had enjoyed the confidence of many of the King and St Laurent ministers and who repaid that favour with largely complimentary newspaper coverage of the Liberal regime, was characteristic of the older generation of Liberals and Liberal supporters.[13] In general, they were not opposed to some degree of social security in Canada, but they identified a dangerous trend towards an ever-more intrusive state. Hutchison was in favour of "the expansion of those social services which are the gift of Liberalism to Canada, but we should stand firm on the proposition that we will go only as far as the means of the nation allow, and we should concentrate most particularly on the task of increasing the size of the pie rather than the process of dividing it."[14] In the heady post-war years, Canadians seemed to be under the impression that the pie was quite large enough but that not everyone was being offered the same size of piece. The St Laurent Liberals had been chastised at the polls for not understanding the point.

Those people who had not experienced Liberal politics from the front lines, but had instead worked behind the scenes at the National Liberal Federation, offered a somewhat different assessment of the party's problems than their political counterparts. Although federation executive Duncan MacTavish thought that "the basic organization does not have to have complete rebuilding,"[15] echoing the ex-cabinet ministers' defence of their own position, there were others at Liberal headquarters who thought differently. One observer at the federation suggested a fundamental restructuring of the body, giving it much more centralized control over elections and policy and thereby forging important links between the national party and individuals, as opposed to between Ottawa and regional bosses. He suggested the same kind of restructuring for the provincial organizations, noting that the Liberals had not made any gains on the provincial level since 1943. The structure, however, should be fully integrated and largely controlled by the centre. He stressed that there should be "only one Liberal Party [with a] greatly strengthened Party executive on every level ... a completely new financial set-up and ... an over-all plan of political action for 365 days of each and every year."[16]

Other commentators, such as National Liberal Federation general secretary and advertising executive H.E. (Bob) Kidd, also identified a need for a complete restructuring of the party. He noted that "local organizations are now looking to the Federation for help and assistance. Before the election it was apparent that the local organizations ... were prepared to accept the responsibility for the politics in their own area. The defeat of June 10th has created a new attitude."[17] Furthermore, he identified the need for greater integration of duties between cabinet ministers and backbenchers through subcommittees and associate ministers, and a stronger Liberal Federation, achieved specifically by implementing the practice of annual meetings, "to keep interest mobilized and maintain contact between the leaders and the rank and file throughout the country,"[18] as ways to avoid the organizational dilemmas of previous administrations.

The organizers, however, were not just concerned with organization. Duncan MacTavish, for example, diagnosed policy and procedural weaknesses beyond the structural flaws noted by others. Critics had complained that the party "should have something positive to say about current problems,"[19] and to this end MacTavish thought it was time to "pause in the development of our natural resources. The party should endeavour to deal with urban problems and lay less emphasis on rural problems. *It should be remembered that the really big issues are personal issues.* Issues which touch on family life and involve personal difficulties for people who are living in the urban areas of Canada."[20] The analyst for the National Liberal Federation also pointed to the importance of policy changes. He argued that it was imperative to return to the social-reform spirit that had characterized the last years of the Second World War, a type of liberalism that had not yet run its course. By implementing coherent programs of health insurance and pensions, the Liberal Party could "act positively to equalize opportunity." This was not to say, he cautioned, that the policies of the past were adequate for the needs of the future, and he stressed that in addition to fulfilling the mandate of a previous generation, the Liberal Party had a responsibility to "be searching now for the next new Liberalism."[21] In marked contrast to the comments made by the ousted cabinet ministers, the elite of the organizational hierarchy suggested that social security needed to be more fully developed if the Liberals were to regain federal power.

A final group of people who encouraged the pursuit of more progressive policies and a more coherent organization had had little or no previous association with the Liberal Party, but they were to become important in its rejuvenation. Tom Kent had emigrated to Canada from Britain in 1954, resigning from his position as assistant editor of The *Economist* to take on the job of editor of the Winnipeg *Free Press*. By 1957 he had succeeded in returning the *Free Press* to a position of prominence in Canadian journalistic circles while at the same time distinguishing himself as a sharp-minded political critic. He was not a journalist in the same mould as Bruce Hutchison, for whom "personalities and traditional partisan loyalties" were key to his sustained support for the Liberal cause.[22] Kent had already drawn the wrath of Liberal stalwarts such as C.D. Howe, "Minister of Everything," and Newfoundland's boss J.W. Pickersgill by criticizing particular policies of the federal government.[23] Despite these disagreements, Kent found himself in closest sympathy with the policies of the Liberal Party, and a mid-October address to a convention of Manitoba Young Liberals cast him as a political player prepared to offer tangible "new ideas."

In his speech, Kent did nothing to tone down any of the criticisms he had levelled against the St Laurent government during the spring campaign, and indeed he went so far as to suggest that the reason the Conservatives had won on 10 June was because the Liberal Party had lost touch with its fundamental principles. He told the youthful audience that "if the Liberal party is what it ought to be, Young Liberals will never hesitate to assert principles." Introducing a theme that he would continue to reiterate through the next decade, he continued: "There'll always be plenty of other people to give weight enough to expediency. The masters of expediency are often successful in the short run. But it's not too pleasant to wake up from their ministrations and find that the Tories have got into office by putting on our mislaid clothes."[24] Most of Kent's speech focused on the need to re-evaluate the fiscal structure of Canada in order to create a freer economy that would tend towards smaller businesses and a more equitable division of resources.

Toronto businessman Walter Gordon was another important source of opinion on the shape of Liberalism for the 1960s. Though he was not officially associated with the Liberal Party in 1957, he had been dabbling in politics and policy development for many years. He was chair of the Royal Commission on Economic Prospects which had just reported dangerous levels of unimpeded American investment in

Canada and set out a program of economic development that would facilitate growth of domestic markets. Foreign investment had long been and would continue to be a particular bailiwick for Gordon, and his royal commission report was a strong nationalist statement destined to ruffle the feathers of the business community. In discussing the future of the Liberal Party with Brooke Claxton, Gordon resolved that it was absolutely imperative that the Liberal Party clearly identify itself as the party of reform. "Some people think the main reforms which we have fought for in the past have now been accomplished," he wrote. "This is true in part as any review of the social security measures introduced by the Liberal Party over the years will show. But there will always be need for reform." In Gordon's mind, the long-term objectives of the party should be clearly outlined. In particular, he wanted the Liberals to commit to complete health insurance and promise to introduce a universal, contributory pension plan to meet the demands of Canadians who "are not satisfied with the old age pension plan in its present form."[25] He was convinced that the Liberals had grown complacent after so many uninterrupted years in power and needed to demonstrate a real commitment to the type of social services that had so long been a part of the political agenda but had never quite been firmly embraced.

Taken together, these several versions of the solution to Liberal woes represented the organizational and political dilemma of the party. Clearly, the defeat of nine cabinet ministers meant that the traditional method of organizing and disseminating information had to be revised, as the National Liberal Federation officials suggested. The policy objectives would also have to be reassessed in the light of the new political situation. It was too late, however, to return to the type of conservative economic management advocated by the King and St Laurent administrations and now being promoted again by many of the ministers from that era. The public rejection of the Liberals demonstrated that they had not responded to contemporary policy imperatives; it was not the rejection of a party that had done too much for Canadians, but instead the rejection of one that had not done enough. Organizational structures also needed revamping, less to answer the concerns of the voting population than to create a system than would carry the Liberals back into office. Since a highly centralized party structure was necessary following the loss of the traditional middlemen in the system, the policy message that the Liberals brought to the people also had to be highly centralized. A shift to promoting progressive social goals was best suited to cultivate a new relationship between Ottawa and the individual, since such goals did not need regional interpretation. Many of the commentators hinted at this dual realignment, arguing for new policies that would fit perfectly with the

new organizational imperatives. There remained the problem, however, of identifying the new locus of power within the wreck of what
was once the Liberal Party.

Leadership conventions, the organization and orchestration of which
the Liberal Party faced in the aftermath of their 1957 defeat, had not
had a long history in the Canadian experience. Leaders had traditionally been selected by caucus, and while the Liberals had gone to convention in both 1919 and 1948, the mechanisms by which a new chief
was selected had generally perpetuated the elitism of an even earlier
period. Veteran Liberal Chubby Power argued that since the majority
of the delegates to a leadership convention were selected by the constituency association, or more specifically the incumbent Liberal, the
process was only one step removed from the caucus decision of the
Laurier era.[26] The rank and file were rarely included in the process,
the party platform was dictated from behind the scenes, and the choice
of one person over another reflected the results of backroom negotiations rather than convention voting. Though the convention of 1958
was not "modern" in terms of the number of serious candidates, the
degree of campaigning, the input from the grass roots of the party, or
the level of media attention, it must be regarded as the transition
between past and present.[27] The national Liberal Party attempted to
democratize its leadership-selection process by inviting a large number
of delegates, who had the dual responsibility of selecting a new leader
for the party and voting on various policy options. There was an
increased number of elites involved in the process of screening the
policy resolutions submitted by the constituency associations, a change
which, while not in itself particularly democratic, demonstrated a shift
to achieving a greater level of accountability. The end result was inevitably a degree of guided democracy, but the appearance of a new
generation of Liberals with a strong attachment to the man elected to
lead their party was to have a lasting effect on the development of
social policy in Canada.

The first step in organizing the 1958 convention was to set up a
variety of policy committees to sift through the resolutions which had
been solicited from the member Liberal associations. The transition to
democratically determining policy goals was destined to be only partial: ultimately, elites of one sort or another would be responsible for
the final selection to be heard by the convention as a whole. George
Marler, MP, was the chair of the resolutions committee for the leadership convention, and he assumed the job of setting up the various
subcommittees to discuss different aspects of Liberal policy at the

convention. Each of these groups would develop the resolutions on the particular subject referred to that group and would then convey the resolutions to the convention at large for final voting. Senator David Croll, a self-styled crusading Liberal for many years past and a one-time renegade member of Ontario premier Mitch Hepburn's cabinet, was the convenor of the session on social security, which also included Mrs A.H. Leiff of the Liberal Women's Association, Ottawa civil servant Maurice Lamontagne, and MP James Byrne. Marler also thought that the former minister of national health and welfare, Paul Martin, might be interested in having some input into the resolutions on social security, since his progressive views on the issue were well known.[28]

Other veterans of Liberal governments were bound to be less enthusiastic about the challenge of redefining social goals. The former Progressive who was reincarnated on the right of the Liberal Party under King, T.A. Crerar, for example, was dubious of the benefits of the policy discussions and hoped that the Liberal Party would "not go off the deep end in a lot of foolish resolutions."[29] The policy groups were designed to address such concerns by screening the resolutions and presenting "only those ... which are of the greatest importance to the country as a whole" to the full convention.[30] Whether the vetting process would be pursued in exactly the way people such as Crerar hoped was, however, unlikely. For the most part, Liberals who had achieved their apex of power under St Laurent had grown weary of the mundane activities of party organization, and they confined their contribution to the convention process to grumbling among themselves. Younger people, or those whose party work had not been onerous in the past, took on most of the policy-committee responsibilities.

The social-security committee was not the only one to be struck well in advance of the actual convention – preparatory work was under way for other policy sessions as well. One of these was to be devoted to a statement of Liberal principles, and Tom Kent was the primary drafter. He struggled to define a philosophy between "conservative" and "socialist" interests that "puts freedom for the individual above all other political considerations" without denying the importance of "the positive right of each and every individual to full opportunities in society." Kent's brand of Liberalism, which "carries with it society's insurance of the individual against misfortune," aligned him closely with Walter Gordon in terms of the importance of a commitment to social betterment.[31] But the centrality of Kent's role in preparations for the leadership convention also placed him at odds with some of the powerful members of the old guard of the party, who found it difficult to accept the assistance of one who had been so openly critical of the Liberal administration in the editorial pages of the Winnipeg *Free Press*.[32] Thus, while Kent's definition of Liberalism heralded the arrival of a new group of advisers into the ranks of the party, the concomitant practical and intellectual changes proved to be considerably unsettling for some.

To those involved in laying the policy groundwork for the convention, it was clear that many issues, such as foreign affairs, would occasion little or no debate but that others, such as whether to support a move to free trade as Tom Kent advocated, were bound to divide people dramatically.[33] In the area of social policy, the Liberal Party had to confront truly conflicting dictates – its own historical commitment to a complete system of social security, and the realities of a rapidly increasing modern budget. Policy makers could not take sides on this issue. Rather, a careful balance was necessary between those who demanded a completion of the social-policy goals of the previous generation, and those who saw this as encroaching on individual liberty. Both opinions would have to find a home in the Liberal Party. Kent knew that "even among so-called socialist parties, there is increasing recognition that over-centralization in the state is dangerous to freedom and that it fails to release the creative individual energies on which human progress depends."[34] Kent preferred to focus on more subtle social-security goals than merely giving more handouts. He saw the need for a "welfare economy – which means (as opposed to socialism) an enlargement of the public sphere not in production as such but in consumption – larger public expenditures on education, health, housing and other services."[35] His work before the convention, however, was largely on the articulation of a modern definition of Liberalism, and it was Senator David Croll who was responsible for putting together a statement on the social goals of the party.

Croll himself had long been committed to the necessity of a comprehensive social-security plan, and the statement that resulted from the deliberations of his committee clearly indicated that he did not think that Canada had yet achieved that goal. Although it was "not necessary ... to recount the unfolding of the grand plan ... through 22 years of Liberal government, [the] fact that the mosaic is not yet complete highlights the complexities of the great task of bringing to the Canadian people the things which a free democracy has and must bestow."[36] In outlining a policy of full health insurance, including sickness insurance for the unemployed who are sick, an extension of old-age security, and a universal, contributory, and portable pension plan, the committee on social security hoped to fill in the gaps in existing programs. The resolutions committee recommended a redesign of the preamble to the party platform, "declaring that not only must there be high employment and social security in Canada but that these must be 'constantly improved.'"[37] The convention seemed to endorse Croll's sentiment that "there is no evil in welfare, and the welfare state is not an evil concept. The problem of our generation is not to demonstrate the need for reforms, but to bring them about and know how to do it."[38]

In drafting the resolutions to be put forward at the convention, the resolutions committee occasionally had to contend with input from people outside of the Liberal Party who had become interested in the contest as a result of the media attention. It is interesting that, despite the emphasis on the role the grass roots of the party played in policy determination, even those outside the party were certain that decisions would ultimately be made by the members of the resolutions committee. National Liberal Federation president John Connolly had encouraged this assessment by already soliciting some views from outside the party, including those of Joseph Harris, the president of Great West Life Assurance Company. The insurance industry as a whole was critical of the hospital-services insurance recently enacted, although Harris himself felt that it "has gone too far to withdraw." On the question of other social-security measures, he only expressed concern that "the basic thinking on welfare should be that no help is available to anyone who is capable of looking after himself. Any other position leads to a letting down of saving and thrift and tends to make a weaker segment of the population depend more and more on government agencies."[39]

As the convention drew nearer, others within the insurance industry began to express concern over what they suspected was happening in the meetings of the resolutions committee. David Kilgour, a vice-president of Great West Life, wrote to Tom Kent to "express the conviction that any Liberal platform that promises to go further down [the national health insurance] road would be very damaging, both to the country and the Party. The current political flavour of talking up a United States social security plan for Canada on top of our other social measures may tempt the Liberals to climb on to that bandwagon as well without any realistic regard of the consequences."[40] Kilgour's disgust with the entire concept of health insurance was well known. In the late 1950s he had toured the country visiting provincial governments in an attempt to convince the premiers that they should not adopt Ottawa's plan for national hospital insurance. His appeals were considered by many to be misguided and directed only at securing the interests of his own insurance industry.[41] Kilgour petitioned Kent that the public really did not want additional welfare measures but instead would rather pocket the money for other purposes. In

Kilgour's assessment, the benefit of living in a democracy was that the people had the choice not to provide for life's emergencies. Since Kent's views on social-security legislation had not yet been articulated at any length, Kilgour was able to state that he had sent the letter "only with the hope that it might be a line of reasoning that would assist in restraining the 'do-gooders' we must contend with."[42] Time would place Kent firmly in line with the do-gooders and leave Kilgour still desperately trying to get a political audience for the views of the insurance industry.

If Kilgour had been wrong in assuming that he had found an anti-social security ally in Kent, he was correct in identifying the locus of Liberal policy formulation. The specifics of the new policy platform, and there were few, came not from the recently defeated party hierarchy, the leadership contestants, or the grass roots but from the new generation of Liberals who had been charged with drafting the resolutions. In many cases these people had only tenuous links to the Liberal Party, but they had replaced the civil servants as the party's policy strategists. At their head, and mainly responsible for designing the left-leaning program that was eventually adopted, was "a small group of writers and intellectuals, the most active of whom were Tom Kent … and Maurice Lamontagne."[43] They were among those who sifted through the resolutions submitted by the various Liberal associations across the country and drafted a program of texts involving the most acceptable of them. Nothing was left to chance. The resolutions that would emerge from the policy committees and plenary sessions at the convention had been selected weeks before in the party's backrooms.

In deciding on a platform, the Liberal Party worked feverishly to give the impression of greater democracy, but in reality it moved only marginally in that direction. The main contenders for the mantle of the party, in contrast, appeared to demonstrate the still-firm attachment to the principles that had guided the St Laurent administration. It was only behind the scenes that one could locate an important transition towards a new brand of Liberalism. While both front-running leadership hopefuls Paul Martin and Lester Pearson were progressive and left-leaning, both had also played significant roles in the Liberal Party under St Laurent and so could hardly be considered new blood. Moreover, the persistent rumour that defeated Finance Minister Walter Harris would throw his hat into the ring clearly demonstrated that the right wing of the party was not dead.[44] Of the two main candidates, Martin had probably always wanted to be prime minister, while those closest to Pearson suspected that if he "had been offered an important international position at the time, he would have taken it."[45]

From the outset, most observers, both inside and outside the Liberal Party, expected that Pearson would win the contest. His well-known handling of the Suez crisis and subsequent nomination for the Nobel Peace Prize appealed to a population "increasingly aware of and frightened by the new dangers in the world," and "his easy personality and ability to get along with all groups and classes of people" highlighted his suitability for the job of leader. He was not without weaknesses, however, by far the most important of which Gordon identified as "his reputation for not being interested in or knowing much about domestic affairs."[46] Interestingly, many of the new recruits to the Liberal Party emphasized the centrality of social policy. Their attachment to Pearson, instead of to well-established social reformer Paul Martin, is therefore puzzling. Because Pearson was regarded as a relative newcomer to politics, untarnished by the arrogance of the St Laurent administration, and a progressive intellectual, many of his followers assumed that his views on social programs would reflect that left-leaning liberalism. He said little to disabuse people of this notion but at the same time did not and was not advised to encourage it.[47] The fact that most of the members of the resolutions committee supported Pearson for the leadership, however, meant that their work was in many ways designed to facilitate Pearson's social-policy reputation.

The leadership convention opened in Ottawa with relatively little fanfare on 14 January 1958, perhaps because there seemed to be little doubt in anyone's mind who would be the winning candidate. In a field that included Paul Martin and Lester Pearson, as well as dark-horse candidates Mayor Don Mackay of Calgary and Portage la Prairie mayor Lloyd Henderson, most commentators expected Pearson to win easily on the first ballot. The pundits were more interested in the type of program the Liberals would adopt at the convention than the leader they would elect. The conservative opinion was that the historic role of the Liberals in forging internal unity and creating the welfare state was outdated, since "neither of these great issues generates any political steam today, [and] neither will decide a future election."[48] For people who subscribed to their view, the purpose of the Ottawa convention was to chart a completely new political course. In contrast, those of a more liberal persuasion were not convinced of the utility of abandoning the party's fundamental traditions. Arguing that the previous generation had "defaulted on liberalism," the Toronto *Daily Star* demanded a return to welfare reform. "Once a reform is won, it becomes an object to conserve," pointed out the editor. "Some Liberals have even said that all the goals are won, that there are none new to achieve. Bosh. That is a cosy conservative attitude. Even the 1919 objective of health insurance is but half achieved: the 1957 Liberal legislation included only hospital insurance."[49]

The Ottawa convention supposedly looked to the grass roots of the party for the policy ideas that would bring them back to power. The National Liberal Federation reported the submission of 170 policy resolutions prior to the opening of the convention, and it intended to introduce the practice of giving Liberal associations the opportunity to present resolutions from the floor, an innovation in party conventions that has lasted to the present.[50] The convenors were most pleased about the fact that "the great majority of the delegates will be attending their first large political gathering. Or, to put it differently, the Liberal Party is giving the green light to the younger members in its ranks, members with a fresh viewpoint and a burning desire to see that social justice is done to all citizens."[51] However, as the convention progressed, it became apparent that it had merely been made to "look as democratic as possible, [as] elaborate plans were laid for the moving of spontaneous resolutions from the floor ... [which] instead of looking spontaneous, looked contrived."[52]

Considerable time in the three days scheduled for the convention was allotted to a parade of the party brass, most of whom appeared more than slightly tarnished after the debacle of the June election. In addresses to the assembled delegates, many members of the Liberal hierarchy attempted to outline policies that would ensure re-election. Few of the old Liberal stalwarts, however, seemed willing to press for substantial changes. Jimmy Gardiner wishfully argued that "the Liberal Party was not displaced in government because it had not been true to its principles, nor was it displaced because of any dishonesty in administration. It was displaced because the Conservative Party promised more and resorted to issues which promote disunity."[53] Others followed in the same vein, defending the practices of the past while attempting to spur the delegates to action for the next election. It was a case of "talking about looking ahead while looking backward."[54] Or, as one Ottawa observer commented, the speeches by the old party politicians showed that they "were like a bunch of pallbearers pretending not to recognize the corpse."[55] However, despite the occasional charges that the party brass was over-represented in the discussions and the decision-making process,[56] there seemed to be a relative deficiency of ideas from either the plethora of ex-cabinet ministers present or the leadership hopefuls.

Observers recognized that Pearson's forte lay in the sphere of international affairs and that he did not "have as much political moxie as

... Martin ... at least not in the domestic issues that are the very nub of federal politics."[57] Pearson devoted most of his nomination address to the general issue of liberalism, mentioning Liberal social-security goals only briefly. Near the end of a twenty-minute speech, he commented that "we must everlastingly insist on the freedom of the individual against the state. We must also recognize the fact that this freedom will be dust and ashes if the individual does not have social security."[58] The speech was not likely to shift any of the voters and most certainly had not clarified any specific policy proposals.

Paul Martin was the more effective campaign speaker, and not surprisingly the ex-minister of national health and welfare devoted a considerable amount to time to the explanation of his social goals. His was a left-leaning brand of liberalism, convinced as he was that "enterprise must be free but it must be free within the limits of responsibility, so that free enterprise for one will not mean slave enterprise for another." The means by which Martin intended to give "the greatest possible scope to human enterprise and individual initiative" was by continuing to make advances in the areas of health and unemployment insurance and disability and old age pensions.[59] It was, by all accounts, a "powerful" political speech, in which "he tried to etch an image of himself in the minds of the delegates – the image of an indomitable fighter who could lead them to victory."[60] Martin had hoped to replicate King's 1919 performance when he swept the leadership convention with his dynamic nomination address. But it was not to be.

It came as a surprise to no one that Pearson won an easy victory over Martin, 1084 votes to 305, but where the party would go from there was still uncertain. In the previous days of meetings, it had sometimes appeared as if "the party [was] trying to out-promise the Tories ... [although] it is proper to say that most of the proposed reforms are reforms the majority of Canadians feel they want and can afford." Even so, the party officials, and particularly those with political experience, were well aware of the fact that "the resolutions are only general directives to guide a future Liberal government rather than rigid mandates."[61] Pearson declared, to much applause and enthusiasm, "our resolutions ... are in startling and stimulating contrast to those of the last Conservative convention, which were born in controversy and frustration, were misshapen and unattractive after birth, and were then quietly smothered in one of the cruelest acts of political infanticide in history."[62] The future of the Liberal resolutions remained unclear.

The choice of Pearson over Martin was never considered a victory of foreign policy over domestic. Rather, casting Pearson as the political neophyte certainly did his drive for the leadership no harm, for, as Norman Ward has pointed out, "it would appear to be established that one excellent way of ensuring that one will not rise to the top of the Liberal party is to start at the bottom."[63] Pearson had also surrounded himself with advisers who were more familiar with social issues than was he. Before the convention, he had expressed the view that the party should remain committed to establishing a complete system of health insurance, although only after the "other urgent commitments permit, and the essential preparations are sufficiently advanced." Moreover, the division of powers demanded that the federal government not take action until the provinces felt that full health coverage was necessary.[64] In his acceptance speech, he was just as careful to take into consideration the reality of federal-provincial relations, and as a result he sounded somewhat more conservative than the drafters of the statement on social policies had been. One of his eight main objectives was that "the autonomy of all the provinces should be strengthened" and that it was the "duty of the Federal Government to give financial assistance to provincial governments."[65] The strategy, apparently, was not to force the provinces into accepting social policies, for which they alone were largely constitutionally responsible, until they were ready. He also carefully distinguished the difference between Liberal social security and odious state interference with individual liberty. The partisan audience thought that Pearson struck just the right note, with fighting words of progressivism and reform, mixed with enough recognition of the responsibilities of power not to alienate any of the more conservative members of the party. The speech was characteristic of Pearson the diplomat and should perhaps have been taken as a warning to those committed to a thorough rewriting of the Liberal platform.

The published resolutions formed the blueprint for the Liberal campaign against Diefenbaker and outlined the new fighting breed of liberalism as well as policy objectives in external affairs, Canadian unity, economic policy, agricultural policy, and social security. The earlier drafts of the resolutions committee were more obvious in the finished product than were the suggestions from the floor of the convention, and so the resulting "New Statement of Liberal Policy" again demonstrated the power of the planners. It also sounded appreciably like Pearson's own acceptance speech, particularly in the section dealing with "liberalism for progress." There were significant overlaps in the personnel involved in drafting the resolutions, writing Pearson's speech, and subsequently putting together the Liberal policy statements.

On the issues of social security, the final statement was similar to that which came out of Croll's committee, but it included assurances that individual initiative would not be impeded by a Liberal government's implementation of further social measures. It recommended, as Croll had before, the early consideration of additional health insurance, the extension of disability pensions and old age pensions, an improvement of family allowances, and the introduction of a new, universal, contributory and portable pension plan. For those concerned that there was already too much of a social net, however, the point was made that "the social tragedies that still disfigure out society are *hard cases* which cannot be fully met by the benefits provided under any realistic general welfare schemes. A sustained drive to end such *special* hardships, in co-operation with the provinces, will have top priority in further Liberal social legislation."[66] It was a more comprehensive statement than the leader had made, but the careful balance between progress and caution demonstrated that there were still internal debates.

In acting so quickly to reproduce the policy statements coming out of the convention, it seemed that the Liberals were once again on a winning tack, armed as they were with a coherent program and a new party leader. It had been a good beginning, but as Blair Fraser wrote in *Maclean's*, Pearson still needed "time to restore order, make himself known to his own workers, [and] put the party machine back on the rails."[67] Perhaps riding high on the wave of enthusiasm from the convention, perhaps still lacking the confidence to dismiss the advice of a key politician, Pearson leapt at the first parliamentary opportunity to demand Diefenbaker's resignation, thereby giving Diefenbaker the excuse to call an immediate election. Jack Pickersgill took credit for the manoeuvre, but had he anticipated the response he would surely have kept his role secret. Constitutional expert Eugene Forsey concluded that the parliamentary strategy demonstrated that Pickersgill had a "total lack of what Borden called 'the commonplace quality of commonsense'" and the realists in the party could only hope that the result of this "first unsound tactic" would be that Pearson would learn to "distrust his overly slick advisors."[68]

The Liberal organization for the election called for 31 March 1958 was in marked contrast to that in place during previous elections. Owing in part to the fact that there was no alternative, the party electoral machine was highly centralized, with senators J.J. Connolly and Chubby Power orchestrating the action from Ottawa. Gone were the days of regional cabinet bosses. Yet, while a new era of electioneering was brought in, it happened not with a bang but with a whimper. Neither of the campaign coordinators was particularly comfortable with his position, the new leader seemed somewhat reluctantly cast in the role of focal point for the campaign, and the party platform was still in its formative stages. Moreover, Diefenbaker's folksy charm, his whistle-stop campaign, and his "agitated eloquence" captured the imagination of the country. With the help of Merril Menzies, the Conservatives had perfected their "One Canada" theme since it first appeared in 1957, emphasizing northern development through the "roads to resources" scheme and articulating a place in the polity for all those on the margins who had been excluded before. In retrospect, the Conservative landslide victory of 208 seats was surprising only in its magnitude.[69]

The election itself demonstrated the internal confusion that seemed to be plaguing the Liberal Party. There had been some important steps taken to rejuvenate the party at their leadership convention, both in terms of personnel and policy, but the party as a whole had still not moved convincingly in the direction of reform. The convention statements provided the basis for the Liberal election platform, advertised as "The Pearson Plan," but they failed to spark any enthusiasm among the voters. As he toured the country, Pearson spoke of finally implementing the mythical health-insurance plan, reducing the age requirement for pensions for working spinsters and widows, introducing a universal portable pension plan, increasing grants to universities, and increasing family allowances.[70] Despite the extravagant promises, social security was not a prominent issue in the campaign, and what little was said fell on deaf ears. Diefenbaker's first term had seen immediate increases in pensions and allowances, and the voters seemed to have a "healthy inclination to give the Conservatives a chance after so long in the wilderness."[71] Pearson appeared to be in a bidding war with Diefenbaker, in a vain attempt not only to secure votes but to demonstrate that the Liberal Party was more committed to social reform and security than were the Conservatives.[72] It was an inopportune time for the embryonic policies of the leadership convention to be paraded before the electorate – the party was still torn between the old and the new, and even those reformers committed to broadening the social net were unsure exactly how it should be done.

The election was a complete rout for the Liberals, as they lost even in their traditional stronghold of Quebec, but it was of fundamental importance.[73] While the 1957 defeat could be excused as a temporary aberration, that of 1958 indicated "that the Liberal party had imperceptibly entered a period of decline."[74] The results destroyed the last vestiges of what remained of the Liberal Party of King and St Laurent. It did not, however, shake the resolve of the reformers who had become aligned with the Liberals in 1957. As Tom Kent explained the results,

"I don't think the public was voting against Mike Pearson or against such element of a 'new look' as had been given the Liberal party at the convention and in the election platform and speeches. What the public was determined to underline was its rejection of the Liberal government as it had become under the old men. On March 31 people were still voting to punish C.D. Howe."[75] To underline his renewed commitment to resurrecting the Liberals, Kent immediately wrote to Pearson: "If it weren't for your leadership I would be very frightened for the future of Liberalism in Canada. With your leadership, we'll come out all right in time. I don't need to tell you, I hope, that the Free Press will do its utmost, and from me to you personally, I will try to be of help in any way you suggest."[76] The complete electoral disaster also encouraged others who wanted to build a progressive, leftish party from the ground up to come out of the woodwork.

Revitalization never occurs quickly. Lethargy and depression are the more likely immediate responses to failure, and so it is not surprising that the first two years following the election of 1958 have traditionally been viewed as a vacuum for the federal Liberal Party – a period of little activity and even less thought. To a certain extent, this is true. The tiny caucus that formed the official opposition to Diefenbaker's behemoth Progressive Conservative majority was largely inexperienced and bore little similarity to the party of either King or St Laurent. But, if the voices of powerful Liberals had been subdued by an electorate tired of their arrogance, they had not been silenced. While the Conservatives went about the business of governing the nation and the CCF toyed with the idea of a political partnership with organized labour, the Liberals, old and new, engaged in a quiet battle for control of the party, the result of which would ultimately dictate the policies that the Liberals would pursue in the 1960s.

Not only were the Liberals internally divided, but they faced a confident and seemingly well-organized parliamentary opponent. In the spring of 1958 the Diefenbaker Conservatives enjoyed a political dominance never before experienced in Canadian government. Their successes were based on a combination of an energetic and charismatic leader, an opposition that had lost momentum, and a political organization that seemed at least to be built from the ground up. At the helm of that political machine was Allister Grosart, president of the National Progressive Conservative Association, who had supported George Drew for the leadership of the party in 1948. Diefenbaker considered him "among a very select two or three organizers in all the political parties," high praise from a man known to carry political grudges.[77] Grosart plotted the areas of Conservative strength, cultivated the image of the leader as a populist who listened to the little man, and built the central organization into a position from which it could respond to the slightest shift in voter concern. Dalton Camp, himself an able organizer, wrote to Grosart that "there is little I can add, I am sure, to the deserved praise which has already been bestowed on you ... You have done an incredible job over the last year in forging an organization in which, in my experience, there has been a total lack of recrimination and pettiness and which, instead, there is a pervasive feeling of confidence."[78]

The same could not be said of the Liberal Party organization. Not only was there a marked lack of confidence, not surprising given the magnitude of their defeat, but there was also a considerable degree of recrimination – and the odd display of pettiness. Those who had been rejected by the electorate in 1957 and 1958 refused to leave the political scene quietly, insisting that neither their decades of service to the party nor their considerable political acumen should be dismissed in the wake of a Conservative victory. The old guard of a Liberal Party that the voters had branded as out of touch with the country spent a good deal of time in the hiatus after the 1958 election discussing the relative shortcomings of the new Pearson party, offering advice, and seeking influence.

For a number of reasons, the old party warhorses were offended by Pearson's early parliamentary performance as leader of the Liberal opposition. Harris had advised him even before the convention officially elected him as the leader that his amendment to the supply motion should deal with external affairs, Pearson's acknowledged forte. Pearson later rejected this advice on the grounds that "he must not look like Anthony Eden any longer," and Harris regretted not having pushed his case more forcefully.[79] Nevertheless, after choosing instead to follow advice proffered by Jack Pickersgill, Pearson played his hand badly. As Harris reported, "Jack is credited with the amendment and the blame. This is unfair as it was an alternative devised after my suggestion was rejected."[80] C.D. Howe was even more blunt in his assessment of Pearson's behaviour. "Mike's excuse for everything is that he accepted the advice of those he gathered around him," he complained. "I hope he will soon appreciate that a leader must decide what advice is appropriate to the occasion, and that his own judgment and responsibility are required."[81]

Pearson's actions indicated to Howe that his problem was more one of leadership than of inexperience. If this was the case, then the group of advisers that Pearson consulted, and the political organization that was built, would have to be all that much stronger and more reliable. Howe had his doubts about this, too. He himself told "Mike that advice from those who have never been elected to office, and are

unwilling to be candidates for office, must be regarded with skepti-
cism." It was a deliberate attack on Walter Gordon, who had not yet
indicated an official attachment to the Liberal Party, let alone any
desire to run for office. Howe did not think that his advice was
accepted by Pearson, although given his view "the team that he had
with him in the last election were about as inept as could have been
gathered together,"[82] he must have anticipated that the leader would
soon see the light.

The older generation of Liberals, however, did not expect to play
much of a role in rebuilding the party, except perhaps from behind the
scenes. The 1958 election had disabused them of notions of continued
power. Howe was "so shocked by the direction of the campaign that
[he] decided to take no part in it, other than to help with the financing." With the party obviously trying to distance itself from the Liberals of old, "not a word was said in defence of our program during
twenty-two prosperous years, and everything was pinned on an
attempt to out-promise Diefenbaker." Howe was left to conclude "that
the party as at present constituted is not looking for help from the
'old guard.'"[83] Jimmy Gardiner also felt alienated after 1958 and did
not bother to attend organizational functions of the National Liberal
Federation. He had "been intentionally or otherwise made to feel that
anyone who has had a successful past in the Liberal party should have
no political future." Gardiner was more specific about who should
carry the blame for what he viewed as an unfortunate turn of events.
As far as he was concerned, Pearson seemed "to be taking advice from
the group in Manitoba who ruined Liberalism in the west while Mr.
St Laurent was leader and if so our route back will be ... a long
one."[84] Liberal journalist Bruce Hutchison echoed these concerns. He
pointed out that, with the definition of Liberalism beginning to
change, many were questioning what the future would bring: "Keynes
and Kent? Debt and deficit? More government and less taxes? A slight
revision of the Regina Manifesto?"[85] The old-guard Liberal predicted
the rapid demise of his party.

Many of this group of Liberals who had learned their political skills
at the feet of Mackenzie King, and honed them under St Laurent,
identified the organization of the party in opposition as the main area
for attention. While they recognized that the central structure of the
party had been failing to function effectively throughout much of the
1950s, most neglected to notice that fundamental changes were necessary in order to deal with contemporary circumstances. "Maybe it's
a good thing that we took a licking," contended one long-time Liberal,
"because now that the deadwood has been eliminated a party can be
formed after the pattern that we used to have in the old days."[86] Since

a political machine had to contend with "a multiplicity of human beings,"[87] a static organization would not be enough – the Liberal Party was challenged to build a machine that would be able to respond quickly to the whims of the voting public, a mandate that did not necessarily mean rebuilding the organization that had proved to be so effective in the King period.

Those who rose to the challenge of rebuilding the moribund Liberal Party were generally the newer recruits. In the fall of 1958, Harvard-trained economist and ardent Quebec federalist Maurice Lamontagne suggested to Pearson that the "organization of the Liberal party ... should be under the direct responsibility of the Leader."[88] He had witnessed the party's neglect of Quebec in the past and thought that it would be more difficult for the leader to follow the same course. But Pearson, despite the high hopes for reform surrounding his selection as leader, was already beginning to demonstrate a characteristic that would grow to infuriate most of his progressive supporters: he invariably recoiled from taking a position. True to form, Pearson neither acted on Lamontagne's recommendation nor dismissed it as inappropriate. The following year, Lamontagne again attempted to explain his conception of party organization, suggesting the establishment of structures that were at once more centralized and decentralized than had been the case before. What he envisaged was one system that would be based in the riding associations, responsible for the dissemination of information, and ultimately accountable to regional organizers. The central structure, the National Liberal Federation, would be freed of organizational responsibilities and would instead devote its energies to "the continuing revision of the party platform ... Study and research could become very important functions of the Federation." Lamontagne further suggested that "we could even have an intellectual or a social leader as president of the Federation."[89] In other words, decisions of policy would be made in Ottawa and subsequently communicated to the different regions, as opposed to relying on information gleaned from powerful cabinet ministers speaking on behalf of their own areas. The grass roots of the party still played an important role in Lamontagne's system, but only in the performance of functions that "required direct contacts and detailed knowledge of people and problems at the local level."[90]

Lamontagne was not alone in advocating fundamental restructuring. Tom Kent advised that the national association be responsible for general policy, research, and publicity and that it should be a democratically elected body. Organization and finance, in Kent's view, should fall to individuals appointed by the leader. His main reason for suggesting these changes was that the existing structure relied too heavily on provincial association, and "we do not effectively mobilize for service ... those Liberals who are most deeply interested in federal issues."[91] The advice was in marked contrast to that offered by the old guard, who advocated the immediate restructuring of provincial associations.[92] However, the appointment of Keith Davey as the national director of the Liberal Party of Canada in the spring of 1961 (a new, chiefly organizational position) represented the acceptance in principle of some of the things discussed two years earlier. A strong supporter of Pearson at the leadership convention, where his lead had been followed by many other young Liberals, Davey was an energetic Liberal, a political organizer of the first order, and largely responsible for revitalizing the Toronto organization in the 1950s when it seemed that the locus of Liberal power was centred in the Canadian periphery. His political skills and his commitment to a truly national party made him an ideal choice as national director.

Though Pearson was not quick to implement sweeping changes in structure – or in policy – he was willing to work in a piecemeal fashion. The first housecleaning had taken place when most of the powerful cabinet ministers were ousted from office by the electorate in 1957 and 1958; there remained, however, a number of party officials who perpetuated the view that, if the structure of the old Liberal Party could only be repeated, victory would again be assured. The newcomers to the party, both elected and behind the scenes, believed that a revitalized brand of Liberalism demanded organizational housecleaning as well. But the work was slow and not a few people resented the changes being made by a group of men who were viewed with scepticism because of their relative lack of experience with the political system.

As far as the executives of the National Liberal Federation were concerned, "a beginning was made [in] October [1959] towards getting the Liberal Party machinery in some sort of order again – and in particular, some steps were taken to straighten out its finances,"[93] which had been left largely unattended through the previous two elections. Second World War veteran General Bruce Matthews became president of the federation in 1959 and he was also named treasurer, with the responsibility to ensure that the party was in the black. The Liberals had spent more money on the 1958 campaign than any other party, a fact that induced some of the younger potential Liberals to participate in the campaign, but the costs left a financial burden on the organization in the aftermath of defeat.[94] While Matthews put the books in order during his term as president and treasurer, the strain of filling both positions eventually led him to resign the presidency. Others gradually lost influence because their abilities and opinions no longer coincided with the kind of party that was envisaged by the "new guard." They left the party neither quietly nor happily. One of the first to go was Bob Kidd, long-time secretary of the federation, ostensibly because of his position as vice-president of Cockfield Brown, the advertising agency of the Liberal Party. Although Kidd maintained that the positions he filled were "negotiated between officials of the Liberal party and Cockfield Brown,"[95] by 1960 the dual responsibilities were seen as something of a conflict of interest. Kidd's departure was also an opportunity to end a long relationship with Cockfield Brown which, according to C.D. Howe, "have not done much for us over the years, except advocate spending money uselessly."[96]

Kidd's dismissal caused some unpleasant rifts to develop between the two generations of Liberals, but the progressive forces had the clear advantage. His long association with the party, beginning as director of publicity in 1944, endeared him to many of the veterans of the King and St Laurent administrations. Upon hearing of the consideration being given to the termination of Kidd's position, Brooke Claxton argued forcefully on his behalf. "Bob had more to do with [organizing and preparing material for the 1945, 1949 and 1953 elections] than any other single person ... it was superbly well done and ... no one could have worked more effectively over longer hours or with greater success."[97] Despite Claxton's intervention, Walter Gordon made clear at a meeting with Pearson in the spring of 1960 that the Liberal Party was no longer in need of Kidd's services.[98] The ease with which he was removed from his position upset Kidd, but no more so than the source of complaint. He confided to Duncan MacTavish that "the inner circles of the party now seem to be dominated by men from Toronto. Remembering the days of 1945 when it was like hunting a needle in a haystack to find a federal Liberal in Toronto – this is indeed a change – and for the better, of course. Nevertheless, the Toronto climate seems to have brought with it a deterioration in internal relationships which may have significant consequences on the party's future."[99] The new people who were beginning to associate themselves with the Liberal Party certainly hoped that changing existing personnel would have an effect on the party's future – they wanted to create an organization that would better reflect the new progressive orientation of the party and would similarly dissociate it from the Liberal Party of old.

Equally important, a carefully designed central organization would facilitate the achievement of the party's new social goals. The emphasis on universal assistance programs and national health insurance suggested that the Liberals were shifting away from policies that demanded strong regional bosses to interpret the needs and desires of their particular constituents. National schemes, designed to benefit all Canadians, did not need any special regional slant. They could be designed in Ottawa and advertised as part of the Liberal agenda from the central offices. These sorts of social programs, in marked contrast to policies of economic development, necessitated a strong central organization instead of strong regional structures. The organizational changes advocated by the new Liberals paralleled and were designed to facilitate the policy shift the same group of people had advanced at the leadership convention.

While the old guard grumbled about their own declining significance, the group of people whom Mike Pearson gathered around him in those dark days of opposition began the work of remaking the party in a new image. In addition to attempting some initial organizational changes in order to give more power to the National Liberal Federation and rely less on the abilities of individual regional bosses, new members of the party sought to redefine Liberalism and its component policies. Walter Gordon, not yet officially affiliated with the party, outlined his conception of economic nationalism in a variety of speeches to Toronto crowds; Tom Kent delivered an early enunciation of his philosophy of social security at the annual meeting of the Canadian Welfare Council, suggesting the importance of universal assistance programs and complete health insurance; and Quebec MP Jean Lesage outlined the new brand of fighting Liberalism, arguing "j'espère vous avoir démontré que le libéralisme n'est pas plus aujourd'hui une idée et un mouvement révolus qu'il n'était au siècle dernier une idée et un mouvement révolutionnaires."[100] Although still lacking a coherent philosophy of social security, the Liberals were at least well placed to be able to make some progress in that direction: Diefenbaker's Conservatives, after adopting hospital insurance as their own, had done little to remould the social policies of the St Laurent government, and the CCF was more concerned with extending its power base through a formal alliance with organized labour than it was with advertising its commitment to social programs.[101] As yet, however, the Liberals had done little work on developing tangible policies. Of much more importance in the early stages of what looked like a long stint in opposition was shaking off the last vestiges of the old guard and supplanting them with a rejuvenated team of Liberals. With that process well on its way, all eyes turned to the preparations for a thinkers' conference in Kingston in the fall of 1960. As Walter Gordon said, "everyone is hoping there will be some imaginative discussion about policies at the September meeting."[102] The party was certainly in need of concrete action in this area.

3 The Planning and Preparation of a Social-Policy Agenda, 1960–63

The progressive members of the Liberal Party had been slowly moving into position in the years following the selection of Lester Pearson as the new leader, but by 1960 they had still not achieved positions of unquestionable dominance. On the one hand, the politicians who had been unseated in the elections of 1957 and 1958 had refused to relinquish their positions of influence within the party without a fight. On the other, there was still a large number of active politicians and political organizers who maintained that the key to achieving power was the development of sound economic policies with only tangential attention given to the formation of the solid social programs that characterized the policy approach of the new generation of Liberals. Two events in 1960 and early 1961 marked a turning point and left those people in favour of the development of coherent and wide-ranging social policies in an ideal position to dictate the direction of the party. Alone, the intellectual think-tank known as the Kingston Conference was not particularly significant because the politicians were instinctively distrustful of the musings of a group of people with only tenuous ties to the formal Liberal Party. However, the ascendancy of the planners' stars was confirmed by the fact that the participants in the subsequent Liberal Rally, a massive grass-roots endorsement of the Kingston Conference, reached their conclusions as a result of firm but subtle guidance by the very people the politicians had most distrusted at Kingston. These new Liberals, who had been fighting for the acceptance of their social policy ideas since 1958, now found themselves in a position of relative power within the party and were able to take advantage of what, in retrospect, was obviously a brief moment in the sun to complete the initial and important drafting of health insurance and universal pensions. Whether that commitment would stay firm once the Liberals returned to office was dependent to a large degree on the headway that the planners could make during the final three years in opposition.

The September 1960 conference of "liberally-minded" Canadians held in Kingston, Ontario, fulfilled a number of different functions in the process of rejuvenating the Liberal Party. It successfully provided the opportunity for free, frank, and informed discussion of the sorts of policy options open to a Liberal government, and it also lured a number of closet Liberals into the party fold. The organizers had hoped that it would generate more widespread interest in the party, but they were less successful in achieving that goal. By essentially excluding politicians from active participation in the conference, a more dominant role for the social-policy planners was also achieved. All of the successes of the Kingston Conference, however, would have been ephemeral if they had not been the first step of the journey that led to the massive Liberal Rally four months later in Ottawa. At that event, the achievements of Kingston were etched in stone.

The idea of holding a national conference was first seriously discussed in the wake of the Conservatives' landslide victory of 31 March 1958, when the need for a re-evaluation of the Liberal future had never been clearer. Only days after the election, John Connolly, the chair of the National Liberal Campaign Committee, contacted Tom Kent and others and suggested a private, informal party meeting of fifty or sixty people to engage in "an extensive discussion of Liberal attitudes and policies."[1] No headway was made on organizing such an event, apart from the board of the party magazine's occasional promotion of a scheme to convene a conference of the party faithful, until early 1960.[2] Mike Pearson had certainly been aware of the proposal early on, but he balked at the enormity of the task of organizing such an event and put off making a decision of any kind for almost two years. By the time he acted in appointing Mitchell Sharp as the organizer of the conference, it was clear that he had not only decided to go ahead with the scheme but had also made up his mind about the sort of meeting that would best serve the needs of the Liberal Party.

Pearson's choice of Mitchell Sharp as the organizer of the conference was an important indication of its non-partisan nature. Sharp's previous connection with government had been on the purely administrative level, as a long-time civil servant and as deputy minister in the

Department of Trade and Commerce until 1957. After that time, Sharp had removed himself from Ottawa and "retired" to private industry with Brazilian Traction (Brascan) in Toronto. Pearson chose him to organize the Kingston Conference for several reasons, not least his own realization that a party-organized affair would not achieve the same goals as one that was being spearheaded, at least officially, by a man with no previous connection to a political party. Pearson approached Sharp early in 1960. "You're not a member of the party," Sharp reports that Pearson began. "You are known, however, to be liberal in your views, and I would like you to organize the conference for me. If I organize it, it will be far too partisan an affair. People will come if you invite them that wouldn't come if I invited them. And I want it to be an open conference. I want thought; I don't want simply partisan reflections."[3]

In limiting the association of the Liberal Party with the Kingston Conference, Sharp was in a position to attempt to woo people into the party's ranks. The most serious efforts were centred on achieving the participation of Claude Jodoin, president of the Canadian Labour Congress, its vice-president Frank Hall, Jean Marchand, president of the Confédération des syndicats nationaux, and William Mahoney, vice-president of the United Steelworkers of America.[4] Clearly, the Liberals were seeking to weaken the ties between organized labour and the CCF and instead assert, as did the president of the National Liberal Federation, that "the Labour movement and the Liberal party have always worked together as a team and I believe there are many who hope this teamwork will not cease now."[5] Although all but Hall attended the conference, the labour leaders did not immediately sever their connections with the CCF in order to form new alliances with the Liberals; in this regard, the organizers of the conference were perhaps more successful in attracting people of less fixed party allegiance.

Sharp sought the assistance of two of his business associates, Michael Mackenzie and Robert MacIntosh, in selecting the fifty or so people who would be invited to participate in the conference. While they avoided elected politicians, the trio hoped to include young "liberally-minded" Canadians who had recently been complaining that the party was completely "bankrupt of ideas" as well as speakers "with an established prestige."[6] Among those in the latter group, Tom Kent's participation in the conference was considered a must. He had resigned his position as editor of the Winnipeg *Free Press* in January 1959 over differences of opinion with the publisher on the need to present the news in as unbiased a format as possible; since then, he had moved on to an executive position with Chemcell, the Montreal-based subsidiary of the Celanese Corporation of America.[7] His position in charge of planning left plenty of time to work for the Liberal Party and, more important still, did not present the same possibility of conflict of interest that editorship of a newspaper had. Kent readily agreed to produce for the conference a paper entitled "Toward a Philosophy of Social Security." Sharp tried to impress on him the importance of the paper, which "should be stimulating and ... [conclude] with some definite policy recommendations. We wish," he continued, "to avoid papers that are too neutral and that do not come down definitely enough on one side or the other of contentious issues. Your paper will be the springboard for later discussion of the subject and it should, therefore, provoke your hearers to express themselves either pro or con."[8]

The exclusion of the politicians, who more than likely would have tried to give the impression that the Liberal Party had a plan when in fact the whole purpose of the conference was to try to come up with one, pleased the likes of backroom planners Tom Kent and Walter Gordon considerably. Both hoped, in Gordon's words, that the result of the Kingston Conference would be "a dynamic, expansionist philosophy and program which [the Liberal Party] will be prepared to go to bat for."[9] The politician most actively involved in the preparations was the leader himself, and he merely responded to the occasional request for advice from one of the planners or participants and did not seem to think that there was any greater role he or the other politicians ought to be playing.[10] Other Liberals, however, were less convinced of the wisdom of the conference. Paul Martin, not unsympathetic to the idea of an exchange of ideas but nevertheless part of the old guard of the party which would be under-represented at Kingston, wanted it made clear that such a conference was designed to posit propositions "beyond the grasp of the pragmatic politician" – Kingston should be in no way binding.[11] This was an obvious point of contention, since many hoped that the ideas discussed as the Kingston Conference would form the basis of a new Liberal Party platform.

When the conference finally opened on 6 September 1960, it was clear to all but those in attendance that any dream of getting the electorate excited about the rebirth of the Liberal Party would have to wait. Although almost two hundred people flocked to Kingston, four times the number on the original invitation list, enthusiastic talk of a party revival was confined to that group. The conference generated little media attention outside southern Ontario, where the Liberal Toronto *Daily Star* heralded the "break with the Liberal Party tradition of St Laurent [when] liberalism virtually disappeared from official doctrine and the party's left wing lost influence" and the Conservative *Globe and Mail* complained that the participants were "foolishly hankering after the future."[12] But the newspaper reports were scanty compared to the fanfare that some of the organizers had predicted.

The press reaction ought to have been anticipated: even if the conference was a success, it was merely the first step in a long march towards the clearly stated political commitment to new policies. The Kingston Conference was just talk – more exciting for the participants because of the large number of generally young, well-respected intellectuals and business people they were able to mingle with than for the specific ideas discussed in the panel sessions. Most of the topics covered in the formal papers, including defence, social security, and Canadian values, had been examined in detail on many other occasions. While there were moments when exciting and innovative proposals were discussed, the conference broke little new ground and certainly came to no conclusions about the direction of Liberal policy.

The papers on social security, an area that had attracted so much attention in the backrooms of the opposition offices and that was seen as a key area of policy redevelopment, were characteristic of the tone of the entire convention. Speaking on the old-age-security system in Canada, former chair of the Canadian Tax Foundation Monteath Douglas argued for a broadening of the concept of old-age assistance in order to extend aid to the destitute below age sixty-nine. Until such improvement of the existing system could be achieved, he saw little need even to discuss the merits of a contributory system, which "would operate for many years to the relative advantage of the less needy."[13] The dean of medicine at the University of Saskatchewan, J. Wendell Macleod, delivered the paper on hospital and medical-care coverage, another issue of growing interest to the Liberal Party. In the same vein as Douglas, Macleod argued that the best way to ensure the availability of health care for all was to improve programs already in existence. He thought that health-care facilities should not only be upgraded in quality but increased in quantity; that there be a greater degree of coordination of services; and that health-education standards remain high in universities. Macleod was convinced that "the solution of the financial problem of the individual or family does not itself ensure high quality care."[14] Given this view, he not surprisingly concluded that the implementation of health insurance was a low priority in the improvement of Canada's health-care system.

It was generally agreed that the most controversial discussion papers were given by Maurice Lamontagne, on his Galbraithian views of economic management, and by Tom Kent. Although Kent's discussion of the philosophy of social security followed some well-worn tracks, he challenged traditional adherence to discrete social-security measures by advocating a comprehensive, wide-ranging program. His main points were outlined in an eleven-point scheme, which included government-financed medicare delivered on a sliding scale related to income; sickness insurance as a means of income maintenance; a restructuring of the unemployment-insurance system to provide increased benefits for prolonged unemployment; employment retraining; regional development; investment in the renewal of urban cores; increased public housing; better education; and egalitarian university opportunities.[15] What marked Kent's paper as controversial was the means he suggested to pay for the increased burden of social services. One of his proposals, and the one that predictably caused the greatest stir, was that advertising be taxed. Although the proposal was "heard without challenge" at the session, sources as disparate as the *Globe and Mail* and the *Canadian Forum* held it up to ridicule and essentially diverted any attention away from Kent's more central call for a sweeping social-security program.[16] Worse still, it provided additional ammunition for Diefenbaker's arsenal of abuse as "again and again he vilified ... Tom Kent, 'a dreamer and philosophic socialist who wants to tax advertising.'"[17]

From the very beginning there had been impediments to policy development at the Kingston Conference that just would not go away. Not only was there no opportunity provided for decisions to be made, intent as the organizers were on providing merely a forum for free and frank discussion, but the politicians, who would ultimately have to hammer home Liberal policy, had always been distrustful of the conference. Despite these roadblocks, a number of people discovered over the course of the week of discussion that they could find a happy home within the Liberal Party; among these were John Turner, Maurice and Jeanne Sauvé, Jean Marchand, and Mitchell Sharp. But a new program had not been agreed upon, and the politicians seemed no more agreeable to the events of the Kingston Conference in its aftermath than they were before it commenced. The old guard reportedly complained that "this free-wheeling conference was dangerous for the party" for, as Paul Martin believed, "many of the papers presented ... directly contradicted party policy and revealed little understanding of the political process."[18] The omnipresent member from Newfoundland and political insider extraordinaire, Jack Pickersgill, was equally concerned that there was not much originality in the papers and that the participants had unfairly painted the St Laurent government as "conservative and managerial."[19] Both Martin and Pickersgill were upset by the Kent and Lamontagne papers, which they considered both an "embarrassment" and inconsistent with the "mainstream of politics," and they most likely were among the people who called for the removal of the two "radicals" from the party.[20]

For the practical and experienced politicians, it would be at the Liberal Rally, a meeting in Ottawa of Liberals from all across the country and all walks of life, that policies would be developed. A huge convention of the sort planned was considered a more appropriate political activity than the intelligentsia-driven discussions in Kingston and possibly a great opportunity to affirm to the public that Liberalism had not forgotten the individual voter.[21] But, significantly, the so-called "brains trust" of the Pearson entourage also looked forward with equal enthusiasm to the Liberal Rally. For the leader, Kingston was part of the preparatory work preceding the grass-roots convention, where the "bulging bushel of ideas, some of them good, some of them not so good," that were the result of the study conference would be somehow combined "with suggestions from the constituencies and other organizations [and] examined by the rally [from which would] flow the Liberal policies."[22] The goal of the planners was to ensure that the convention endorsed the program discussed at Kingston, thereby curtailing criticism from the old guard that the policies were too impractical and not desirable for the average Liberal voter.

By the opening of the rally in January 1961, two of the most instrumental social-policy planners had solidified their relationship with the Liberal Party and were in a position to take an active role in the event's policy discussions. Not only had Tom Kent resigned as editor of the Winnipeg *Free Press*, but Walter Gordon had spent much of 1959 and 1960 delivering public addresses on his commitment to an independent role for Canada in world affairs. He did so in the hope of eliciting Pearson's agreement on the subject, which was his precondition for any formal role in the Liberal Party. In July 1960 Pearson finally and firmly stated that he supported Gordon's views, and as a result Gordon agreed to become chair of the policy committee for the rally.[23] With Gordon at the helm, it was obvious that Kingston would not be forgotten since he made clear to Pearson that "it will be important that the people responsible for preparing the report of the Policy Committee for the rally should be at the September Conference and should be listening to the discussion with their coming task in mind."[24] Thus, in early October, he asked Kent to "put forward some specific suggestions as to what should be done about pensions and other forms of social security" and brought in Maurice Lamontagne, Maurice Sauvé, and Robert Fowler to assist in organizing the convention.[25]

The little ad hoc policy committee had its work cut out for it. The Liberal Party had always occupied the middle ground of Canadian political ideology, and as a consequence it had to appeal to people fairly widely dispersed across the centre of the spectrum. With a recent Gallup poll indicating that national support for the Liberals had increased from 37 per cent in March to 44 per cent in November, skilful draft resolutions were necessary in order to maintain the support of all sections of the Liberal coalition.[26] Kent recognized the importance of carrying along the "unadmitted conservatives, who won't argue about objectives but don't want to be committed to doing anything much about them."[27] Despite his image of progressive leadership, Pearson has to be considered part of this group since he had demonstrated all too frequently his inability to commit to policy objectives or campaign strategies for fear of making a mistake. In order to ensure resolutions that were broadly acceptable, the policy-committee members consulted widely as they worked on draft statements for discussion at the twenty-one policy sessions scheduled for the rally.

One of the most important policies for consideration was the Liberal approach to health insurance. While the Gordon-led committee members had definite views on the direction they believed the party ought to be heading, they also consulted the Canadian Medical Association and prominent Liberal organizers. The CMA was not taken seriously since it had long been a proponent of an insurance scheme financed by doctor-sponsored plans, and at a recent meeting, the results of which were made available to the rally's planners, it had undertaken to restate the composite view of the member physicians in light of the increased political interest in such plans.[28] The Liberals were committed not to a physician-sponsored scheme but to a government-sponsored one, and so it ignored the underlying principles the CMA wanted incorporated into the rally's resolution. There remained key debates over the extent of the government involvement, however. Robert MacIntosh, one of the Kingston organizers, proposed a plan with a significant annual deductible, reimbursement to the patient after services had been paid for, and a per-head payment to physicians for treating indigent patients. There was relatively little to distinguish this plan from that proposed by the CMA, and the more liberal Gordon opposed all its components, preferring to focus the debate on whether the plan should be a contributory insurance-type scheme or a straight medical-aid program.[29] There was no question that it would be universal.

The resulting policy resolution, written by Kent, who ended up doing most of the actual drafting of all of the resolutions, was broad and vague and oddly naive. But it set the Liberal Party on a course from which there would be no turning back. The Liberal "Plan for Health" started with the proposition that "many people still face medical costs, outside the hospital scheme, that are financially crippling to them." The CMA and MacIntosh plans simply did not provide adequate coverage of the population. The Liberal scheme would be universal, physicians would be remunerated out of general tax revenue on a fee-for-service basis, and prescription drugs would be included. The paper stated that "the scheme will be worked out with the provincial governments under the provisions of the BNA Act," but at the same time it gave a commitment that "the plan should not be delayed, or stalled until after a report from another Royal Commission. A new Liberal government will be ready to put this health plan into effect quickly, but with the administrative care that a sound system of this sort requires."[30] The naivety of the drafters was evident, for, as time would show, speed of implementation and provincial consultation and agreement were incompatible goals.

Unlike the Kingston Conference, which opened with little fanfare, the Liberal Rally had attracted the attention of the media even before it got under way. The press expected the recommendation of significant tax cuts, a tangible move to the left to stave off attack from the New Party (successor of the CCF and precursor of the New Democratic Party) and a clearer statement of policy than any since Pearson had taken over the leadership in 1958.[31] The more than one thousand delegates were also excited about the prospect of making real decisions about the direction of Liberal policy, and they had particularly high hopes for the session dealing with health – all the more so considering a national health-insurance plan had been supposedly part of the Liberal platform since the election of Mackenzie King as leader in 1919. In his opening address on 9 January 1961, Pearson gave the impression that the hopes of all involved would not be dashed: he forecast that the three-day meeting would be one of the most constructive in Canadian history and that "we will leave no doubt as to where we stand."[32]

As the planners had anticipated, nothing attracted more attention than the Liberal "Plan for Health" and seventy people crammed into the plenary session to discuss the resolution of the policy committee. A policy subcommittee, headed by Torontonian Dr Boyd Upper, was then charged with the responsibility of moulding the comments of participating delegates into the framework provided by Gordon's initial planners. The real point of contention was the nature of remuneration for the physicians. Some delegates questioned the government plan to pay the physicians, arguing that such a scheme bore too close a resemblance to the socialized medicine that the Saskatchewan CCF was offering, and pushed instead for a system by which the patient would initially pay for services and then be compensated. The arch-conservative Toronto *Telegram* claimed that the lengthy plenary deliberations threatened to degenerate into a fist fight, but rally chair Paul Hellyer was delighted with the discussions and stated that "the longer the deliberations the more people care – and the more people care, the better will be the policy statements."[33] By the final day of the rally, there was virtually unanimous approval for the nine-point "Plan for Health," which included all of the points that Gordon's group had hammered out before, guarantees that financial responsibility for medical bills would depend on ability to pay, and a commitment to universality.[34]

In preparing for the rally, the policy committee had devoted a great deal of time and energy to ensuring that the proposal for national medicare would appeal to all sectors of the Liberal Party and be accepted as a strong component of the revised platform. While this was, in the planners' minds, second in importance only to a plan to decrease unemployment, they also drafted policy statements on scholarships, job training, and urban renewal, all of which were to become important elements of the Liberals' social-security program. They had not, however, anticipated the delegates' interest in other areas of social policy. The policy committee had included a brief statement on the need to reduce the pensionable age for widows and unmarried women from sixty-five to sixty, but in an effort to limit its own range of social programs it had not included any other statements on pensions. The delegates to the rally were not content with the working paper and pushed for a much more inclusive pension policy. The result of the deliberations was a far broader statement, quite vague in its wording. The resolution that eventually emerged was: "The pensions presently available to many older persons are inadequate. This deficiency can be remedied either by a direct increase in monthly payments under the present old age security system or by a new contributory scheme, if this can be worked out with the provinces on a sound actuarial basis. A major objective that should be given high priority is to lower the starting age of old age pensions to 65."[35] The concerns of the delegates were to have a profound effect on the focus of the Liberal Party's social program.

The Liberal Rally, anticipated by the old guard as an appropriate expression of the will of the grass roots and destined to erase from the collective memory of the party the foolish notions discussed by the intellectuals as the Kingston Conference, actually *confirmed* the policy direction established at the conference. The rally's participants endorsed the fundamental Kingston ideas, particularly in the areas of social policy, and even went farther in articulating progressive old-age-pension policies. But this was not merely coincidence. The Kingston participants recognized that the only way to make their ideas relevant was to have them endorsed by the grass roots that the politicians put so much faith in; as chief policy planner Walter Gordon noted, the rally might "have been a ghastly failure without all of the preliminary work that went into the policy issues."[36] The ad hoc policy committee had worked feverishly to turn the Kingston ideas into concrete resolutions that would appeal to the Liberal delegates, and in that they had been successful. Robert Fowler still felt that "the statements we produced [at Kingston] were better than those that came from the Rally," and the entire committee realized that it still needed to work with the resolutions that emerged from the rally and "change them to some extent and sharpen up the language,"[37] but the rally had transformed the Kingston proposals into tangible, and palatable, plans. The ability of the policy planners to take advantage of their newfound preeminence within the Liberal Party and force the Liberals to articulate clear and coherent social-policy objectives would play an important role in the party's return to power.

The period between the close of the Liberal Rally and the eventual return of the Liberals to power in 1963 was one of frantic activity for the policy planners. For slightly more than two years, those people who were committed to the formulation of progressive universal social programs were in their prime within the Liberal Party and those programs received enormous and concerted attention. Yet the positions of Tom Kent, Walter Gordon, and the various other figures associated with the left wing of the party were not inviolable. Constant activity was necessary to ward off the threat presented by other parties and, perhaps more important, to keep the more reluctant Liberals firm in their resolve to implement national health care, welfare reform, and universal pensions once in power. It seemed a never-ending battle against the enemies of hesitation, obfuscation, and bafflegab, but the social-policy planners had earned their political legitimacy both through the strength of personal integrity and commitment and through their dominance of the Kingston Conference and the Liberal Rally. They were thus well positioned, or at least as well positioned as they would ever be, to design programs, force their inclusion in the official Liberal platform, and tie the Liberal Party to progressive social policies so tightly in the collective mind of the electorate so as to make virtually impossible any backtracking once in office.

The first matter of business was to turn the rally's statements from expressions of possible policy direction into official Liberal election promises. Pearson was evidently not going to be much help in this process. He privately conceded that the resolutions would be of little use in articulating policy and publicly, according to Gordon, gave the appearance of wanting to drop the "whole thing like a hot potato."[38]

This was characteristic of Pearson, who seemed virtually incapable of committing to a position for fear of alienating its critics. He was especially wary of destroying his image as "a responsible public figure who would not indulge in a competition of promises."[39] But the early indications were that the delegates' resolutions on social policy had struck a sympathetic chord with Liberals across the country and with a broad cross-section of society as well. At the annual meeting of the Manitoba Liberal Association, Kent offered a distillation of the social goals of the party agreed to at the rally which was received enthusiastically. Expressing the importance of "counting costs" in meeting the Liberal agenda of health insurance, pensions, university scholarships, and low-income housing, he stressed that the evaluation of "what we can afford to do" included "what we can't afford to leave undone."[40] An even more ringing endorsement of the rally's resolutions came in the form of an unsolicited national-opinion survey conducted by McLaren Advertising. The survey found widespread sympathy for a government-sponsored health-insurance plan, especially in urban areas and west of Quebec. Quebeckers were more likely than any other group to prefer a provincially run scheme, while others tended to favour a joint federal-provincial program. The survey also indicated that social policies were the area in which the Liberals could take the most advantage of perceived party differences.[41] Despite its flaws, the survey validated the direction the social-policy planners wanted to take the party.

Obviously, a universal pension scheme needed to be outlined, since the rally's participants had made known the centrality of such a program to the grass-roots view of social welfare, but the planners continued to devote their initial attention to health insurance, which was considered the more complicated of the two plans. Gordon, Kent, Sauvé, and Boyd Upper, the rally's health-policy chair, set to work defining provincial participation, universality, and funding, disagreeing only occasionally on the question of timing. Gordon, a progressive Liberal but nevertheless a scion of Toronto's financial establishment, argued that it would be "impractical to introduce the health plan until the economy proceeds to expand again." Kent insisted that there ought not to be "'ifs' and 'buts'" attached to Liberal promises.[42] Upper felt that there was "a certain critical element becoming manifest in the electorate about giveaways and welfare."[43] Still, it was a close-knit committee, with all members in agreement on the necessity of concerted action in the field of national health insurance.

The real problem was in getting the Liberal ideas out of the backrooms, which were still backrooms despite being occupied by new people, and into the public forum. This became increasingly important as the other two major parties were seen to be making tangible advances in the social-policy field. Diefenbaker's Conservatives, characteristically, made the clumsiest and most hesitant moves, but they were actually achieving progress. Just before the opening of the rally, Diefenbaker announced the establishment of a royal commission on health insurance and named his old friend and fellow Conservative Emmett Hall to head it.[44] The Conservatives had decided to act, or at least discuss the subject, at the urging of the Canadian Medical Association, which favoured federal-government involvement in the delivery of health insurance only to the extent of "grants in aid for the indigent or catastrophe situation."[45] Quite suddenly, health insurance had become an issue which the Conservatives regarded as "of extreme importance to the progressive development of Canada's National Health Program."[46] Although Minister of National Health and Welfare Waldo Monteith still tried to avoid "the degree of overexposure which my predecessor achieved so successfully," by the autumn of 1961 Diefenbaker began to stress the importance of "continually [updating] the measure of social justice which makes the opportunity of free enterprise truly available to all of our people."[47] The Conservative Party needed to develop its social-policy platform in order to appeal to the electorate: it was no longer sufficient to remind the voters of the pension-policy mistakes of the Liberals in 1957.[48] The Conservatives belatedly offered some tangible proof that they recognized the centrality of social security but, given the then-astronomical unemployment rates of over 7 per cent, they persisted in placing control of the Unemployment Assistance Act at the top of their agenda and argued in cabinet about the necessity of contributory pensions.[49]

It was in the party on the left of the Canadian political spectrum that the most changes were occurring – changes largely to the structure of the party itself but ones that would affect the way the public perceived its approach to social policy. The old CCF, which remained strong in its birthplace of Saskatchewan, had been experiencing decreasing popularity at the national level since Diefenbaker took the country by storm in 1957. His own Saskatchewan roots, his fiery oratory, and his grass-roots commitment to the "little man" cut deeply into CCF strongholds and caused worry that the three-party Canadian experiment would come to an end at the national level if decisive action were not taken immediately. To this end, there had been a movement afloat since the late 1950s to reorganize the federal CCF into a more broadly based party. The Winnipeg Declaration of 1956 had laid much of the ideological foundations for more moderate CCF policies,[50] and with it in place there was renewed pressure to create a more broadly based coalition of support.

After years of preparation and negotiation the formal consummation of the marriage between the old CCF and labour organizations occurred at the Ottawa Coliseum in the summer of 1961. In preparation for this event, the official national CCF had ceased to exist after 1959 and instead the group of politicians who looked to M.J. Coldwell as their leader adopted the moniker "New Party" despite there being little to distinguish the "new" from the "old" until after events at the founding convention. The more than two thousands delegates, composed of farmers, union members, socialists, and the "liberally-minded," had high hopes for this latest attempt at restructuring and recasting Canada's left-wing political party – as high, almost, as the sweltering mid-summer heat inside the cavernous Coliseum. Different groups had conflicting goals for the convention, and not all were met, but most significantly the congregation was successful in its most pressing problem – the seduction of the ever-popular premier of Saskatchewan, Tommy Douglas, as the new national leader. Douglas was the CCF's most successful politician, he commanded the respect of Canadians from all political parties, and his evangelical fervour, commitment to the essentials of social democracy, and ability to turn a comment into a catchphrase set him apart as one of Canada's most popular and colourful public figures ever. With Douglas at the helm, and only with Douglas, the New Party might possibly come to power. Despite Hazen Argue's bid to win the leadership against Douglas, the results were never in doubt since labour and the kingpins of the CCF – David Lewis, Stanley Knowles, and Coldwell – were firmly in Douglas's corner. The convention voted 1,391 to 380 in favour of Douglas. The decision to adopt the label of the New Democratic Party (NDP), while certainly more of a compromise than the decision about the leader, was another major result of the founding convention.[51]

The policies that the NDP adopted, to which opposition political observers paid close attention, drew different responses, but most Liberal planners saw little in the NDP's program that threatened their own party's social-policy course. So busy were the NDP delegates electing a leader and a name, and deciding on approaches to federal-provincial relations and national defence, that nothing was decided about either a national health plan or a contributory pension scheme, both issues being left to the national council to consider at a later date. The founding convention did not provide the opportunity for publicizing the party's policies nationally, and in any case, of those policies that had been debated at the meeting, there seemed to some observers "little in the platform in which the liberals would take exception."[52] Other commentators expressed delight with the "salutary example of democracy in action" as delegates directed the party with their votes, and for the most part the convention was seen as a "triumph for the moderate majority over the small, but tenacious, left-wing minority," one that resulted in a "defensible program without diluting its [the left's] principles beyond the point of recognition."[53] But even as it was being made clear by the actions of the founding delegates that the NDP was moving towards the political centre and thus encroaching on traditional Liberal territory, Liberal insiders remained convinced that it "doesn't offer the voters an alternative to the Liberal and Conservative parties. It is simply an immature Liberal party, not quite certain where it is headed, badly split by ideological disputes. The men who brought it into being, the men at the top, are political adventurers and masters of expediency, barren of profound political convictions."[54] Few would really accept the dismissiveness of this view, but Tom Kent was alone in wishing that the party on the left would hire an expert speech writer "with vitriol but not dogma" who would "play with our doubts and wobbles, our cross-currents and contradictions, our undigested mixtures of progressivism and conservatism [and therefore] provoking us ... to make up our minds."[55] Complacency, even in the face of a direct threat, was the more common Liberal approach.

The most serious offender was the leader himself. Mike Pearson had an almost pathological unwillingness to make decisions, although whether this was genetic or strategic is somewhat unclear. A few of his close associates have argued that Pearson was in fact a shrewd and experienced manipulator who played his advisers off against each other.[56] While his habit of consulting widely allowed him to convince his advisers that he relied on their assistance, and in the minds of some indicated a non-partisan approach to politics, it also masked his own fundamental reluctance to commit to one position and his insecurity as leader of the party.[57] Whatever the reason for his leadership style, Pearson's refusal to decide upon a particular approach – especially on issues of social security – was infuriating to many and served only to steel the resolve of his most progressive advisers.

There was nothing out of the ordinary about the difficulty the social-security advisers had in forcing the leader to come out publicly and strongly in favour of the sorts of programs that had been agreed upon at the Liberal Rally. Speaking to the Canadian Club in early spring 1961, Pearson ignored the planners' advice and spoke vaguely and defensively about Liberal social goals; he then was forced to explain to Kent why he had "put the emphasis with regard to expanded public activity in a rather different place than you would have done, even though we are both in agreement on the principles and objectives of such activity. I did this deliberately because I think it is important for me at this stage to counteract the impression which the Tories are actively and intentionally trying to create that our proposals are merely examples of give-away irresponsibility."[58] Kent was not moved by the explanation, arguing that Conservative charges of "give-away irresponsibility" were only a "stick to beat us with, and that one is weaker than most."[59] But Pearson remained unprepared to commit the party to a course of social-security advances and his failure to align himself with the progressive members of his own party threatened the ability to plan for the next election. It took a "free and unhurried discussion" between Pearson, Lamontagne, Gordon, and Kent regarding "the fundamentals of strategy" and the incontestable reality of an approaching election as Diefenbaker moved into his fourth year in office before the leader began making more categorical statements about Liberal social policy.

An address given on national radio in October 1961 marked the first time Pearson clearly identified the social objectives of the Liberal Party. On this occasion he stated:

And because growth and expansion can be achieved, a new liberal government will move promptly forward in the social welfare policies that we first introduced to Canada. We will ensure, through a medical care plan, that no Canadian family goes without adequate health services or is financially crippled as a result of costly illness. We will develop, on a contributory basis and in co-operation with the provinces, better pension arrangements. That's one of the essential ways, I believe, to adapt ourselves to modern science. Most people nowadays have more years after retirement. But too often, they are years of unnecessary misery and loneliness for our older citizens themselves, and a burden on their families. So it is an obligation of a responsible society to make possible retirement without worry. But I don't believe we can do that on a simple hand-out basis. We need sound government plans to which the individual himself contributes. That's Liberal policy.[60]

The articulation of Liberal social goals was clearer than it had been in the past, and the programs were no longer obviously contingent upon a strong economic outlook for Canada. As Pearson explained to a prairie audience, the achievement of a national pension plan would be done "steadily and responsibly, as fast as all the other obligations of Canadian governments at all levels for health, for education, for economic development, for defence, and all the things that make a better life for all Canadians."[61] Social policies were described not as a second tier of Liberal promises but as an important component of the first.

A somewhat more aggressive approach on Pearson's part was exactly what had been needed to spur the planning behind the scenes.

Already, the party had set up a leader's advisory committee to orchestrate election planning, its work being directed by tireless National Director Keith Davey, who wanted to stress a "simple positive programme" that emphasized the merits of a new Liberal government. A national health-insurance plan and better pensions were key parts of the platform "that everyone will know about and stick to."[62] Significantly, this strategy was in marked contrast to that employed in earlier elections, when policy had moved from the ground up with very little control exerted by the national level. The next election was to be fought from the centre, and policies were to be designed by those central-election strategists within the Liberal Party in such a way as to appeal to all the electors, without need for specific regional interpretation.[63]

Even farther behind the scenes, but of key importance to the development of these programs which were to be explained on the hustings across the country, a group of advisers worked to put flesh on the bones of the social proposals that had been being tossed around for the previous three years. Pensions had become the bailiwick of the most influential politicians in the party and it was to this subject that the planners first turned their attention. Although there were those, like Kent, who consistently advocated a comprehensive approach to social policy and argued against sweeping health insurance, education and housing grants, and welfare increases "under the blanket of bigger pensions ... for all," even he ultimately had to concede to the "practical politics" of promising a plan that would be relatively easy to achieve.[64] Thus, committed to a contributory pension scheme, Pearson gave a small committee drawn from business and provincial politics the responsibility of examining the question of pensions and reporting back to the party on the most effective way of implementing a new program. David Stanley, of Wood Gundy, was the chair of the group, which included G.R. Conway, M.P. O'Connell, P.F. Oliphant, and Andrew Thompson. Walter Gordon's hand in selecting the members of the committee, and therefore his key position in the determination of pension policy, is obvious: the first three were to gain ignominy as the "whiz kids" in the 1963 budget debacle.

The plan that this group devised was contributory, with a percentage of the earnings of each worker being paid by both the employee and the employer, initially at a rate of about .5 per cent of actual earnings from each. Each employee would be eligible to receive one-third of his or her earnings during their most prosperous years, up to a maximum of $500 per year. Moreoever, the pensions were to be completely portable, compulsory for all employers and wage earners, and open to the interested self-employed, and the rights to the pension would not be lost if a person suffered unemployment. Since the plan would not be fully operational for ten years, and would not apply completely to people currently between the ages of sixty and seventy, the Liberal Party announced its support for an increase in the old age pension of $10, to a new minimum pension of $75 per month for single people and $135 per month for married couples.[65] Although the implementation of a pension plan obviously involved achieving the agreement of the provinces, it would not be a joint federal-provincial initiative. The Liberal Party had underlined its attitude towards intergovernmental relations at the 1961 rally and in further statements made by Pearson: the federal level would cease to participate financially in permanent joint programs, and would provide compensation to provinces through a reduction in federal direct taxes and equalization payments, and would set up guidelines for contracting-out of new programs.[66] The federal-provincial aspects of the pension plan were to be worked out in accord with this new view of "co-operative federalism."

The reaction to the plan was enthusiastic. The preliminary outline was presented in a small pamphlet on the Liberal pension plan, timed perfectly to deflect attention from the January 1962 Speech from the Throne which announced the Conservatives' initiative in contacting provincial premiers in order to get what they considered the necessary constitutional amendment for contributory pensions.[67] Despite its having been drafted in the new backrooms of the Liberal Party, the experienced politicians set aside any misgivings they might have felt towards the new brains trust and expressed delight with the outline of the plan. Martin found it so superior to other proposals that it would put pensions "out of reach of political maneuver or mismanagement" and "eliminate the ... cynical competition of seeking voters by making pension promises to the older people of the country."[68] Even in business circles, "the reaction has been generally favourable; the policy has ... been regarded as a practical and responsible approach to a difficult national problem."[69] But the job of the planners was far from over; with pensions out of the way, attention had to turn to devising approaches to the other Liberal social-policy proposals.

The group of people brought together to compose a Liberal health-insurance policy were, significantly, the same group as had produced the report on contributory pensions, a fact which suggests that their expertise lay in service to the Liberal Party rather than in superannuation. Tom Kent and Walter Gordon joined to round out the committee that was charged with the responsibility of determining whether public or private insurance carriers would be used, the necessity of deterrent fees, and the extent of the coverage. Pressed for time, as it became clear that an election was imminent, and without the luxury of previous investigations into the subject, the committee produced a report that was unsatisfactory in comparison to the clarity of the pension proposal. The policy objective was clear: "to wipe out the fear of heavy medical bills" and "to attract people into medical practice and research, so that better service can be provided for all." It was the details of the plan that remained murky. The proposed scheme promised to use existing administrative machinery to finance, out of general tax revenue, insurance for physician, diagnostic-service, and prescription-drug fees as well as pay sickness-insurance benefits. Whether a means test would be required, whether private insurance companies would continue to provide health coverage, and how provincial jurisdiction over both insurance and health service would be affected were questions that remained unanswered.[70]

Nor was there any time left to refine the social-policy objectives into anything that would provide the electorate with a concrete plan of action. After weeks of threatening, Diefenbaker finally dissolved Parliament on 18 April 1962, calling an election for 18 June. With the campaign under way, the Liberal strategy was to provide voters with definite proposals, focusing on health and pensions as the cornerstones of Liberal social policy, and thereby demonstrate "the contrast between the [Conservative] record and the action a new Liberal government would take."[71] Kent cautioned against the defensive approach, arguing that the previous Liberal administration should not be held up as an example of what was in store under Pearson: "there is no profit in defending what the public has already voted against."[72] This tactic was in marked contrast to that of Diefenbaker, who believed that a lack of major issues favoured the party in power and thus campaigned almost exclusively on his record.[73]

For the Liberals, the plan to emphasize specific policies meant that the physical structure of the campaign would be different from that pursued in previous elections. The renewed emphasis on social policies that would be implemented identically across the country allowed the party to demand that each local politician follow the same, centrally administered formula and not rely on his or her ability to interpret the national agenda for regional consumption. Pearson's national tour was itself a carefully orchestrated event, with J.J. Connolly, publicist Richard O'Hagan, and Tom Kent having primary responsibility for ensuring that the Liberal platform was appropriately conveyed.[74] This "team" around Pearson also promised to be a central feature of a Liberal government, since the politicians boasted that they would introduce "a task force of brains to solve current difficulties."[75] But, despite the new approach to campaigning, the arsenal of new social proposals, and the early indications that the Conservatives would go down to defeat, public sympathy began to turn in favour of the much-harassed Diefenbaker, and apparently neither Pearson nor his policies inspired support. Both major parties failed to achieve what they had hoped: the Conservatives were reduced to a minority position and only 116 seats, and the Liberals again failed in their attempt to regain power despite doubling their number of MPs to 100. The NDP was unable to reap the promised benefits of a coalition with organized labour, winning a mere 19 seats. Only the Social Credit in Quebec achieved more than was expected, electing 26 members and therefore holding the balance of power in Parliament. It had been, as Pearson complained, a "very rugged and exhausting" campaign.[76]

With Diefenbaker reduced to a minority government, the Liberals could find some solace in the inevitability of an early election, and as a result they merely tinkered with the existing machinery and strategies.[77] The Liberal Party of 1962 seemed firmly committed to changes in social policy and even the leader had begun to campaign on this issue. In the area of policy development, it was, as usual, Kent who offered an assessment of what needed to be altered in order to turn the next election into a winning effort. He firmly believed that Liberals were convinced of the necessity of the programs the ad hoc advisory committee had devised for pensions and health insurance, but he felt equally strongly that the somewhat cautious approach currently advocated – cautious, at least, in contrast to the mandate provided by the 1961 rally – was acceptable only if "the party said fairly definitely what it would do."[78] It was the definition that had been missing in the 1962 election campaign, an especially critical mistake in the light of Ontario's recent inquiry into the feasibility of provincial portable-pension schemes and Saskatchewan's attempt to introduce province-wide medical insurance. Both the provincial Conservatives and the NDP were making tangible advances in the social-security field; the national Liberals had to specify how their proposals surpassed the provincial plans. Keith Davey's investigation into the success of the central management of the campaign yielded similar assessments of "what went wrong." In general, the central direction was positively regarded by local politicians, although those in the west were most likely to argue that "there could have been more regional representation on the National Campaign Committee and more thorough solicitation of regional ideas prior to the Campaign," a complaint which suggested a growing sense of alienation in regions that had traditionally been both consulted on policy issues and rewarded for their support. But most telling was the sentiment that "we had succeeded in bringing the Tories to their knees but we failed to move in for the kill – that is, we failed either to be 'specific' or to present a positive alternative."[79] It was exactly this sort of ambiguity that the Liberals had to avoid the next time around.

The health plan, which had been cobbled together in the aftermath of fairly extensive analysis of the pension problem, clearly needed work, and it was to this task that the advisers turned their post-election attention. After identifying three possible approaches to health insurance, including full government coverage over a specific annual amount per family, full coverage of costs exceeding 3 per cent of family income, and full coverage for those over age sixty-five and under age sixteen, the advisory committee members were given a week to reach their individual decisions.[80] The resulting draft statement on "health care as needed" was a compromise of sorts but clearly a victory for those favouring quick and decisive action. The new Liberal government would immediately introduce full coverage for children through secondary school, the aged over sixty-five, and those out of work for two months or more, and it would cover all physicians' bills above the first $25 for those between the ages of full coverage. The committee estimated that the plan would cost the federal treasury something over $200 million the first year, but "with full employment and the sort of annual economic growth that was usual in Canada before 1957," the halcyon era of Liberal domination which the planners of the 1960s used as their economic ruler, "federal revenues from present taxes rise – because peoples' incomes improve – by about $500 millions a year."[81] An additional tax increase would not be necessary.

The needs of physicians, expressed both through the Canadian Medical Association and through individual representation to the Liberal health committee, had not been forgotten. Not only would patients be free to see the doctor of their choice, but physicians themselves would be under no compulsion to practise within the confines of the government plan. They would receive their remuneration on an agreed, fee-for-service basis, which was left undefined pending the negotiations with the medical community that would follow a Liberal election victory. The same promise of "full consultation" was true for the provinces. The report stressed that "there will be no restriction on the freedom of action of the provinces. A province that wants to set up a different type of health plan will be able to do so. It will, in any event, receive from the federal government the costs of the services ... described. Additional services can be financed, by provinces that desire them, from provincial revenues or by means of a premium."[82] The Liberal plan also included a form of sickness insurance paid through the existing unemployment-insurance scheme to cover loss of income during bouts of illness, an increased scholarship and grant program in part designed to increase the existing pool of Canadian physicians, and proposals to broaden the plan at some indeterminate point in the future to provide even more comprehensive health coverage.

The plan was not without its critics. The insurance industry mounted a massive attack against any further shifts in the direction of government-administered health insurance. With David Kilgour, president of Winnipeg's Great-West Life Assurance Company, as their spokesperson, and the Saskatchewan doctors' strike as their catalyst, members of the Canadian insurance industry increased their efforts to nip government involvement in health insurance in the bud. In a widely distributed speech to the American Life Convention, Kilgour warned that "there are politicians in every party and well-meaning, if utterly ill-informed, people in all walks of life who are anxious to put the show on the road without the slightest assurance that it might not do irreparable damage to both our medical care, and our national and provincial financial health."[83] He identified three "elements" that represented Canada's only hope of preventing "any further precipitous action" in the health-insurance field: the necessary increase in taxation, particularly in a period of financial austerity, would require government "to take a very sober look before leaping into the very deep water of medical care"; the final report of the Hall commission would have to be received and studied before any government would dare to take any action; and finally, and obviously most closely tied to the Kilgour's own professional interests, the "very many serious people in all walks of life [who] are thoroughly alarmed by the narrow ledge upon with the voluntary system apparently stands in this field and are determined to do something about it."[84]

The Canadian Chamber of Commerce was one such group. It vehemently opposed further government commitments in the social-security field, believing that "existing commitments are substantial and are recurring and increasing" and that a "dangerous situation exists with an increasing proportion of the national income required to meet government expenditure of which welfare payments are an ever-increasing part."[85] As far as the business association was concerned, "the adequacy of voluntary health care prepayment and insurance plans give substance to its firm opposition to any form of compulsory national health insurance or socialized medicine." The chamber was further convinced that "a compulsory plan is not only unnecessary but would impose an unbearable additional strain on the finances of the country."[86] This was merely a reiteration of the points made in the Chamber of Commerce's submission to Hall's royal commission, but because the organization was deeply disturbed by the Liberal platform an additional audience for its concerns could do no harm.

The Liberals remained undeterred by these tactics. Having admitted the need for prepaid coverage on a universal basis, Kilgour proposed providing coverage for the people regarded as "non-insurable" out of the premiums paid by other people. As Kent noted, "when he feels compelled to retreat this far, the battle for a health plan is no longer in doubt; it's going to be won."[87] He went on to explain to the leader the aspects of Kilgour's plan that made it untenable, most importantly the fact that it failed to take into consideration the ability to pay, an issue that "matters a bit too much [to the Liberals] to be violated for the sake of keeping the insurance companies in business."[88] Kent's counter-attack was reasoned and mindful of the economic implications of a national health plan while at the same time remaining true to social principles to which the party had made a commitment.

The Liberals did not have much time to prepare for the federal election that Diefenbaker called for 8 April 1963. Events had moved quickly following the Christmas recess. The long-simmering Conservative cabinet crisis came to a boil over Diefenbaker's chronic indecisiveness about nuclear weapons, dividing caucus enough that Social Credit was able to pass a motion of non-confidence. The 25th Parliament thus ended abruptly on 6 February 1963, and all parties scurried to begin campaigning.[89] The Liberal pension scheme had been untouched since the 1962 campaign, although the advisory committee on national health insurance had managed to clarify the Liberal position on that component of the social-policy agenda. Indeed, in contrast to the Conservatives' position on social policy, the Liberal schemes seemed carefully constructed. The Conservatives were saying little about health insurance but had focused on pensions to the extent that the interdepartmental committee on social security had examined alternative approaches.[90] All that the committee could agree upon, however, was that there were certain benefits to the pension plan envisaged by Ontario's committee on portable pensions.[91] Thus, in embarking on the second election campaign in less than a year, the Liberals felt that they needed only to present their platform to the electorate in a clear and comprehensive manner.

The election of 1963 was not won or lost on the issue of social security; the cabinet crisis served to deflect attention from that subject and focus it instead on defence, foreign affairs, and the personalities of the leaders.[92] Given the chaos within his own party, Diefenbaker should have faced defeat from the outset, but adversity served only to enhance his natural flair on the hustings. "The way John Diefenbaker is behaving," the Ottawa *Citizen* pointed out, "it's as though he had found the politician's Eldorado, the fount from which he could draw inexhaustible reserves of energy, optimism and self-confidence ...

There he is, night after night, cavorting on the platform as though it were in the springtime of his career, slaying dragons left and right, chuckling about his difficulties with his cabinet, sentimentally reminding his audience that he is one of them, a humble farm boy moved by some predestination to come forth and protect the 'average man.'"[93]

Pearson, on the other hand, seemed barely able to keep up. The campaign organization was virtually identical to that of 1962, and the message Pearson and his team provided was equally similar to the broadcasts of the previous year. Diefenbaker's magnificent performance on the campaign trail, where the Liberals complained that he acted not "unpredictably but in an unpredicted fashion,"[94] forced Pearson and his group to resort to desperate manoeuvres in the dying days of the election. Pearson's advisers wanted him to make nine pledges – one on each of the remaining days before the vote – and to commit the party to "60 days of decision" in which the corresponding legislation would be brought before the House of Commons. A national contributory pension plan was one of the main pledges for the first two months of Liberal government. Health insurance, a much larger problem in the eyes of the politicians, had to wait, but it, too, was promised on the hustings. The combination of Diefenbaker's early bumbling, Pearson's more decisive-sounding campaign promises, and an electorate eager for change, served to win the Liberals enough seats to form the next government. With 129 seats to the Conservatives' 95, the NDP's 17, and Social Credit's 24, the Liberals had fallen short of their goal of a majority victory. For the first time in six years, however, they were back in a position of power, and their social policies balanced on the precipice between promise and reality.

4 Early Obstacles to Pension Reform, 1963

The Liberal Party seemed much more united in 1963 than three years earlier. The distance between the St Laurent and the Pearson administrations was great enough, both in terms of time and ideology, to suggest to Canadians that they had elected a government committed to implementing important social policies as a matter of national responsibility. While it was certainly true that some Liberals had endorsed pension- and health-insurance plans merely as a strategic way to win back the public support and return to office, there were other planners and politicians who recognized social security as an inherent right of citizenship. As a result, the national government appeared ready to play a more active role in the lives of individual Canadians, no longer resigned to let ten different provincial administrations design ad hoc mechanisms of protection or leave peoples' ability to attain basic health and welfare benefits to the whims of uncontrollable economic fluctuations. The Liberal Party's more activist stance on the social-security front had been obvious in the backrooms of opposition and represented a philosophical victory at least for the left side of the party.

Regardless of appearances, however, the gains that had been made by the social-policy advocates in the last few years of Liberal opposition were deceptive and served only to camouflage some fundamental weaknesses. At least part of the problem was that the Liberal's social policies had been, to a large extent, designed in a vacuum. Despite Tom Kent's most earnest efforts to force the politicians to elaborate clearly the details of the pension and health programs, most campaign promises had been relatively vague and restricted to guarantees of Liberal action without specifying the course that action would take. Moreover, since there had been little contact with provincial governments and only cursory meetings with extra-parliamentary lobbies, the Liberals were uncertain of the strength of their opponents. In power, the Liberals needed to be both united and committed to the policies they had advocated on the hustings, for it was as the government that they would face their fiercest critics. But, with the achievement of power and the shift in focus from appealing to the electorate to providing sound government, many in the party reverted to their old opposition to expensive social programs. The first few months of office resulted in the emergence of party divisions that had been hidden since the late 1950s; the lure of an escape to more traditional policies proved too attractive to ignore.

Furthermore, as a minority government, the Liberal Party was in a strategically weak position. The new prime minister slept fitfully on election night 1963, wondering whether he would "prove equal to the heavy burdens of governing without a majority."[1] The demands of minority government were such that the Liberals had to retain the support of another group in Parliament, a state of affairs that raised questions about the feasibility of implementing some of the more imaginative pieces of the Liberal policy agenda. In 1963 the Liberals' numerical weakness in the House of Commons forced the party into making a number of decisions that seriously threatened the position of the social-security advocates and, therefore, the future of the programs themselves. This, combined with the realization that there was strong opposition to the implementation of national social-security schemes, served to derail the best laid Liberal plans.

On the advice of people eager to capitalize on the obvious indecisiveness of the Diefenbaker administration, Pearson had concluded the 1963 campaign by promising that a Liberal government would begin with "60 days of decision." In retrospect, many people felt that they should not have promised that so much would be accomplished in the first two months. Pearson had stated that he would call Parliament at the earliest possible moment, thereby ensuring that the clock started counting off the sixty days almost immediately. Tom Kent, however, maintains that the pledge made the difference in winning the election, and he gives Keith Davey full credit for the inspiration.[2] The goal was to create in the voters' minds the sense that the Liberals would bring new energy to government. Those first two months, however, were anything but a demonstration of the strength of Liberal administration.

Instead, because of its minority position and its own self-imposed deadline, the Liberal Party appeared divided, particularly in regard to social-policy objectives.

The first act of a new prime minister is the creation of a cabinet and Pearson had no more difficulty than usual. Saskatchewan was the only province that failed to elect a Liberal, and although the party's strength was clearly in Ontario and Quebec, there was a wide array of political talent, both old and new, from which to chose cabinet ministers. The twenty-seven people he ultimate settled upon were regarded favourably by the press, and heralded by John T. McLeod in the Toronto *Star*, as "the most impressive array of brains ever assembled in a Canadian Cabinet."[3] Even less staunchly Liberal newspapers echoed the praise, despite there being few surprises in Pearson's choices. Walter Gordon was the new finance minister, a selection that had seemed a foregone conclusion since 1959; Paul Martin found himself at External Affairs; Lionel Chevrier became minister of justice. There did seem one flaw, however, and it did not go unnoticed. Walter Gordon, who was to be profoundly affected by the choice of cabinet ministers, recalled that "the over-all impression of the first Pearson government was that the 'old guard,' who were not wholeheartedly in sympathy with the party's new policies, many of whom had not contributed very much to the electoral victory, were to predominate. In a way, it was a triumph for seniority over the new spirit which had been created in the Liberal Party."[4]

It was an observation that others made as well. For example, the Ottawa *Citizen* announced that "Prime Minister Pearson has chosen experience over youth and service over promise ... Wherever Mr. Pearson had a choice, he appointed the men he knew and trusted over the glamorous rookies."[5] Keith Davey, another of the new young Liberals, made a similar complaint: "Quite frankly, I thought [Pearson] had forgotten about our new politics when he appointed such dreary, old guard politicians."[6] Others saw the choice of cabinet ministers as "a deliberate attempt to straddle the centre until the government can win a clear and comfortable majority," leaving in question whether the Liberal Party intended to move to the right or to the left.[7] It was a safe cabinet, not a progressive one.

National Health and Welfare Minister Judy LaMarsh, a young lawyer from Niagara Falls who first won a seat in a by-election in 1960, was a surprise to many. As the minister responsible for guiding the implementation of the proposed pension plan, not to mention a national health-insurance plan, through the stormy waters of federal-provincial relations, LaMarsh obviously had her work cut out for her. Despite her long service to the party and her not inconsiderable political skills, her appointment raised questions about Pearson's commitment to social policies. Pearson thought that Health and Welfare was an appropriate position for a woman, perhaps focusing more on the "social" aspects of social security than on the potential for serious constitutional and political battles. In the days before the prime minister announced his cabinet selections, LaMarsh herself was reasonably confident that Pearson would want to follow established precedent and include a woman in his cabinet. One woman, however, was as many as Pearson would allow, or at least that was his explanation to Pauline Jewett for why she was not offered a cabinet post. That Pearson seemed not to understand women was widely acknowledged by his colleagues. If that was the case, his choice of the Department of National Health and Welfare for the novice LaMarsh seems to underline the fact that he did not understand domestic politics either.[8] But with Kent's assurance that he would be able to work with LaMarsh, and indeed counter her impulsiveness, Pearson made the appointment.[9] To the great relief of the civil servants who had suffered through the Diefenbaker administration, Kent subsequently became "coordinator of programmes," a position that allowed him an opportunity to influence the fledging government from behind the scenes.[10] The enthusiastic reaction to his appointment contrasted greatly with the reception he had received from some members of the press following his previous posting as "speech writer." Grant Dexter of the Winnipeg *Free Press* had then complained to Pearson that "as far as liberalism is concerned ... Tom had been one of the most destructive people in the country."[11] The advice to remove Kent went unheeded, and in 1963 he was firmly entrenched as the chief bureaucrat in the Prime Minister's Office.

The cabinet was sworn in on 22 April 1963, and with the need to make good on their promise of sixty days of decision, the ministers quickly got down to work. One of the most pressing problems was the pension plan.[12] The interdepartmental committee on social security, composed of senior civil servants, had already met several times by the middle of May, and its output seemed to increase with the change of government. Pleased by this phenomenon, Pearson wrote his son, "Moral [sic] is really higher now – especially in the civil service. We have a very efficient managerial govt."[13] The work done on retirement insurance moved out of the realm of preliminary discussions in May, and after reaching decisions on the nature of the graduated benefits and the type of contribution, the committee forged ahead on outlining the details of administration. The benefits, based on contributions on the first $500 earned per month from both employer and employee, would range from a maximum of $167 to a minimum of

$10 per month, would be available in full at age seventy and at a somewhat lesser level between the ages of sixty-five and sixty-nine, and the plan would be implemented over a transitional ten-year period. Owing to the "fact that the contribution rate will be relatively low at the time the plan is initiated and raised gradually over the years," there was an opportunity for "adjustments to be made gradually by private pension plans."[14]

When the new cabinet ministers received the reports of the committee, however, they were not unanimous in their approval. The old divisions between left and right, action versus delay, were again apparent. At a cabinet meeting on 9 May 1963 "some said that it would be unwise to indicate a target date for the entry into force of the plan in the Speech from the Throne. The scheme should not be introduced in Parliament until the government had a compete grasp of all its implications and a good knowledge of how it would work out in practice." Others thought that such study could conceivably continue far into the future and would serve only to dissociate the Liberals from pension reform. "Some form of words," they thought, "should be found for inclusion in the Speech from the Throne which would clearly bring out the firm intention of the government to accomplish its promise ... Discussions could begin at once with the provinces."[15] Typically for the Pearson Liberals, cabinet did not reach a decision either on the particulars of the plan under discussion or on the course of action to be pursued.

Such impediments were not enough to stop the progress of those in cabinet who were committed to the implementation of a nation-wide pension scheme. As minister responsible for overseeing the details of the plan, LaMarsh found herself allied with Walter Gordon and Maurice Lamontagne in cabinet and with Tom Kent and Keith Davey behind the scenes. Yet she had not been an active participant in the work on either pensions or health insurance in the opposition years and was at a disadvantage in her new position.[16] Much of the groundwork fell, as a result, on her deputy ministers, J.W. Willard in Welfare and Donald Cameron in Health, Tom Kent, and cabinet colleagues who were more familiar with the territory. Although all were undoubtedly well-meaning, there was evidence from the outset that Judy LaMarsh was not to be the sole proprietor of the Department of National Health and Welfare. Gordon, for example, issued an invitation to the Canadian Life Insurance Officers Association to meet with government officials to discuss the pension plan – and informed LaMarsh after the invitation had been made.[17]

Gordon's involvement in the design of the plan, and his obvious commitment to immediate implementation, caused more extra-parliamentary concern than LaMarsh's activities. Holding the powerful position of minister of finance, and with considerable influence over the prime minister, Gordon represented a real threat to all who were opposed to the national plan. He was that rare combination, never before seen and never to be seen again, of a finance minister dedicated to costly social-security measures, and not a few people found the mixture distasteful. "As I am sure you know," one concerned constituent warned Pearson, "a great many of us who are well versed on pension costs are alarmed by Walter's apparent determination to barge ahead with contributory pensions regardless of cost and quite contrary to his assurance to me a year or so ago that there would be no interference with existing plans of an adequate nature."[18]

There were other problems on the horizon. Since the Kingston Conference and the Liberal Rally, the national Liberal Party had theoretically been committed to the early implementation of a system of universal health insurance. The plank had been significant, if not adequately explained, in the election platforms in both 1962 and 1963, but it took a back seat to pensions in the immediate aftermath of electoral victory and in the flurry of activity surrounding the sixty days of decision. Even those Liberals dedicated to the quick implementation of social-security legislation disagreed over the ordering of these two priorities. LaMarsh was more committed to medicare than to pensions, and Kent, her chief aide in pushing through the proposed legislation, was also a relatively latecomer to the pension field.[19] Moreover, as Liberals were so often reminded, health insurance had been purportedly part of their platform since the leadership convention of 1919. Activity at the provincial level, which had increased considerably in the early years of the 1960s, served as a glaring and sometimes painful reminder that the Pearson Liberals would have to take some kind of action soon or finally make the decision to leave the difficult and rocky field of health insurance entirely in the hands of the provinces.

The Liberals in Ottawa had watched with interest the disputes over medical insurance in the provinces. Their proposal for a nation-wide scheme of compulsory health coverage came warily, with full recognition that they were embarking on a treacherous path. Saskatchewan had only recently begun to recover from the full impact of its divisive doctors' strike, and the Ontario physicians seemed ready to carry on the fight.[20] The medical profession was a powerful interest group, and although in Canada it had not achieved the degree of financial and governmental influence that characterized the American Medical Association, Pearson's Liberals were aware of the need to have them on side in order to secure the success of any national health-insurance program.[21]

The difficulty of implementing health insurance suggested that action on a national pension plan was much more viable in the early weeks of the new Liberal administration. The federal government had access to the numerous reports already issued by Diefenbaker's Conservatives and private organizations, and it could also be much more convinced of the universal acceptance of at least some degree of public involvement in the administration of a contributory pension plan. As Judy LaMarsh later recalled, the pension issue "was the first thing to start with ... because it would be self-funding and we didn't know how much money there would be to start with Medicare."[22] Of the two major social policies envisaged during the period of opposition, the Canada Pension Plan seemed by far the easier to accomplish and the least likely to upset the momentum of the Liberals' sixty days of decision.

The Liberals adopted an aggressive position on pensions, designed both to appear decisive and to pre-empt possible provincial legislation in the same field. Kent secretly advised the prime minister to plan on informing the provincial premiers around the middle of June of his intentions to legislate shortly on the Canada Pension Plan. There would remain a number of issues requiring federal and provincial attention, including the portability and solvency of private pension plans and the need to protect employers in provinces that already had some form of compulsory pension contribution from making double provisions for their employees, all of which would be topics of discussion at a formal federal-provincial conference. So, too, would the issue of "insurance benefits for widows below pension age but with dependent children, for orphans, and for disabled people." Kent advised Pearson to inform the premiers that "the federal government would be willing to add such benefits to the Canada Pension Programme and then withdraw from existing federal provincial joint programmes; or it would consider improving those programmes; or it would consider, it the provinces preferred, withdrawing from the joint programmes without adding such insurance features to the Canada Pension Programme, and so leaving the field to the provinces."[23] This was an approach to federal-provincial relations that demanded provincial compliance rather than offering the opportunity for consultation, but it reflected the depth of the commitment of many of the Liberals to their own social-policy design. Before the letters were sent, however, the Liberals faced a near-fatal crisis.

Two months before the government's budget was presented in the House of Commons, Kent had received the prime minister's agreement that "it should be a 'fairly stand-pat budget'; more thorough reforms would come, but not earlier than the fall."[24] What Gordon produced was, in fact, a budget "of restraint, both in terms of rhetoric and reality,"[25] and given its content no one expected it to cause the frenzy of parliamentary debate that ensued for the next several weeks. New Democratic Party MP Douglas Fisher opened the floodgates with the accusation that Gordon had relied heavily on the services of econo-mists brought in from outside the government – a taboo in drafting a secret document such as a budget. In fact, Gordon relied on the same assistants – M.P. O'Connell, Geoff Conway, and David Stanley – whom he had engaged to draft the original pension and health plans. This controversy was followed by adverse public reaction to the pro-posed 30 per cent tax on sales of domestic corporations to non-residents; opposition to this measure was so strong that it was ulti-mately withdrawn. The business community was almost entirely against Gordon's brand of economic nationalism, and his star within the Liberal Party began to dim appreciably.

The reaction that Gordon received from his parliamentary col-leagues during this period of both personal and professional trauma left little question in anyone's mind that his position in the party was beginning to change. On one level, letters of appreciation and support poured in to his Ottawa office, demonstrating, as one correspondent noted, that "the grass roots are with you."[26] One MP noted on a local radio station that "as a social document it is perhaps unique among Canadian budgets," but its merits seemed to be lost on most of the more senior members of the government.[27] Left-leaning Liberals in Parliament began to feel threatened by the NDP as they watched their party beginning to be pulled in a more conservative direction, and they settled into a mood which was "definitely despondent."[28] Pearson did not support Gordon publicly during the debate over the budget, a decision apparently made because Diefenbaker had not entered the fray.[29] In his stead, Mitchell Sharp addressed the Commons, using notes Tom Kent had prepared for use by the prime minister. It was an ironic choice of defenders, and one which suggested that many in the party did not believe that Gordon's budget was defensible. Buckling under the incessant onslaught he faced in the House of Commons, and the lack of support he found behind the scenes, Gordon offered to resign towards the end of June 1963.[30] Pearson did not accept the resignation, but he again demonstrated his tendency to make all sides believe they had the prime minister in their corner by asking Sharp if he would be willing to take over responsibility for the Department of Finance.[31] Robert MacIntosh, who attended the Kingston Conference but cut his ties with the Liberal Party as it became more obvious in the early 1960s that Gordon had the leader's ear, no doubt spoke for much of the business community when he later wrote that if "Pearson understood that it was Sharp and not Walter Gordon who brought economic competence to the Liberal Party, the direction of the economic policy would have been somewhat different in the years 1963 to 1965." "Somewhat different" undoubtedly meant "better," and while such a shift in personnel would have perhaps shortened the death throes of the left wing of the party, it was not yet to be.[32] However, even without the official acceptance of the resignation, as far as Judy LaMarsh was concerned, "the retreat from Walter started right then, and it really was ... shocking to the Party, because Walter was kind of the golden boy who'd raised the money and persuaded Mike to run and got support for him, and ran the campaign, and was unfailingly charming and courteous and effective."[33]

The appearance, at least, of Walter Gordon being deserted provided an opportunity for more conservative members of the party to voice their opinions. A left-wing commentator argued that the first session of Liberal government was something of an "ideological testing ground" which would clarify "whether the party has become an earnestly liberal and progressive force or is still the business-oriented bureaucracy of the St Laurent-Howe period."[34] The battle for supremacy between left and right interpretations of Canadian Liberalism, which had been waged throughout the years of opposition, seemed suddenly to shift in favour of the latter, after three years of relatively solid dominance by the social-welfare proponents within the party. Senator T.A. Crerar advised Pearson on damage-control measures in the wake of the budget debate. "It appears clearly," he wrote, "that so far as the public is concerned Mr. Gordon should be removed from Finance. So far as it is possible to judge, there has been a heavy loss of confidence in his judgement; and this in the most sensitive Department of your administration would be most hurtful to the Government."[35]

Crerar's view of Gordon had been repeated by advocates of more traditional Liberalism since his arrival on the political scene with Pearson's election as leader. Calls for his removal were louder than ever as a result of the budget, but Pearson was not quite ready to take action. He worried about the support Gordon could muster among the younger generation of Liberals in cabinet and beyond. "Mr. Gordon," he replied to Crerar, "notwithstanding the way in which the budget was handled and certain of its provisions, has a very strong position in the Caucus and in the Party and a forced withdrawal from the government at this time, under pressures which reflect on his personal integrity as well as on his ability, would bring about a serious split in the Party."[36] It was not Pearson's confidence in either Gordon's budget proposals or the social objectives he pursued that kept him in the cabinet in 1963; rather, it was fear of creating an obvious division between competing interests within the party.

Desperate to demonstrate that they could act quickly and decisively, the Liberals made early mistakes which had a particularly negative effect on the completion of a social-security net. While Gordon's budget did not threaten the life of the minority government, the opposition's concerns about outside advisers and the withholding tax did cause embarrassment for the Liberals. More important, the criticism raised internal concerns about Gordon's position in cabinet and cast doubts on the viability of his projects in the social-policy area. His failure to produce a satisfactory budget suggested that there might be similar problems with the proposals for a contributory pension plan and national-health insurance which he had played such an instrumental role in initiating. Kent tried to mend the damage by reminding his colleagues that "the pension plan is the only item in our programme so far that comes home to any large number of people as directly beneficial to them."[37] Nevertheless, the immediate effect was to produce the feeling that the progressive Liberals were "now in the doghouse"[38] and to encourage Gordon to work at luring to Ottawa people sympathetic to his ideological views. As if feeling besieged by his current colleagues, Gordon began in the middle of July to pressure Al Johnson, the deputy minister of finance in Tommy Douglas's Saskatchewan CCF government, to come to Ottawa.[39] Gordon no doubt realized the ramifications the budget debate would have for his hopes to implement progressive social policies and thought it wise to shore up defences by bringing in one of the masterminds behind Saskatchewan's medical program. Only time would tell whether the groundwork that the current crop of social-policy planners had already completed on specific social policies would survive the attacks from the increasingly powerful conservatives in the Liberal Party.

In addition to being more divided on social policy after the budget fiasco, the Liberals had to face the provincial responses to a national pension scheme. Activity in Ontario suggested that the provinces would be anything but willing to let the federal government dictate the terms of a portable pension plan. The Ontario government had demonstrated its interest in implementing a provincial scheme as early as 1960 when Premier Leslie Frost appointed a commission to examine the nature of existing pension plans, "identify the principal difficulties, dilemmas, issues and problems encountered in achieving portability of pensions," and suggest suitable resolutions to those problems.[40] Frost named George Gathercole, long-time deputy minister of finance for the province of Ontario, to chair the commission. The results, which made wide use of information from the Dominion Bureau of Statistics and private industry, were to be put before a select committee of the legislature during its 1961 session.[41]

In its first report, Gathercole's group noted the social and economic factors that made the inquiry desirable, and it also demonstrated an awareness of both changing circumstances and expectations which surpassed the general thinking of the national Liberal Party. The summary report, presented in early 1961, pointed out that industrialization had caused such profound changes to the Canadian economy that new means of providing security had to be designed. It pointed out as well that "while most individuals are preoccupied with short-term security, and while many are quite unrealistic in their expectations for the future, sentiment is growing in support of the view that one's standard of living upon one's retirement should bear some reasonable relationship to one's standard of living while at work." In conjunction with this was the "widely-held belief that government has a responsibility to promote the well-being of its older citizens."[42] With the initial studies complete, the Conservative government in Ontario, now headed by John Roberts, drafted its pension benefits bill and opened the doors to comment from representatives of business and industry.

The Ontario proposal anticipated the formation of a private company to work in cooperation with existing insurance companies to provide compulsory insurance through their auspices, thus quieting the initial concerns of private business.[43] Hearings held in September 1962 demonstrated that the government had been relatively successful in offering a balanced solution to competing demands. Although the Canadian Manufacturers' Association argued that the economic climate was not favourable enough to justify compulsory increases to pension benefits beyond the levels already reached in private pension plans, other groups, including the Canadian Life Insurance Officers Association, felt that if there had to be compulsion the Ontario plan was more palatable than the national Liberal plan was rumoured to be. Even the Ontario Federation of Labour allowed that "the general intent of the legislation meets our approval not as a cure-all but as a significant step toward necessary social objectives."[44] Despite some confusion over the relative merits of the Ontario plan compared to the American Social Security system, there seemed to be a general degree of satisfaction with the scheme.[45]

Most participants in and commentators on the Ontario pension deliberations felt that a provincial scheme was second best to a national portable-pension arrangement. Premier Robarts's dislike of Diefenbaker was well known, and looking forward to a change in prime minister, he had confided in early 1962 to Pearson "that the government of Ontario would concur in and facilitate proper and reasonable plans by your government resulting in a contributory social insurance program becoming a reality."[46] Representatives of the Life Underwriters Association of Canada, the Canadian Bankers Association, and the Canadian Life Insurance Officers Association all echoed the need for uniformity of legislation, national portability, and, therefore, a nationally implemented pension scheme.[47] However, what all seemed to envisage was a national plan along the same lines as Ontario's Pension Benefits Act, not a scheme that replaced free-enterprise principles with government sponsorship.[48] Thus, early in the 1963 session, the Ontario Conservative government enacted its pension legislation and then watched for parallel legislation at the national level.

Ontario's tactics were obvious from the outset. With its much clearer grasp of the issues involved in implementing a system of portable, contributory pensions, Ontario immediately put pressure on Ottawa to "explore the possibility of co-ordinating any new Federal plan with the new Ontario Act."[49] Similarly, George Gathercole reminded John Robarts that the insurance industry was "strongly in favour of [Ontario's scheme] over the Liberal proposal and expressed the hope that you will not yield on it."[50] Robert Clark, author of the Diefenbaker-sponsored report *Economic Security for the Aged in Canada and the United States,* urged the new Liberal administration to "forego its plans for a contributory programme with graduated benefits if provincial governments will enact legislation of the Ontario type which meets minimum federal standards."[51] If the federal Liberals were intent on implementing their own form of national pensions, they would have to take the initiative away from Ontario – and conceivably deal as well with Quebec, where pension studies were also under way.

Obviously, Quebec presented a problem, although most federal politicians seemed blissfully unaware of the extent to which the province had investigated the pension question.[52] But on a more general level, even people no longer in active politics, such as Senator T.A. Crerar, identified the issue there as "a protest against the centralizing tendencies that have been clearly manifestest [*sic*] in Ottawa, particularly since the end of the last war."[53] The onset of the Quiet Revolution with the election of Liberal Jean Lesage had done nothing to shake Quebec's opposition to its loss of power to the national government and, if anything, relations were more strained than might have been expected with parties of the same colour in power at the two levels.

Maurice Sauvé and Tom Kent agreed that it would be most beneficial if there was an immediate meeting between Pearson, Gordon, Guy Favreau, and Maurice Lamontagne from Ottawa, and Lesage, Paul Gérin-Lajoie, René Lévesque, and Pierre Laporte from Quebec, to discuss "all aspects of federal-provincial relations."[54] They also recognized the importance, at least as far as Quebec was concerned, of being able to contract-out of joint federal-provincial programs. Quebec was already suspicious of what the cooperative federalism espoused by the new government entailed, considering that "Ottawa wishes 'to aid the provinces to fulfill their obligations' at the same time that it searches in the name of 'national unity,' of the 'common good of Canada,' of efficiency and uniformity, to share with the provinces the domain of their sovereignty."[55]

Quebec had been working feverishly on its own system of contributory pensions since the announcement in the Throne Speech that it was the intention of the federal Liberals to enact national legislation. While some studies had been made in the early 1960s, often using information made available through the Ontario Portable Pension Commission, by the spring of 1963 Quebec had only a "half-formed resolve to move in the same field" and the federal government's plan was much more advanced.[56] However, an interdepartmental committee was immediately set up under Claude Castonguay, a consulting actuary, to examine the financial implications of the Quebec plan. It submitted its report on 21 June 1963, concluding that a provincial government-sponsored pension plan would serve to provide a $1 billion fund within five years, much needed money as Quebec embarked on its massive projects of modernization. From the outset, Quebec's interest in a provincial pension scheme had less to do with providing benefits to the elderly or "maître chez nous" than with the need to fill the provincial coffers. The summer of 1963 also saw the completion of a more general report on pensions, begun the fall before under the directorship of André Marier. He argued that the Canada Pension Plan "was merely an attempt to resurrect a 'moribund' Confederation" and reiterated the view that the revenue benefits of a provincial scheme were necessary in order to complete the objectives of the Quiet Revolution.[57]

With the two largest provinces moving rapidly towards implementing their own pension legislation, the federal Liberals faced a difficult challenge in fulfilling the promise of a national scheme. The fact that the cabinet was itself divided over how best to approach the problem meant that the challenge fell squarely on the weakened shoulders of the social-security advocates. Paul Hellyer, for example, the new minister of national defence, complained in mid-June that he disagreed with the shape of the Canada Pension Plan, prompting a challenge from the prime minister that he come up with a better system. Hellyer did just that, but it failed to obtain cabinet approval since it did not fulfil the letter of the election promises regarding pensions.[58] The Canada Pension Plan resolution, as it was originally conceived, was announced on the sixtieth day of decision, barely sneaking under the wire of self-imposed activity during the "Votes and Proceedings" of 21 June. By pushing ahead with its plans, the federal government had clearly adopted a strategy of bravado in the face of mounting opposition to a national pension scheme, partly to camouflage the internal divisions that the pension issue had uncovered.

The day before the resolution was announced, Pearson had written to all of the provincial premiers outlining the federal government's intentions. Benefits for survivors were not included in the pension provisions as a result of the constitutional question, and a full discussion of the implications of joint federal-provincial programs in the field of old-age assistance and disability insurance was put off so as not to "delay immediate steps for the improvement of benefits for older citizens."[59] Ignoring the advice of federal officials, who counselled a "new approach in the assistance field prior to further increases in old age security payments" as a means of changing the national role to one of "encouraging improved standards rather than setting detailed limits and conditions," the government pressed forward with separate legislation on pensions.[60] Furthermore, the ministers refused to be drawn into the preliminary discussions suggested by the Canadian Pension Conference, an association drawing its membership largely from the insurance industry, preferring to play their hand carefully. Judy LaMarsh did forward the group a "firm but carefully reasoned statement" explaining the basis for the federal proposals, but she made no effort to consult with these self-styled "experts."[61]

Ottawa's reluctance to discuss the details was partly aimed at keeping the provinces in a state of uncertainty: the national Liberals would therefore have the upper hand at least in the initial stages of negotiation. However, the approach was also made out of necessity since the cabinet itself was not clear on the details of the Canada Pension Plan. In cabinet in the middle of July, the ministers finally agreed on their proposals for universal contributory pensions. There was to be a $10 monthly supplement to the Old Age Security payments, to commence on 1 April 1964; registration for the Canada Pension Plan was to be conducted by the Unemployment Insurance Commission beginning 1 May 1964; on 1 October 1964 National Revenue would start to collect contributions at the rate of 1.5 per cent of assessed earnings, which would continue at this level for the initial ten-year period and thereby make possible the recovery of the $10 flat-rate increase in the first year; graduated benefits, with the option of reduced benefits at age sixty-five, were to begin to be paid 1 January 1966; and the benefits would be calculated on the basis of the ten best consecutive years in which contributions had been made.[62] They also agreed that the minister of national health and welfare would make public the federal position on the Canada Pension Plan in the House of Commons on 18 July 1963.

The aggressive approach adopted by the federal Liberals not surprisingly drew criticism from the provinces. Representatives of the Ontario insurance industry demanded that the federal government "lead towards uniformity" by adopting Robarts's legislation, which would have the benefit of ensuring that the national Liberals' "election pledges will have been fulfilled."[63] More disquieting, however, was Quebec's unexpected reaction. Premier Lesage thought that any joint meeting of federal and provincial representatives should "consider the heart of the matter, namely, the principle of a contributory old age pension program, and not only its means of implementation." He went on to advise the federal government that he had "certain reservations to express" on the Canada Pension Plan, and he announced his intention to do so "on the occasion of the suggested conference as well as to inform [Pearson] then more precisely of Quebec's plans in this field." Moreover, he insisted that "no Bill on this matter should be discussed in the Parliament of Canada before the holding of this conference."[64] Such a response came as a surprise to Pearson. The Liberal leader had been wary about eliciting the sort of reaction from Quebec that Diefenbaker had experienced on the pension issue, and so he had sent Lionel Chevrier and Maurice Lamontagne to Quebec City to outline the Liberals' proposed plan in a confidential manner early in May. They reported that the premier had raised no objections. Kent remembers that Lesage himself viewed the meeting differently and claimed that the two federal ministers had been so vague that he assumed the federal plan was only in its formative stages and that there was nothing for him to respond to. Lesage was apparently disappointed enough with his spring meetings with Chevrier and Lamontagne that he refused to meet with any federal ministers in the future. If it were not feasible to talk directly to the prime minister, he would be content only dealing with Kent or secretary to the cabinet Gordon Robertson, and the conversation would probably be more congenial. Apparently, Lesage and Pearson "did not communicate easily. Lesage was precise and decisive, and he regarded Pearson as unclear and evasive."[65] Perhaps Lesage had had a change of attitude, perhaps there had been some degree of misunderstanding at the meetings earlier in the spring, or perhaps, as Kent later postulated, Lesage dealt a heavy blow to the federal proposals because the government itself appeared weak.[66] Regardless, there could be no doubt that the federal-provincial negotiations were not likely to go as smoothly as hoped.

Cabinet did agree to a few changes to the proposed Canada Pension Plan prior to Judy LaMarsh's announcement in the House of Commons on 18 July 1963. The ministers lowered the maximum assessed-earnings base from $6000 to $4000 and agreed to raise the initial rate of contribution from 1.5 per cent to 2 per cent.[67] LaMarsh advised the Commons that the Canada Pension Plan was "the only type of pension plan that can be made available to all Canadians," and she said that contributions would be compulsory for all employers except in cases of self-employment where it was not "administratively feasible." Her statement was designed to avoid the opposition of the provinces as much as possible. She made clear that

the Canada Pension Plan is *not* intended to be comprehensive in any other sense; it is not designed to provide all the retirement income which many Canadians wish to have. This is a matter of individual choice and, in the Government's view, should properly be left to personal savings and to private pension plans, subject in the latter case to such degree of supervision as the province may think appropriate. The recent Ontario legislation is the first example in Canada of an attempt at close supervision of private plans. [Under the Canada Pension Plan] there will be scope for the continuation and extension of private pension plans to provide benefits over these minimum levels.[68]

The Ontario government believed that Kent was responsible for writing the statement read in Parliament, although LaMarsh apparently "takes full responsibility for it, saying quite frankly that this was the way she felt."[69] Regardless of the author, however, opponents of the plan lost little time in expressing their concern, suggesting that its implementation would result in "a rising tide of cost, a draining of [Canada's] sources of capital, accentuated budget difficulties, higher costs of production, [and] rising taxes."[70] The Canadian Life Insurance Officers Association maintained the position that the implementation of the proposed legislation would "be a serious misfortune for Canada and Canadians."[71] In Ottawa the Conservatives bemoaned the loss of the spirit of "cooperative federalism" they had tried to engender while in office, and they predicted that the centralizing tendencies of the new administration were destined to produce "violent protests in response."[72] The New Democratic Party chose a different approach at its annual convention in August, pledging its support for a social-security policy that would represent "a radical departure from free enterprise welfare practice," with pensions "related to the cost of living" and with no penalty for "lack of personal market value."[73]

Somewhat apprehensively, therefore, cabinet agreed that "the Minister of National Health and Welfare prepare a draft letter to be sent to the Ministers of Welfare of all provinces, inviting them to Ottawa, with their officials, for a meeting on September 9th–11th with the Minister and appropriate federal officials, to discuss matters relating to the Canada Pension Plan."[74] On 5 August 1963 Pearson invited the provincial governments to send a delegation headed by the appropriate minister to Ottawa to discuss the technical aspects of the plan as well as deal with the questions of policy which had obviously arisen.[75] While all provinces agreed to send delegations to the conference, clearly they were not planning to rubber stamp the federal plan. Pearson was convinced that Robarts would ultimately accept the national plan, but he recognized that Lesage "was determined to assume full responsibility for all social security in Quebec." This made LaMarsh uneasy, for "the future of federalism in Canada would be in serious jeopardy if the Provinces were entitled to contract out of essential pieces of federal social security legislation." Although the prime minister assured her that contracting-out would not be allowed unless the province "provided its own people with comparable benefits," discussion of the provincial schemes was added to the conference agenda in the hope of reaching an agreement that would "accommodate a Canada-wide approach as set out in the Canada Pension Plan."[76] It all gave the impression of a "pension race" by Ontario, Quebec, and the federal government, with, as the Montreal *Gazette* said, "too much ... being done too soon by too many."[77]

The federal government seemed curiously uncertain about the best approach to take with the provinces on the pension issue. On the one hand, the federal politicians appeared intent on acting brashly, summoning the provinces to Ottawa to discuss a national plan which did not even have the unanimous support of the cabinet. On the other hand, Pearson in particular seemed hesitant to make a public issue out of pensions, perhaps concerned that too much publicity would tarnish the sheen of the national proposals. These two approaches – aggressive and cautious – were incompatible, and ultimately the former negated any of the benefits of the latter. This was particularly true in the case of the Ontario provincial election, where both tactics were attempted simultaneously.

In mid-August 1963 Premier Robarts called an election for 25 September. Early in August, Keith Davey provided Ontario Liberal leader

John Wintermeyer with some unofficial assistance in preparing a campaign-strategy paper, and at that time the Ontario organization encouraged him to direct their campaign. As far as Walter Gordon was concerned, whether Pearson allowed Davey to accept the position depended on whether "you want to make a major issue of the pension plan." If Pearson did not want to "take on the financial community, the right-wing press, some of the provinces, [former National Liberal Party President] Bruce Matthews, and perhaps one or two members of your Cabinet," then it would be best to keep Davey in Ottawa and not encourage a pension debate in the provincial election.[78] The Ontario Liberals and the national Liberals would have a better chance of retaining their autonomy if Davey stayed on his traditional political turf. The fact that, in the end, Davey remained at national headquarters suggests that Pearson was not willing to have the Ontario campaign centre around the Canada Pension Plan. Whatever the earlier desires of the federal Liberals had been, however, within two weeks Pearson declared that "the Canada Pension Plan was assuming the proportions of a major political issue."[79] A province-wide poll indicated that 20 per cent of the population deemed pensions to be the major issue of the Ontario campaign.[80] It was too late for the national Liberals to adopt a cautious approach to pensions.

The Ontario campaign brought unwanted attention to the national pension plan. Quebec became even more of a problem. Lesage announced the provincial scheme for contributory pensions in the National Assembly and issued an absolute rejection of the Canada Pension Plan as an infringement of provincial rights. The federal government's next move was uncertain: the options, as far as Kent was concerned, were either to drop the universal contributory pension plan altogether in favour of more generous increases to Old Age Security as a means of fulfilling the pledge for "Better Pensions for All," or to make provisions for the Canada Pension Plan not to apply in Quebec.[81] Although "bottom-liners" such as the governor of the Bank of Canada preferred the former approach, the latter plan was the more acceptable strategy, provided that LaMarsh agreed. However, it depended on Ontario accepting the plan, for administrative chaos was certain if the two largest provinces opted-out.[82]

The question of when to announce that the federal position had changed somewhat also caused concern. An announcement prior to the opening of the conference would eliminate the problem of appearing to succumb to provincial pressure, but it might be considered "discourteous to the provinces to produce a major policy announcement just before the conference." Waiting to make the statement until after the Ontario election, however, would stop Robarts from claiming that his political pressure had ensured the increase to Old Age Security benefits, but on the other hand such a delay would make the national Liberals appear weak and indecisive. Kent suggested that the earlier the announcement was made the better, either before or at the beginning of the conference, since the federal government would be able to claim the initiative and a fight with Quebec would be headed off.[83]

A few days before the conference convened, Pearson informed cabinet of the course he wished to follow: at the same time that LaMarsh made her opening statements to the conference, he would issue a press statement indicating that the $10 supplement would be detached from the Canada Pension Plan. It was a tactic with which John Wintermeyer agreed and of which Jean Lesage was to be informed prior to the convening of the conference.[84] Gordon said that this increase could be initially financed through an increase in personal income tax and, after 1964, through the proposed increase in the sales tax on machinery and building materials. Although some of the ministers doubted the wisdom of making changes to the pension plan, since it would be effectively "admitting that nothing could be gained by negotiations between Ottawa and Quebec," Pearson said that "the government could not hold the line until the end of the month."[85] Ultimately, the cabinet agreed to the proposals made by the prime minister, and LaMarsh began her final preparations prior to the opening of the conference.

The decision to inform Wintermeyer of the intentions of the federal government proved to be unwise. The Ottawa Liberals had hoped that Wintermeyer might be able to use the information to his advantage in the Ontario election campaign by calling for an increase to the old-age pension and then emphasizing his power with the national government when the increase was announced at the federal-provincial conference.[86] The information, however, was leaked to the press, and that, combined with the Ontario Liberals' strategy of focusing their campaign on the pension issue and with the invasion of federal Liberal politicians during the contest, forced Robarts to take the offensive.[87] He announced that, despite not being invited, he would attend the federal-provincial conference of ministers of health and welfare in order to clarify Ontario's position on pensions. Meanwhile, Quebec demonstrated its commitment to implementing its own plan by sending only "observers" to the conference. It was an inauspicious beginning to the discussions.

As agreed in cabinet, the meetings began in Ottawa on 9 September 1963 with a statement from LaMarsh outlining the federal proposals for the Canada Pension Plan and Ottawa's intention to separate the increase to Old Age Security from the contributory pension plan. Pearson issued a simultaneous press release that it was "the substance of this social advance for the people of Canada that is important, not the form in which it is achieved" and that the federal government had no intention of "entering into a competition with the provincial governments."[88] Robarts was then reluctantly given the floor and the opportunity to correct any of the misconceptions about Ontario's views on pensions propagated during Wintermeyer's campaign. He emphasized that a national scheme was preferable but noted that there were a number of outstanding problems which had to be dealt with before Ontario could agree to the Canada Pension Plan. Robarts was particularly concerned that neither the national nor the provincial legislation should violate existing union-negotiated plans; that benefits from private plans in excess of the government benefits should not be imperilled; that "neither plan should inhibit the capital investment necessary for the development of the economy"; and that "benefits under any second deck (Canada or Ontario plan) should be related to contributions."[89] In closing, he indicated Ontario's willingness to cooperate by saying that he was prepared to recommend amendments to the Pension Benefits Act so that Ontario could participate in a national scheme, although he was careful not to make specific reference to the Canada Pension Plan as it stood. Privately, Ontario Provincial Treasurer James Allan assured LaMarsh that Ontario would without doubt agree to participate in a federal pension plan, although again, not necessarily the Canada Pension Plan as currently drafted.[90]

The federal representatives, who found the Ontario delegation somewhat unusual in its composition since it included an employee of an insurance company, were left confused as to the provincial position.[91] LaMarsh noted "a division between the political side and the officials; Mr. Allan said that he thought the Ontario pension legislation would be adjusted to take account of the Canada Pension Plan, but his officials seemed to want major adjustments in the Federal plan." But there was little doubt that "Ontario had dominated the conference," with Robarts essentially taking the initiative from the federal Liberals and probably securing his own re-election in the process.[92]

The Quebec observers behaved as expected but were obviously a greater problem for Ottawa. In his opening statement, Quebec official Carrier Fortin left little doubt that, if pushed, his province was more than prepared to fight the legislation on constitutional grounds. Not only did the provinces have "prior rights" in the pension field, but Quebec "was ready to take over old age security and old age assistance if the federal government were willing to provide the province with the necessary funds."[93] Interestingly, Quebec did not participate in the discussion on the extent of funding, despite its own desire to create a large fund for financing other government initiatives. LaMarsh made clear that the federal legislation was "designed as a welfare measure – not a fiscal measure, nor a means to control capital investment. It is primarily concerned with the needs of our old people, and those who will be retiring in the future ... We regarded it as undesirable in the present state of the economy to withdraw hundreds of millions of dollars in payroll taxes from the private sector of the economy in order to build up large reserves within the public sector."[94]

Quebec's reticence during these discussions indicated its commitment to its own plan, regardless of the conflict with the stated aims of the federal scheme.[95] However, the president of the Privy Council, Maurice Lamontagne, detected "signs that the provincial government was beginning to feel that it might get into a difficult political situation if it continued with its plan for a funded contributory scheme involving initial rates of contribution significantly higher than the Federal rate," and so in order to structure its provincial scheme Quebec needed to know Ottawa's intentions.[96] Despite enormous concerns about financing pensions, the Quebec delegates were also influenced by the burgeoning sense of nationalism. As *Le Devoir* had warned a week before the conference began, "à moins qu'il ne capitule dans une cascade de 'pis-aller' ... le gouvernement du Québec va se rendre compte qu'il est engagé dans une bataille décisive, permanente, de plus en plus dure et sur tous les plans, bataille qui ne prendra fin que par l'éclatement de la fédération ou l'adoption d'une constitution entièrement nouvelle, de type réellement confédéral."[97] The provincial delegation's most positive contribution to the conference was over the issue of portability, since the Quebec "observers" offered their assurances that every effort would be made to ensure that the two plans were completely compatible and that there was relative ease in moving from one to the other.[98]

The concluding communiqué was inevitably somewhat different from the one drafted by the federal representatives prior to the meeting. While little had been agreed, much had been discussed. All aspects of the Canada Pension Plan were examined, including size of benefits, rate of maturation, scope of coverage, and the size and investment of the accumulated funds. Apart from Quebec, there was general agreement that a national contributory plan would be beneficial, and that a constitutional amendment should be made in order that it might include benefits for disabled people, widows, dependent children, and orphans. Ottawa and the provinces also agreed that two technical inquiries would be undertaken, one with representatives from Ottawa and Quebec City to discuss the interrelationship between the two plans, and the other with representatives from Ontario to discuss how its pension plan could be coordinated with federal legislation.[99] These were the only conclusions of the meeting which all could agree were fit for public consumption, but new relationships had been forged, others were broken, and the battle lines were becoming more obvious.

When Judy LaMarsh announced at a press conference following the federal-provincial meeting that the Ontario position was still unclear, she did so on the basis of Robarts's reluctance to state whether Ontario was willing to take part in the Canada Pension Plan.[100] Robarts was not pleased with the implication that he had not been cooperative with the conference delegates, and he issued a press release himself, pointing out that "I made a long statement setting out with utmost clarity our position and accepted, in principle, and offered my full support in devising a scheme which would be right for all of Canada, and which at the same time would protect our people in Ontario."[101] It was clear that Ontario was a major obstacle to federal legislation, but since representatives from others provinces believed that Robarts would eventually come around, there was still a degree of optimism.[102] Al Johnson, one of the key members of the Saskatchewan delegation, even began to consider the possibility of the move to Ottawa that not only Walter Gordon but also his deputy minister Robert Bryce had previously been encouraging, partly on the basis of his new view that federal-provincial relations was "clearly not only interesting but terribly important as well."[103] The federal government could even justify the separation of the $10 increase from the Canada Pension Plan on the ground that it reduced the urgency to rush into pensions "before there has been ample time to give it the benefit of full discussion and enquiry," despite the public perception that the Liberals were "bowing to political pressure rather than responding to an urgent social need."[104] But the results of the Ontario election dampened the reasonably high spirits of the Pearson government. As had been expected, Robarts was once again elected with a majority government, and Pearson was concerned about the fact that Wintermeyer had campaigned heavily on the issue of the Canada Pension Plan and had been defeated on it. The lack of commitment from Ontario and Quebec's continued opposition to a federal plan forced the prime minister to the conclusion that there was "little value in pressing adoption of the Plan in Parliament until the Government was assured that Ontario was prepared to participate in it."[105] For the time being at least, the federal government's plan for a national contributory pension went on the back burner.

5 Changing Liberal Tactics and the Completion of Pension Negotiations, 1963–66

Quebec's absolute rejection of the federal plan, and Ontario's threat to do the same, demonstrated the failure of Ottawa's strong-arm approach at the September 1963 federal-provincial conference and forced the Liberals to change tactics. To proceed unilaterally could do serious, permanent, damage. Instead of dictating terms to the provincial governments and therefore keeping pensions in the public eye, the federal politicians and advisers now adopted a more cautious approach, characterized by a conciliatory attitude on certain key points. They also worked to keep pensions out of the media limelight, leading commentators to suspect that pension policy was no longer "high on [the government's] list of priorities."[1] Even provincial bureaucrats who were in favour of a national pension plan worried that the Liberals had lost their desire to initiate legislation. As Saskatchewan Deputy Minister of Finance Al Johnson warned Tom Kent, "it would be a political catastrophe for the Liberals to back down on this one."[2] Though the new approach hinted at weakness, it did allow the national government some privacy in which to shape its policy. The Liberals desperately needed to reach a consensus on the items in the Canada Pension Plan they would be willing to negotiate and on those elements that were not open for debate. If there was ever to be intergovernmental agreement, there would have to be unanimity over both strategy and structure at the centre. With more federal-provincial conferences approaching and extra-parliamentary lobbies continuing to make forceful representations, the Liberals struggled to define their position. While they ultimately demonstrated a remarkable depth of commitment to the concepts of universality, portability, and accessibility, the structure of the Canada Pension Plan would change dramatically as a result of pressure from the provinces.

Promises made at the conclusion of the September federal-provincial conference dictated that national representatives meet with their counterparts from Ontario and Quebec to discuss the various impediments to a national pension plan. Ottawa's goal this time, however, was to explore the provincial intentions rather than attempt to impose a national agenda on the reluctant provincial governments. Ontario was the first problem: cabinet considered it impossible to engage in useful technical discussions with Quebec regarding portability and compatibility before Ontario's demands were known.[3] Although Pearson and Robarts tentatively agreed that a meeting between them might be a good way of reaching a better understanding of "the goals at which we are driving," the complexities of the issues involved in pension legislation suggested that officials were better able than politicians to tackle the problem.[4]

While Kent accepted that bureaucrats should be responsible for the initial exploratory negotiations with the provinces, he wanted first to ensure that they clearly understood the superiority of the federal position. Kent worked hard, perhaps too hard, to convince the Ottawa civil servants that, no matter what they learned about pension proposals in either Toronto or Quebec City, the Canada Pension Plan was vastly better than the provincial alternatives. He stressed that Ottawa's plan was "a well-balanced marrying of insurance and welfare principles, a sensible compromise between them," and that it therefore differed from provincial proposals not merely in structure but in overall conceptualization.[5] That such reminders were necessary suggested that not everyone accepted the Kent version of Canada Pension Plan benefits and that even Kent might be slightly shaken in his conviction. The provinces were fiercer opponents than had been expected. Meanwhile, the Ontario Conservatives worried about Ottawa's position and remained suspicious of its motives. Robarts's advisers were particularly concerned that Pearson intended to make Ontario the scapegoat if the federal proposals were rejected. Their concerns were magnified by the fact that "Ontario has legislation which must be dealt with [and] Mr. Pearson can now afford to wait."[6]

The first Ottawa-Ontario meeting was held in early October, with civil servants from the departments of national health and welfare, justice, and insurance representing the federal government and insurance industry maven Laurence Coward of the Canadian Pension Conference heading the Ontario delegation. The Ontario delegation began by calling for a public inquiry into pensions as a strategy to force the federal government to "disclose a suitably amended plan."[7] Despite a modicum of cabinet enthusiasm for the idea of an inquiry, Ottawa's negotiators pressured Ontario into agreeing to a federal-provincial conference to discuss the possibility of amending the federal proposals on contracting-out, partial funding, and benefit rates. This was better than nothing. Pearson then proceeded to inform the House of Commons on 4 November 1963 that he intended to agree to the request made by "many of the provinces" for the inclusion of pensions on the agenda for the November federal-provincial conference and that he would not proceed with further action in Parliament until after the Christmas recess.[8]

A second informal meeting between representatives of Ottawa and Ontario further clarified the latter's position. The major bones of contention for Ontario were Ottawa's proposed infringement on private pension plans and "current capital formation" and the fact that Quebec's plan allowed investment money to remain in the province.[9] Although they did not reach an agreement, the federal representatives at least had determined that Ontario opposed the principle of opting-out, had no intention of opting-out itself, and wished Ottawa to continue negotiations with Quebec in order to convince the province to remain part of a completely national plan.[10]

Ottawa had, in fact, already arranged informal discussions with representatives of the Quebec government. The discussions were not designed to convince Quebec to join the Canada Pension Plan, though federal officials initially clung to the naive hope that this might still be possible. However, the early discussions indicated that there was not even a remote chance that the Quebec government would choose to forego its own plan, so convinced was it of both the economic and the nationalist benefits of implementing a separate pension scheme.[11] The federal officials found themselves in an increasingly uncomfortable position as they recognized that one of the reasons that Quebec distrusted the Canada Pension Plan was that as yet no study of the economic implications had been undertaken; however, they were unwilling to rectify the situation, arguing that "anything produced by [the Department of National Health and Welfare] will not be received as a completely objective analysis."[12] The only option was to begin discussion on the eventual coordination of the two plans, and the sticking points were clearly going to be the details of the transitional period and the contribution rate and benefits. Quebec wanted a longer transition than the Canada Pension Plan allowed, although shorter than proposed by Ontario, a funded system rather than a pay-as-you-go one, and somewhat lower benefit rates.[13] Since neither group of officials had the authority to reach a formal agreement, such details had to wait for discussion at the full federal-provincial first ministers' conference scheduled for the end of November.

The negotiations between representatives of both Ontario and Quebec had gone relatively smoothly because the federal officials were more interested than they had been in the past in ascertaining provincial positions, the degree of commitment at the provincial level to the idea of a national pension plan, and areas for discussion. They had not dictated a national plan, but at the same time they had acknowledged that there were some subjects which were not open for debate. The meetings had been low-key and did not attract much press attention, allowing the participants the luxury of privacy and a brief reprieve from the incessant questions about their intentions. But, if the governments themselves benefited from some privacy, the groups opposed to a national pension scheme also profited from the hiatus. Labour unions were not alone in fretting that "the forces lined up against the plan are formidable."[14]

The Robarts government had been relatively receptive to those "forces" and had included representatives of insurance companies in both its internal studies and its delegations to federal-provincial conferences. The Ontario government, therefore, was inclined to heed the advice of the industry's spokesmen, who were becoming increasingly active in their attempts to derail the national legislation. The president of the Canadian Life Insurance Officers Association warned that the cost of a compulsory pension scheme "could be very heavy for our children and grandchildren" and called for the appointment of a "committee of experts," presumably meaning insurance people, to examine the question. He was joined in this suggestion by other members of the insurance industry and leaders of the Chamber of Commerce.[15] Lester Pearson, unlike his provincial counterpart, did not give much weight to the extra-parliamentary opposition, perhaps because the federal government owed less to the insurance industry in terms of political power than did the Robarts government. That did not mean that the federal officials were blind to the concerns of the business community, for they were "particularly concerned about the reaction of employers, who will have to bear half the cost and who will have to act as administrative agents for collection purposes."[16] But such worries were an impetus for more clarification and the need to "improve the cooperation of the federal and provincial authorities" rather than reasons for dropping negotiations altogether.[17]

Joint action on the pension front would clearly be impossible without one participant or another making considerable concessions. As it stood in the fall of 1963, there were at least three different versions of the goals of pension policy. Private insurers, whose voices were given credibility by the Ontario government, continued to view pensions as a means of securing private capital accumulation. Public plans were attacked on largely irrelevant actuarial bases and described as fundamentally reorienting the direction of capital formation. Ottawa's plan, originally designed along a pay-as-you-go basis, was in fact designed to avoid the accumulation of a large fund and thus had little impact on private investments. It was not, as the insurance industry failed to notice, a scheme designed along profit-based insurance principles but rather a public program intended to provide benefits. It had nothing to do with actuarial predictions. The third approach to pensions was promoted by Quebec, which envisaged the accumulation of capital through a funded program but took those funds out of the private sphere and placed them under governmental control. Cooperation between the proponents of the three plans was impossible; there would have to be concessions somewhere.[18]

As the November federal-provincial conference approached, Kent became increasingly concerned that little had been done to clarify the government's position. Despite the round of informal discussions, the federal delegation had made "very little real preparation of policy" and had failed to consider "the issues that [will] arise as soon as the [formal federal-provincial] conference is in motion. We haven't thought through our responses to the proposals that we know will come from the Provinces," complained a "bitter" Tom Kent, "tired of being the goat who does a lot of work for nothing." The fact that more attention had been given to the wording of the opening statement than to the position the federal government would take in subsequent discussions was nothing more than "intellectual masturbation, a way of using up time and energy because we are afraid of the real thing – which, in this case, is to make the hard, practical decisions on policy and strategy."[19] Kent was always direct in his advice to Pearson and others, but he had rarely betrayed such feelings of resentment about the process of political decision making. A career in diplomacy had not prepared Pearson for making the sort of hard decisions Kent demanded of his leader, and a career in journalism had not trained Kent in the art of pragmatic politics.

Despite Kent's misgivings, Pearson's opening statement to the conference made it clear that there were certain elements of the pension plan on which the federal government was adamant. He warned: "I do not want to invite you to discussion with any misconception of our position. We have heard many suggestions as to the form that a federal pension plan should take. Some of those suggestions are unacceptable. To be worthwhile, the Canada Pension Plan must satisfy certain minimum needs of those people who are unable – because of their age, or the nature of their occupations, or the level of their incomes – to make any additional provision for their retirement. We will be prepared at this conference to define what we regard as the essentials. Outside of those essentials, you will find us fully willing to consider any idea."[20]

Pensions were only one piece of a much larger conference agenda, since the representatives of the two levels of government were essentially confronted with the task of reshaping the nature of Canadian federalism in the wake of widespread dissatisfaction with the financial agreements worked out under the Diefenbaker administration. The smaller and poorer provinces were, not surprisingly, concerned with strengthening the federal commitment to equalization and anxious about the proliferation of shared-cost programs through which the federal government could essentially set provincial spending priorities. Health services, public welfare, and pensions were all identified as areas that would benefit from cooperation between the two levels of governments. Many of the premiers raised objections to the concept of opting-out as foreign to the proper functioning of a federal state, but whether their concerns were based on theories of federalism or jealousy of Quebec is questionable.[21]

One session of the conference, chaired by the prime minister, studied and discussed the proposals for a national pension plan. The strategy was that he should lay down the eight elements of the Canada Pension Plan that the federal government was not prepared to negotiate and then hear proposals from the provinces on the negotiable elements. The complexity of the issues involved dictated that there was more explanation than discussion, and also that the Ontario and Quebec premiers would participate the most because they were most familiar with the details.[22] If there was any doubt about Quebec's intention to opt-out of the national plan, even if it were suitably amended, they were removed by an informal canvas of Quebec representatives,[23] and since there remained some important disagreements over how best to coordinate the two schemes, the federal government looked to the other provinces for support for its conception of funding and maturation rates.

On the first issue, there was naturally considerable provincial enthusiasm for the Quebec idea of a funded plan, which anticipated access to the money for investment in other provincial priorities. Because the Old Age Security increase had been separated from the pension plan, the federal proposals would involve the accumulation of a small fund.

During the discussions, LaMarsh hinted that half of this "should be invested in the obligations of participating provinces."[24] The premiers viewed this new possibility of a partially funded plan with heightened interest.

On the issue of maturity rates, Quebec continued to argue that its scheme would take at least twenty years before it was fully functional, while Ottawa demanded a much shorter period. The question hinged on different conceptions of government responsibility. The shorter maturation period would build up benefits faster than a private pension plan could achieve and, therefore, would be a deterrent to investment in private plans. As LaMarsh explained, "the purpose of public pensions is to provide an adequate minimum measure of security for those people who cannot make any significant supplementary provision for their retirement." To provide assistance where it was needed most, she argued, "a public pension plan cannot be based on the individual equity principle which produces full pensions only in 40 or 50 years. Pension rates designed to be adequate in the long run, under such a scheme, would be seriously inadequate for many years."[25] Although it recognized that immediate retirement assistance might infringe somewhat on the claims of private insurance companies, the federal government was prepared to stand firm. Ontario was still unconvinced. Robarts publicly questioned the actuarial soundness of the federal plan and asked whether the country's youth realized the future burden of the Canada Pension Plan. His motives were somewhat suspect, however, given the degree his government had involved the insurance industry in its own examination of pensions. Ultimately, little was decided at the conference, but at the same time, everything indicated that the Canada Pension Plan was still within the realm of possibility.

The first six months in office had been difficult ones for the Liberals: between the budget fiasco and the exhausting round of pension negotiations, there had been little time to enjoy the perquisites of power. Both the Conservatives and the NDP were quick to prey on the weaknesses of the government. Stanley Knowles claimed credit for his party for the separation of the Old Age Security increase from the Canada Pension Plan fund and then bemoaned the postponement of further negotiations on the latter. He identified the main problem with the Liberal administration as its inability "to make decisions" and its unwillingness "to stick with those it has made." He claimed that the Gordon budget and the pension delay demonstrated this fatal flaw.[26] Although rumours of a merger between the minority Liberal Party and the NDP had been being bandied about since November, Douglas dismissed the possibility until he was more convinced of genuine Liberal commitment to social programs. As far as he was concerned, "its performance in recent Parliaments is evidence of its half-hearted, too-late acceptance of necessary change, [and] its reluctance to give really effective leadership in the field of economic and social policy."[27] Other left-leaning commentators were also quick to criticize the government for its failure to lead the country in a suitably progressive direction.[28]

The Conservatives' concerns differed from those of the NDP, but they too were obviously dissatisfied with the first few months of Liberal management. Tories focused on the pension plan as a source of particular discontent. It was not the snail's pace of the negotiations, or the delay in implementing the national scheme, that bothered them but rather the direction the talks were taking. The Conservatives accused their Liberal counterparts of being pro-provincial rights, too eager to make concessions to the provinces and unlikely to reverse the trend. While this was an approach that Conservatives detested, it did open up the possibility for them to "take a firm stand on the right as the party committed to a strong central government in Canada." This would mark a "return to authentic Canadian conservatism."[29] The Conservatives, however, were in a greater state of disarray than the Liberals and demonstrated internal divisions over fundamental policy directions. For example, not all Conservatives agreed that the Liberals' policy of "cooperative federalism" was their greatest crime: Ontario Progressive Conservative Party organizer George Hogan appealed to the younger party members to encourage the party to adopt a program of cooperative decentralization of the federation, which was described by its opponents as suspiciously similar to cooperative federalism.[30]

The Liberals themselves were aware that their progress in the first session of Parliament left them open to criticism from the other parties, and in the unstable condition of minority government they were eager to rectify the problems that had been identified. Those included a lack of adequate preparation prior to the introduction of major policies and the continuing tendency to make major decisions at the last moment without careful consideration.[31] The National Liberal Federation also suffered from financial woes, making it virtually impossible for Keith Davey to centralize the activities of the party and oversee campaign preparations as he wished.[32] Having barely recovered from the last campaign, the Liberals were deeply anxious about their minority situation, and by the autumn of 1963 Jack Pickersgill for one felt that an election was "imminent."[33] More worrisome was the fact that the NDP had renewed its promise to enact national health insurance, all but forgotten by the beleaguered Liberals, and pressed for still faster action on the pension plan. Even the Conservatives were reassessing their social-policy goals and considering a shift to a more active level of state involvement.[34]

As the Christmas recess neared, rumours of a cabinet shuffle increased. Kent reasoned that change was necessary to make the cabinet a more effective policy-making body, and he suggested altering some of the minor cabinet posts. He made it clear, however, that "after a period of doubt, I now think that the Minister of Finance is so far rehabilitated as to present the next Budget."[35] Nor did he advise replacing Judy LaMarsh in Health and Welfare, although others suggested shifting Guy Favreau to that position. As Montreal businessman John Payne pointed out, "it would be good to have a French-Canadian handle social legislation at this time as he could take the federal case to the people of Quebec."[36] When the changes were ultimately announced early in the new year, they were largely designed to increase the francophone presence in cabinet after Lionel Chevrier's late-December resignation, and not surprisingly there was "some criticism of the Prime Minister for not removing Walter Gordon and Judy LaMarsh, two of the less successful ministers during the first session."[37]

But the problems facing the Liberals could not be rectified by changing a few cabinet members. Pearson recognized that it would be "hard to re-establish complete confidence in some areas where we have lost it." Moreover, he accepted that some policy decisions had been made without enough prior consideration, a mistake he identified as "a hangover from the motif of the campaign." Liberal policies, however, did not really concern the leader, who believed that the party, "since the 1960 Kingston Conference, has been loaded with policy – economic as well as social." There was a much more serious role for the Liberal Party to play, a much more demanding objective for which to strive. He set out his thoughts on this matter to friend and Liberal senator W.A. Macdonald:

I am convinced that the real issue in Canadian politics today, and for some time past, is national leadership as a united force which must transcend partisan policy and tactics ... This national approach which you so eloquently described can be based on an appeal to Canadian pride in Canadianism – hence our emphasis on cooperative federalism, on full partnership of the two founding races with full appreciation of other ethnic cultures and values. Good, competent government must be built on a new sense of unified, national purpose. Definition of the issue and agreement on the appeal, no matter how simply stated, are of little practical value without their sensitive and sensible translation to the public in national, rather than partisan terms.[38]

Pearson went on to identify the problem of the first few months of his administration as being the inability to translate Liberal Party policies into the language of nationalism and to speak directly to the individual rather than focusing on partisan politics, regional interests, or ethnic identification. He told Macdonald he intended to rectify the situation. In private, and confided to a friend, this was Pearson's strongest statement yet on the responsibility of the federal government to provide a purpose for a nation struggling to bridge the schisms of regionalism, biculturalism, and provincialism. While his public statements were more guarded, and less specific, he attempted to bring home the idea that "a nation's progress must be evaluated at a higher level than that of gross national product," stressing that there were "other elements such as responsibility, the will to act, courage and the quality of our citizenship."[39] It was a faint imitation of President John F. Kennedy, but behind the rhetoric remained the private conviction that the nation, and the federal government, were in need of policies that transcended party labels.

Pearson also recognized that a different approach to policy formation had to be mirrored in a new approach to the organization of the federal government and the national Liberal Party. In his post-New Year message to his ministers, the prime minister stressed that their behaviour had to change in order to elicit the voters' identification with the national government. The government must be seen as a "team" between elections. Pearson wanted to see more consultation between ministers, there being "nothing that can damage the reputation of the Cabinet more than separate, conflicting statements of Ministers," and similarly he wanted to "co-ordinate our public appearances and speech subjects." The prime minister argued that this form of cooperation should not merely exist at the cabinet level but that MPs should also be consulted before any government action was undertaken that might affect their constituents.[40] He claimed that his objective was an administration committed to broad universal goals, not one dependent upon cabinet interpretation of diverse regional demands. This was in marked contrast to the ministerial form of government that had characterized earlier Liberal regimes and indicates, as Herman Bakvis has argued, a shift from a cabinet focus on specific departments to an emphasis on supra-departmental concerns such as social welfare.[41]

While it was a major achievement to be able to point in the direction that the federal government should be proceeding, there was a long way to go before any policies demonstrating a national purpose, unanimously endorsed by cabinet, could be implemented. Cabinet agreed to strike a committee on social security to examine the whole question of the Canada Pension Plan, with Pearson maintaining that pension proposals must be presented to the provinces as soon after the holiday as possible.[42] Meetings in the days between Christmas and New Year produced agreement on a few compromises that the federal government was willing to make in response to the provinces' pension demands, thus putting the ball temporarily in the provincial court. The committee agreed to the use of a retirement test in order to avoid providing pensions for people under seventy who were still employed; it accepted the possibility of increasing the maturity period from ten to fifteen years; and it proposed a partially funded plan.[43] The members advised explaining to the provincial premiers that Ottawa would be willing to open up half of the Canada Pension Plan fund, "to be invested in the obligations of, or obligations guaranteed by, participating provinces ... In deciding what securities to buy, the administration of the plan would be aided by an investment committee, and it would be this committee's duty to consult with the provinces wherever practicable."[44] The committee members were by no means proposing unconditional provincial access to the fund. Although some ministers feared that a retirement test was akin to a means test, that the federal government was making huge concessions on the length of the maturation period, and that the whole scheme was far too expensive, cabinet ultimately agreed to send the proposals to the premiers.[45] Negotiations demanded concessions, and the most telling sign that this approach was working was Roberts's decision to delay certain provisions in Ontario's Pension Benefits Act pending further action by the federal government. The premier's officials advised him not to implement any provincial legislation that would unnecessarily hinder the implementation of a "revised Canada Pension Plan."[46]

Reactions to the new federal proposals were mixed. Saskatchewan expressed concern about the reduction in benefits, the increase in the maturation period, and the implementation of a retirement test as well as the fact that "some provincial governments" seemed to have had more input than others.[47] Premier W.S. Lloyd did not doubt that Ontario was the culprit behind the increase in protection for existing private plans and the subsequent lowering of benefits and extension of the maturation period. Ironically, Saskatchewan and Ontario united in their opposition to the retirement test. George Gathercole of Ontario pointed out that the United States and United Kingdom had found such testing would be overly "cumbersome" and described the federal proposal as a "retrograde step."[48] In general, Gathercole thought that the federal government had ignored Ontario's concerns and made concessions only to Quebec, not altering "the fundamental character or basis of the plan" which had irritated Ontario in the first place.[49] Nova Scotia's Robert Stanfield complained that the Canada Pension Plan negated the possibility of a more extensive re-evaluation of the social-security system, and he did not believe that the plan would have as great an impact on Nova Scotia as it would on larger, more prosperous, provinces.

The federal failure to examine thoroughly the economic dimensions of contributory pensions continued to plague negotiations. Like Stanfield, the premier of Manitoba, Duff Roblin, was interested in how the scheme might benefit his province, particularly given the restrictions on the use of the investment fund.[50] He also continued to press for a comprehensive study of the plan's economic implications. Pearson maintained that "the question of the economic effects had been given a great deal of study by Government economists and ... this was all that was required." Deputy Minister of Welfare J.W. Willard, at least, disagreed and urged LaMarsh to appoint a delegation for the purposes of examining the questions. Several people had already been approached, but none had been willing to conduct the study – the governor of the Bank of Canada, Louis Rasminsky, did not think he was an appropriate choice; Robert Bryce from the Department of Finance said the same of himself and frankly declared that "his appraisal might be negative"; John Deutsch's Economic Council of Canada was busy with other endeavours; the Department of National Health and Welfare was not equipped to "do this matter justice."[51] There seemed to be no obvious solution to the problem, although one has to wonder why the acknowledged need for further inquiry did not immediately result in the appointment of a royal commission.[52] The responses at the 1963 conference to the new federal plan were sufficient to demonstrate that even those provinces initially receptive to federal action on pensions still believed there were some important obstacles to overcome. In Quebec, however, Lesage was reportedly "overjoyed" that Ottawa was allowing its plan to be partially funded as headlines screamed "Ottawa ready to take up Quebec idea."[53]

Although the provinces were by no means unanimous in their support of the proposed revisions to the Canada Pension Plan, they were certainly more enthusiastic than the insurance industry. Since a close relationship had already developed between the representatives of the industry and the Ontario Conservative government, most of the protests against the federal revisions were directed to Robarts and his ministers.[54] The managing director of the Canadian Life Insurance Officers Association warned the premier that although "some of the rough edges have been smoothed out, we are still deeply concerned about the long range implications of the proposal," largely because of the "concentration of a huge fund in the hands of the federal government."[55] The national government itself was not immune to appeals from insurance people, most notably from the vociferous president of Great West Life Assurance Company, David Kilgour, but since neither LaMarsh nor Gordon were particularly receptive the industry found Ontario much more amenable to its concerns.[56] The fact that Ontario almost necessarily had to be a part of the Canada Pension Plan in order for it to be operational meant that there were multiple veto-points at the agreement stage and therefore lobbying Toronto was just as effective as lobbying Ottawa. Indeed, the insurance industry had a greater chance of stopping the implementation of the pension plan by influencing Ontario's decision than it had by attempting to change minds at the federal level.[57] The insurance lobby had little effect on the federal plans to proceed with discussions and, if anything, merely reaffirmed Ottawa's resolve to achieve a national, contributory pension plan.

The federal officials proceeded cautiously, as was their strategy, but the approach seemed increasingly to avoid dealing with the difficult issues the pension plan raised. The whole question of opting-out received renewed attention at the federal and provincial levels of government, both in terms of its philosophical acceptability in a federal state and because of the possibility that Ontario could follow Quebec's lead and undermine the national initiative. The federal cabinet had first seen a draft copy of the pension bill in February and, despite warnings by the drafting officials that "a great deal of additional consideration will be required before it is ready to be placed before Parliament" and opposition from cabinet ministers such as Paul Hellyer, it did little in the following weeks to answer the provinces.[58] Perhaps convinced that the results of a national poll indicating that 72 per cent of Canadians were in favour of a federal pension scheme would encourage reluctant provincial premiers to reach an agreement on the Canada Pension Plan, cabinet tinkered with superficial rather than substantive changes to the proposed bill.[59] The Liberals were thus courting their worst nightmare – that Ontario could chose to implement its own pension plan.

Cabinet made no changes to its pension proposals until early in March 1964, when it increased the contribution rates to the Canada Pension Plan by .25 per cent in each of the years 1980, 1990, 2000, and 2015. Walter Gordon was opposed to the more substantial increases requested by the provinces and only agreed to consider means by which self-employed people with low incomes might better be included in the plan.[60] The federal ministers also gave more careful consideration to the coverage of federal employees in non-participating provinces. But these were not the sort of changes that were of great enough significance to satisfy Ontario. Rumours were beginning to reach the federal government that forces in Ontario were at work not only to withdraw the earlier tentative support for the national initiative but also to "concentrate the pension debate into an anti-Quebec issue."[61] The rumours were not unfounded. Conservative Party organizer George Hogan warned Robarts that he was "being maneuvered into the position of leading the national opposition" and counselled a change of tactics to focus on the "features of the federal plan which adversely affect Ontario vis-a-vis provinces which opt-out," thereby making Lesage into the "villain" of the negotiations.[62] This sort of attack would undoubtedly kill the Canada Pension Plan, threaten the precarious balance of French-English relations in Canada, and force Quebec into an even more isolated position. Cabinet considered an explicit provision in the draft Canada Pension Plan bill that it would automatically not come into force if both Ontario and Quebec opted-out, but this was too extreme for the majority of the ministers.[63] Kent assured the prime minister that the only "technical" reason the pension plan could not be set up for eight provinces was that "the paperwork involved in keeping track of transfers would multiply many times," but he also noted that the real danger in Ontario refusing to join a national scheme was on a political level.[64]

The few weeks before the federal-provincial conference convened saw slightly more activity in Ottawa than had been the case in the preceding months. The long-awaited report on the financial implications of the national pension plan finally appeared and, fortunately for the government, concluded that the Canada Pension Plan would not impair business growth in Canada.[65] The premiers also received a white paper outlining the details of the federal pension proposals.[66] Moreover, Kent tried to encourage the federal delegates at least to think about their responses to questions raised by the provinces. He was particularly adamant that they decide in advance whether "we intend to stand firm" on reserving 50 per cent of the funds for provincial investments, or whether Ottawa would succumb to the pressure to increase the proportion to 90 per cent or 100 per cent. Kent argued against increasing the amount, because he believed that "provinces which accept the federal plan are not doing so for the sake of co-operation with the federal government [but] they are recognising the fact that a great many people move between provinces and therefore a federal plan can better serve the public, who are the constituents of both levels of government." He also pointed to the inequity of the federal government taking primary responsibility for contributions and benefits, then "having little or no interest in the investment of the fund."[67] The commitment to allowing the provinces access to only 50 per cent of the pension fund was perhaps taken in order to give at least the appearance of strength and unity at the national level. After the previous federal-provincial conference, the task was, in Kent's words, "to go on resisting concessions. At the political level, this attitude was strengthened by the Pearson government's sensitivity, after the budget, about any course of action that could be labelled as 'another retreat.'" In retrospect, however, Kent felt that "we had lost control of the situation when, in September [1963] we had not accepted the necessity of making the plan substantially more funded."[68] Whether the federal government, having already conceded much more to the provinces than was its original intent, would be able to stand firm at the negotiating table was yet to be seen.

The federal-provincial conference of 1964 took place from 31 March to 2 April in Quebec City. The opening day was difficult for the federal representatives. There was little room for agreement on the future of shared-cost programs and, therefore, on the very nature of the fiscal and jurisdictional relationship between the two levels of government.[69] The second day of the conference, however, was a total disaster. The terms of the Canada Pension Plan occupied most of the debate on that fateful April Fool's Day and, despite Kent's call for "no retreat" and Pearson's reiteration of this sentiment, "retreat" became the watchword of the day. In response to Robarts's criticism of the federal government's understanding of cooperative federalism the day before, Pearson "said that every province was in exactly the same position as regards contracting out, [although] the attitude of other provinces becomes of even greater interest to the federal government if one has already come out."[70] Robarts maintained that Ontario intended to have a universal contributory pension scheme regardless of what happened to the Canada Pension Plan, and he led the premiers in questioning the consequences of Quebec opting-out. The discussion was premature, since Lesage had not yet explained the details of Quebec's position.

The premier of Quebec said that "he felt bound by the unanimous resolution of the Quebec Legislature calling for a provincial program," but he also declared that "the present similarity between the federal bill and the Quebec plan was such as to assure portability."[71] But, throughout the proceedings, his advisers and cabinet ministers René Lévesque and Paul Gérin-Lajoie were "muttering" to him.[72] Whether they suggested that the premier announce the details of the Quebec pension plan, or whether that had been the intention all along, is unclear. Regardless of its genesis, the disclosure was a bombshell. The

Quebec plan was to cover all employees and self-employed persons compulsorily; its benefits began at age sixty-five; contributions were to be based on that portion of a person's income between $1,000 and $6,000 (and so were more substantial than those anticipated under the federal proposals) and were graduated within that range; and survivor benefits were included, as was legislation for the preservation of rights existing under private pension schemes. The reserves built up under the plan, moreover, were at the complete disposal of the provincial government.[73] Joey Smallwood, the outspoken premier of Newfoundland, asked whether it would be possible for a province to join either the Quebec Pension Plan or the Canada Pension Plan, expressing the views of the delegates so aptly that many others since have taken the witticism as their own.[74]

There was no question that the scheme Quebec intended to introduce shortly in the legislature offered considerably more benefits than the federal plan. It was fully funded and fully available for provincial initiatives, and the benefits were higher and covered a much broader proportion of the population; the Quebec plan even included benefits for widows and orphans, something that the federal government was constitutionally precluded from doing. Tom Kent remembers that the "response in the conference was electric ... and [there was] just no question at that moment the Canada Pension Plan was dead."[75] Until this point, the federal officials had been working on the assumption that only a plan of their design could be considered a national program. They had neglected to consider that provincial proposals might retain all of the key components of the Canada Pension Plan and be structured in a more agreeable fashion. So much effort had been devoted to ensuring that the two plans were similar enough to ensure portability that it appears that the federal negotiators had failed to investigate the details of the Quebec Pension Plan.

Having embarked on the conference with a commitment to make no financial concessions, the federal officials were not in a position to do much to appease the provinces. However, they did offer one carrot which was to have a significant effect on the future of federal-provincial relations in Canada. Robert Bryce, Gordon Robertson, and Tom Kent, frantically trying to save the conference, proposed the establishment of a tax structure committee, composed of representatives from each of the provinces and the federal government, to review the whole fiscal structure.[76] Many of the premiers called it "revolutionary."[77] Although Lesage was not convinced of the utility of such a study, certain that it was yet another federal stalling tactic, "there could be little doubt that an inquiry so structured would result, a year or two hence, in some realignment of taxes favourable to the provinces."[78] Speaking briefly to reporters following the announcement of the formation of the tax structure committee, Pearson clarified "that the time has come when we should consider ... an examination in depth of our tax structure in its relationship to the responsibilities of the two levels of government that have been laid down in our constitution, but which have naturally altered over the years."[79]

At the press conference following the final session in Quebec City, Pearson, Robarts, and Lesage each made statements and answered questions separately, underlining by their actions the failure of the talks and the complete absence of agreement, even if the words spoken were in a vaguely conciliatory tone.[80] As veteran reporter Charles Lynch noted: "It can be argued that Mr. Lesage's comments were at least more honest than those of Mr. Pearson and Mr. Robarts – if the conference was a donnybrook, better to say so than to try to cover it up with diplomatic clichés. It seems possible, however, that Mr. Pearson, Mr. Robarts and the other premiers had honourable reasons for trying to heal, or at least conceal, the extent of the breach with Quebec. Mr. Lesage has his own reasons, obviously, for revealing it."[81]

The federal delegates who left Quebec City following the federal-provincial conference were a dispirited bunch. Nothing of substance had been accomplished, much had been lost, and there seemed little likelihood of success. Worst of all, the damage not only threatened the future of the Canada Pension Plan, a national social program on which the federal Liberals had placed a great deal of emphasis over the preceding two years, but seemed to tear at the very fabric of Canadian unity by pitting provinces against each other and against the federal government – the exact opposite effect that a piece of national social security was supposed to have. The federal ministers present at the conference returned home to lick their political wounds: Favreau, Lamontagne, Gordon, Allan MacEachen, and Harry Hays had all urged a plan of standing firm in the face of opposition at the Quebec conference, and they likely agreed with LaMarsh who was seething with "disillusionment" over Pearson's retreats during negotiations.[82] The civil servants, on the other hand, wasted little time worrying about the political future of the Liberal Party or the leadership qualities of the prime minister and instead gave serious thought to rescuing as many of the national objectives as were possible from the ashes of Quebec.

Both Robertson and Kent spent that first weekend in April putting their thoughts on paper. Robertson regarded the conference as a "serious failure" that irrefutably deepened the "wounds within Confederation" by further isolating Quebec from the other provinces.[83] The only possible solution in Robertson's mind was for the federal government to turn over one or two points from the personal-income and corporate-tax field as "an immediate demonstration that the federal government recognized the growing needs of *all* the provinces."[84]

Kent also tried to make some sense of the options still open to the national Liberals. He felt that what was needed was "to pull off a 'coup.' We have to achieve something that will change the atmosphere, that will translate us from the vicious circle to a virtuous circle in which, because we look good, we can get things moving and therefore look better." His concerns were as much driven by the need to get the Pearson Liberals out of the doldrums of the first two sessions as they were by the need to remedy the situation with Quebec. He proposed coming up with some formula for pensions "whereby the Quebec plan will not be entirely separate from ours (and therefore Ontario won't have an excuse to go it alone)." If the federal government were to open up some tax room for the provinces, it would strengthen Lesage's hand in relation to those in Quebec who were pushing provincial rights even more strongly (some proposed, for example, that Quebec be allowed to manage its own family-allowance scheme) and perhaps enable the federal government to "buy" from Quebec its consent on pensions.[85]

Both Kent and Robertson stressed the need for the federal government to abandon the "no concessions" approach, and both agreed that the only area for retreat was tax sharing. They had reached their conclusions independently, and they hoped that the prime minister would accept their advice as the only solution possible. Kent, who had heard from Maurice Sauvé that Quebec intended to go ahead with its pension plan and tax increases if the federal government did not make an offer soon, could not wait for Pearson's response. He met with the prime minister, discussed the plan he had set forth in his memorandum, and received the necessary permission to make a secret journey to Quebec City (with Sauvé in tow) to hash out the details with Lesage, Claude Morin, and René Lévesque. Since he was negotiating without the consent of cabinet, Kent's challenge was to determine what was possible and then bring that information back to Ottawa. What he achieved was an agreement in principle on Quebec's right to contract-out of existing national programs such as extended family allowances and student loans, its cooperation with the tax structure committee in return for increased federal-tax abatements, and a commitment from the province that it would find a way for the federal government to provide, in the case of pensions as well as other social programs, a basic national minimum.[86]

The two men returned to Ottawa the following day, jubilant that such progress had been made through informal negotiation. The more onerous task of convincing cabinet to accept the details of the arrangements was left to the diplomatic skills of the prime minister. As Kent explained to Pearson in a long memorandum detailing the nature of the discussions in Quebec City, the major concession to the provinces was the increase in tax points from the 1 per cent provided in the current tax-sharing agreements to 3 per cent. It was "enough, but only just enough, for Lesage to accept as politically satisfactory and fiscally sufficient for him to avoid raising taxes and blaming the federal government." Having conceded that, the federal government was then in a position to force Quebec into an agreement over pensions, which Kent felt was "crucial to the 'package.' We are not prepared to make the arrangements on tax-sharing etc., unless agreement is achieved on pensions also." What had been discussed in Quebec was the provision of a "foundation" pension to be based on some of the best features of the national and provincial plans – the federal government would insist on the ten-year maturity period but was willing to move on the issues of contribution rates and funding. Kent explained that "under this plan, Quebec (or any other province) might legislate its own pension plan but would incorporate, identically, the basic federal plan ... In effect, we would be taking a limited part of the 'contribution' (or payroll tax) field, and leaving room for the provinces to occupy more of it. A province that did occupy more would be free either to administer both our part and its own, or to have us administer both."[87]

It is amazing that, so few days after the failure of negotiations at the first ministers' level, a thoughtful, conciliatory, and workable arrangement could be designed unofficially. Away from the spotlight of a federal-provincial conference, there was little to be gained by grandstanding. Kent recognized the benefits of Quebec's plan and could accept it as fulfilling the main conditions of the Canada Pension Plan – it was both portable and universal. Behind the scenes, it looked less like a federal retreat, and neither negotiating team depicted it as such. Nor did the cabinet ministers called together to meet Kent and Sauvé on their return. The assembled ministers included Walter Gordon, Paul Martin, Guy Favreau, Maurice Lamontagne, Allan MacEachen, and Mitchell Sharp. Judy LaMarsh, the minister of national health and welfare and therefore the one most directly effected by the details of the negotiations, was notable by her absence. Incredibly, she had not even been aware of the secret mission to Quebec City.[88] At first, Gordon was reluctant and wanted to think about the proposals overnight before reaching his decision. This is understandable given the criticisms he had already weathered in the House of Commons over governmental retreats and the fact that he would again be responsible for explaining the financial implications of the new deal to an over-eager opposition in Parliament. However, "while the proposals would be a bit messy ... [his] immediate reaction was that this would be a small price to pay if it were necessary to keep Quebec within Confederation."[89] Ultimately, all agreed, and they assured the negotiators that productive discussions could continue and the rest of cabinet would be brought on side. The stage was set for the arrival in Ottawa of Claude Morin and Claude Castonguay to iron out the details of the pension scheme.

It quickly became evident that it would be impossible to agree on a federal "foundation" plan to be applicable in all provinces, with further augmentation left to the discretion of the provincial governments. There were too many differences between the Canada and Quebec pension plans as proposed to facilitate this sort of arrangement. Instead, the parties agreed to combine the two into one compulsory scheme which made funds available for provincial investment, had a maturity period of ten years and contribution and benefit rates that were slightly higher than those Ottawa had envisaged, and included a constitutional amendment ensuring the delivery of survivor benefits.[90] Kent argued strongly in favour of this compromise. Ontario was still enough of a problem that Keith Davey suggested taking the pension question to the grass roots and calling a referendum, but Kent thought that the agreement with Quebec was good enough that it was "hard to see Ontario or any other province making very much difficulty." Moreover, "the changes from our present plan are largely improvements from the public's point of view," and given that "Quebec would be making appreciable sacrifices: reducing her fund ... charging her low-income people more, and sacrificing some pride to meet us," Kent advised the federal government to "make this deal if we can."[91]

On 15 April, just four days after the negotiations between federal and Quebec representatives over the pension scheme, the Quebec cabinet accepted the terms, and the following day Pearson's cabinet followed suit. Gordon and Kent both counselled speed in informing the other provincial premiers of the main points of the pension arrangement and in setting up the tax structure committee. Kent suggested that the new formula for tax sharing, to supersede the existing agreements in effect until 1967, should be announced after Lesage unveiled his own provincial budget, which would allow time for "an improvement in the general atmosphere" and not look like a "concession to achieve that improvement."[92] Gordon urged that Robarts be dealt with more personally than the other premiers, "to make him feel that he is being kept in the picture. I think," he prophesied, "he really is receptive to an appeal to hold Canada together."[93] Gordon was probably the best judge of Robarts's mood, since they had long been associated and it was common when "a difficult financial aspect of national policy arose which directly affected the Ontario government, [for] Gordon [to] fly to Toronto, discreetly enter the Premier's office and seek a resolution to the problem."[94] Pearson had in fact kept Robarts informed by telephone of the progress of negotiations following the initial pension agreement between Ottawa and Quebec.[95] The other premiers received a letter outlining the agreement and a commitment from the federal government, in light of the necessity of improving educational facilities, to offer "an additional abatement of the federal personal-income tax of 2% commencing in January 1965 and a further 2% in January 1966, in addition to the increases at those dates already provided in our law."[96] Telegrams were soon flooding in expressing appreciation of the "expanded policies" of the federal government and the "lead towards strengthening of national unity."[97] It was the first positive sign for federal-provincial relations in a long time.

Walter Gordon had been right about Ontario, however. Used to being a key province in negotiations with the federal government, Ontario representatives were disappointed with the role Quebec had played in the determination of national policy. As George Gathercole complained, "the province that contracts out possesses the right to be consulted; those that contract in unless there is an explicit provision providing for consultation are not consulted, or at least not in an effective way."[98] Robarts agreed that Ontario had been outmanoeuvred by Quebec and resolved to "build a base of new competence in the Ontario government" as a means to combat the forces in Quebec and "the 'Tom Kent Liberalism' prevailing in the nation's capital."[99] Although the federal politicians believed that it was "improbable" that Ontario would "insist on any major changes," they realized that "there is a price for Ontario's acceptance." Since Quebec wanted to retain its rights to change the Quebec Pension Plan unilaterally, "Ontario must not thereby be put in the position of sacrificing, on form or in fact, rights which Quebec retains."[100] In cabinet, Pearson noted that "it now seemed necessary to devise formulae which would safeguard the right of Ontario or any other province to withdraw from the Canada Pension Plan at a future time. In doing so, however, it was important not to make it look as if the Canada Pension Plan were shaky and uncertain."[101]

With full recognition of the need for careful manoeuvring, Tom Kent wrote to the chief pension negotiators in Ontario and Quebec. He noted that "the federal legislation must not restrict – either legally or in practical effect – the exercise of provincial jurisdiction,"[102] and he went into more detail for Laurence Coward of Ontario on this point. Kent clarified that "this means, in particular, that the provinces should not be faced with a 'once-and-for-all' choice. A province that does not exercise its jurisdiction now must not thereby be in a restricted position, if it wants to pass its own legislation at some future time, compared with a province which legislates now."[103] To both provinces, he stressed the need to avoid any uncertainty in the legislation, and he also outlined a proposal to allow provinces to decide in the future whether they wanted to implement their own provincial pension plan without altering the comprehensive character of the Canada Pension Plan. Subsequent negotiations with Ontario resulted in a tentative agreement by which neither the federal nor the provincial government could make substantial amendments to their respective legislation without giving the other government considerable notice.

Ontario requested, and received, a further constraint on the scope of federal control over the pension plan. On 11 June 1964 Ontario and the federal government discussed the procedures to amend the Canada Pension Plan in the future. The proposal was that "the federal legislation should provide that 'major amendments' would not take effect until the first day of January of the third year after notice of them is given to 'relevant provinces,' and 'amendments of substance' would take effect only if consented to by two-thirds of the 'relevant provinces' having two-thirds of the total population of relevant provinces."[104] Quebec could decide to be considered a 'relevant province' for the purposes of agreement on amendments, provided it, too, agreed to give notice to the federal government three years prior to enacting changes to their own provincial pension legislation.[105] Cabinet reluctantly approved the proposals, but only with the understanding that Pearson and Robarts would be responsible for reaching a final settlement, "at which time the Prime Minister would endeavour to obtain an agreement more favourable to the federal government."[106] Later negotiations did not result in any relaxation of the restrictions placed on the federal government, but they justified the lack of provincial concessions on the ground that "the constitutional and political facts are that ... federal freedom to move on pensions is limited by the provinces. The proposal merely recognizes the facts." Moreover, the Liberals realized that "the Ontario government is under very strong pressure from people who do not like the plan at all ... [so] we cannot expect [Robarts] to be accommodating ... unless we provide safeguards which enable him convincingly to say that he really has not sacrificed his future power."[107]

There were more negotiations through the summer of 1964, and some rewriting of the pension legislation was necessary as it made its way through Parliament in 1965, but the major components of a national contributory pension plan were in place shortly after the Quebec City federal-provincial conference.[108] The federal government had made many concessions in order to secure the future of the Canada Pension Plan, and ultimately it implemented a plan that bore little resemblance to the scheme the Liberals had contemplated during the opposition years. Instead of being tied to increases in the old-age-pension benefits and establishing a non-funded scheme, the Liberals had altered their course and agreed to meet the provincial desire for access to the accumulating funds. Ottawa had also compromised on the question of benefits, contributions, and the rate of maturity. If the outlines of the pension arrangement had been changed, however, the goal of a national, comprehensive, and contributory plan remained the same.

The Pearson Liberals' approach to pensions was characterized by a strong commitment to the central components of the Canada Pension Plan: universality, portability, and equality of benefits. If the resolve at the elite level of politics was sometimes weak, strong cabinet ministers such as Judy LaMarsh, Walter Gordon, and others continued to appeal to their colleagues to support the plan. Behind the scenes, Tom Kent worked furiously to see the implementation of universal pensions. Both groups were willing to accept minor regional differences in the implementation of the plan as long as its fundamental qualities remained intact. Quebec's decision to implement its own pension plan was, therefore, not an indication of the failure of the federal initiatives, but rather a reasonable interpretation of the national goal of "better pensions for all." By adopting an approach to negotiations that entailed centralized direction over major objectives but allowed decentralized discretion on implementation, the Liberals achieved more than merely a beneficial social program.[109] They were also one step closer to identifying the general social well-being of the population as a key responsibility of the national government.

The achievement of the Canada Pension Plan legislation also demonstrated the successful transformation of the national Liberal Party. By accepting the national responsibility for a fully portable and universal pension scheme, the Pearson Liberals had shifted their administrative emphasis away from the national economy and towards the well-being of the individual citizen. Unlike the economic-policy objectives that dominated the thinking of previous Liberal administrations, national social programs were ideally suited to a centralized vision of general goals combined with more regional discretion at the implementation stage. The Canada Pension Plan demanded a central, national vision, but at the same time one that could be flexibly interpreted. Moreover, different provincial interpretations of the fundamental pension objectives did not negate the fact that the plan was national in scope. The national government had a new role to play: identifying social needs and designing a template for their solution.

The change in the nature of national government did not happen by accident. As Pearson himself said, the new Liberal Party believed in a form of "politics which, based on the individual citizen, [had] become in its principles and its ideals and in its practice, more non-partisan and more co-operative in national effort and in promoting national welfare; politics which will reject sectional and selfish interests in the interests of the country as a whole."[110] In remaining true to such a course, and interpreting it broadly enough to allow for significant provincial input, the federal Liberal Party succeeded in implementing one of the most important pieces of social legislation yet seen in Canadian public policy.

6 Federal-Provincial Negotiations over Health Insurance, 1964–65

The progressive Liberals who drafted the Liberal Rally resolutions of 1961 had considered a national health-insurance scheme to be the primary social objective of a new Liberal government, and while they had not ignored other pressing social issues most thought that a commitment first made in 1919 had probably gestated long enough in the public consciousness and needed immediate action. However, the combination of grass-roots enthusiasm at the rally and the expectation that pensions would be relatively easier to achieve than health insurance ensured that a contributory pension scheme topped the Liberal agenda. Much to the surprise of the policy planners, however, the process of achieving a national pension plan had been a gruelling one, both during the planning stage while in opposition and particularly during the period of intergovernmental negotiation. The obvious conclusion that they had been naive going into social-policy development had serious implications for the other components in the Liberal social net: some people were fearful of embarking on another round of difficult negotiations, others were sure that there were important lessons to be gained from the Canada Pension Plan experience, and still others preferred a return to a more piecemeal approach to social policy. But just as pensions had been considerably modified through the process of negotiation without altering the long-avowed central tenets, the planners, too, had undergone something of a metamorphosis. They recognized that their health-insurance tactics would have to change in light of the new intergovernmental environment, but at the same time they remained convinced of the centrality of social security not only to the wefare of the nation but also to the very nature of Pearsonian Liberalism.

By the summer of 1964, even before pension negotiations were completed, it was obvious that events were conspiring to force the Liberals to act on their long-standing promise to introduce medical-insurance legislation. With little more than a year of experience in office and in federal-provincial negotiations, the progressive social-policy advocates were nevertheless immeasurably more political than they had been in opposition. Most assumed that the course of pension negotiations was characteristic of all forays into provincial jurisdiction over social policy and thus regarded intergovernmental negotiations as key and likely combative. Ottawa needed to have a clear approach to the provinces before negotiations even began. But the internal dynamics of the party also had an effect on the progress of medicare, and the now more experienced planners and politicians sought to ensure that the Liberals themselves were not guilty of derailing the achievement of health insurance, particularly given the reluctance of some to embark on a new round of negotiations while pensions were still being hotly debated. The group of left-wing Liberals were thus convinced that, if an internal commitment to proceeding with the health-insurance scheme as envisaged in opposition could be achieved, and a clear approach to possibly contentious intergovernmental negotiations devised, the future of medicare would be assured. They had taken their cues from the experience of the Canada Pension Plan, and that experience shaped the initial approach to the second component of the Liberal social-security strategy. That health insurance did not quite mirror pensions, and that the most serious impediments to implementation would be found in the heart of the Liberal Party itself, was not yet apparent.

The degree to which the Pearson Liberals had to be pushed into acting on health insurance attests to the all-consuming nature of pension negotiations. Despite the characteristic caution of the prime minister himself, the social-policy planners as a whole had long been committed to the concept of universal state-sponsored medical insurance. The toll taken by the Canada Pension Plan, however, was high, and even the most vociferous advocates of health insurance, including Minister of National Health and Welfare Judy LaMarsh and key bureaucrat Tom Kent, found themselves foundering in the abyss of difficult pension debates. As the wits in the civil service penned, "The CPP's up in the air/ Let others turn to medicare!"[1] The long and acrimonious physicians' strike in Saskatchewan, pursued in a vain attempt to stop the provincial medicare legislation, was not sufficient to turn the federal government's attention to its own stated health-care objectives. Nor was Ontario's investigation into a private-enterprise version of health insurance, later adopted in Alberta and British Columbia, enough to force Ottawa to take pre-emptive measures. Only the submission of the report of the Royal Commission on Health Services resulted in federal activity. In fact, while cognizant of activity at the provincial level, when the Liberals discussed health insurance at all prior to the summer of 1964 it was to put off deciding anything until the Hall commission concluded its studies.[2] But the combination of provincial activity and the conclusion of the royal commission, along with the concommitant politicization of the public on the issue of health insurance, spurred Pearson's government to action.

Tommy Douglas's Saskatchewan CCF government had the strongest record in the health-insurance field. It had been part of the party's platform when it was first elected in 1944, and the provincial hospital-insurance scheme of 1948 was the first step towards full medical insurance. More than ten years elapsed before the provincial government took the next step.[3] The Douglas administration began working on medicare in earnest in the spring of 1959 when it established an interdepartmental committee to investigate the options. The committee reported in November 1959, recommending a plan that would be prepaid, universal, and government-sponsored. Administered by a public body accountable to the legislature, it aimed to be acceptable both to those providing the service and to those receiving it. Appointing University of Saskatchewan president emeritus W.P. Thompson as the chair, Douglas announced the formation of an advisory planning committee to design a medical-insurance system that would embody the proposals of the interdepartmental committee.

There was every reason to believe that the Saskatchewan physicians intended to resist a government-sponsored health insurance program. The Saskatchewan College of Physicians and Surgeons (SCPS) collected over $60,000 for a public-relations committee to combat the government proposals during the 1960 provincial election and the Canadian Medical Association added another $35,000.[4] But, despite the doctors' best efforts, the voters returned 38 CCFers and only 17 Liberals – a sweeping endorsement of the CCF medicare plan. The members of the Douglas government recognized, as did their associates in organized labour, that "the Saskatchewan medical plan is going to be so important in terms of creating a precedent that it must be the best program possible."[5] However, wanting to take action quickly, at least in part because of Douglas's 1961 decision to move to the national political arena, the government hurried the Thompson inquiry and succeeded in securing an interim report in the summer of 1961.

Based on the majority proposals contained in the interim report, the CCF government, now led by Woodrow Lloyd, drafted legislation and the bill passed into law with relatively little legislative dissent on 18 November 1961.[6] The comprehensive, pre-paid health-insurance plan, financed through premiums and calling for physician remuneration on a fee-for-service basis, was to come into operation on 1 July 1962. When the SCPS announced that its members were considering the withdrawal of medical services until such time as the act was repealed or they were permitted to ignore it, Premier Lloyd described the issue as "whether the people of Saskatchewan shall be governed by a democratically elected legislature responsible to the people, or by a small, highly organized group."[7] Others cast the debate in more vitriolic terms but, in the initial stages at least, the physicians' position seemed to attract a considerable amount of support both within Saskatchewan and across the country. The tide quickly turned, however, when furious last-minute negotiations failed to achieve a settlement and the doctors of the province went out on strike 1 July 1962.

The government immediately took emergency measures to ensure the safety of the population. Those doctors who broke ranks with their profession and continued to provide services were spread around the province, and other physicians from the United States and Britain raced to the scene to offer their assistance. The government was in the unenviable position of being responsible for the cessation of medical care yet unwilling to bow to the demands of the medical profession. In the early days, it was clear to one observer that Premier Lloyd was "worried as to how long a government can hold out in a situation where the population is being subjected to panic conditions."[8] Although not everyone supported the CCF position in Saskatchewan, the physicians came under increasing attack from all quarters: medical practitioners in other parts of Canada and the world criticized the "blackmail method" of their Saskatchewan colleagues, the press outside of Saskatchewan increased their attacks on the SCPS position, and opinion in Ottawa was that "the doctors have left the rails, inflicting damage nationally and internationally on an image fostered and developed by centuries of good work."[9]

The beginning of the end was apparent when Dr. H.D. Dalgleish, head of the SCPS, agreed to withdraw the demand for the suspension of the Medical Care Insurance Act as a condition for negotiations with the government. Utilizing the advising and mediating talents of Lord Taylor, a British physician and Labour peer, the two sides negotiated what became known as the Saskatoon agreement and signed it on 23 July 1962. Although the government agreed to allow patients to assign their reimbursement rights, providing a role for voluntary agencies that had not earlier been anticipated, the agreement was essentially a victory for the Saskatchewan CCF.[10] The Saskatchewan physicians had capitulated and "accepted the fundamental principle of a Government-sponsored, compulsory Medical Care Plan for the Province."[11]

Despite the shaky start, Saskatchewan's medicare system, once fully operational, ran smoothly and functioned as well if not better than the most optimistic predictions. Physicians' incomes did not suffer and their numbers surprisingly increased in the province, the fund accumulated a surplus in the first year and cut the original premiums in half, and, most important, medicare was popular with the public.[12] Yet other provinces did not leap at the opportunity to emulate Saskatchewan's initiative. In mid-1963 Alberta introduced its own scheme, but the Social Credit government of Ernest Manning was an unlikely source of state-sponsored health insurance. Instead, "with a minimum of interest and certainly no contention," the Alberta legislature passed a bill calling for a non-compulsory plan providing health insurance through private carriers and with selective assistance for low-income groups.[13] There was little similarity between the neighbouring provinces' medical-care plans – as Allan Blakeney commented, "we in Saskatchewan aimed at making medical care available to all citizens, regardless of their ability to pay. Evidently this was not the aim of the Alberta medical care plan."[14] In 1964 British Columbia followed Alberta's lead and introduced voluntary health coverage through private carriers and the doctor-sponsored Medical Services Incorporated, despite unrelenting opposition from the provincial NDP leader Robert Strachan.[15] Neither province opted for a scheme in any way similar to Saskatchewan's, or one that anticipated the recommendations of the Hall commission.

The Ontario government had also demonstrated some early interest in the question of health insurance. The Robarts government did not approach the issue in the same way Tommy Douglas had done in Saskatchewan; both Liberals and Conservatives sensed that Ontario physicians would oppose compulsory state health insurance. Nevertheless, the premier encouraged a thorough investigation into the health-insurance options open to a province committed to the ideals of free enterprise. The preliminary meeting between representatives of various medical and insurance groups and the Ontario minister of health in November 1962 was designed specifically to solicit advice on how best the government could implement a universally available, non-compulsory health-insurance scheme that would be offered through multiple carriers. Suggestions for alternative designs were not entertained. This first meeting resulted in the striking of a series of committees to investigate various aspects of the issue, including the mechanics of providing health insurance, medical fees and benefits, and the problem of the indigent. All of the investigative activities were coordinated by an advisory committee vested with the responsibility of keeping the minister informed of the progress. Significantly, David Kilgour, whose life work seems to have been attempting to derail government-sponsored insurance schemes, was named to the advisory committee.[16]

The subcommittees provided a model for an acceptable free-enterprise medicare system. In general, they advised a system of two provincial health-insurance contracts, each universally available through private carriers and organizations which chose to offer health insurance to their members or employees, with premium rates not exceeding a stipulated maximum. In every other respect, the carriers were free to operate in "exactly the same way as at present, and in particular, to offer plans of coverage which may be greater or lesser in extent of benefits or coverage than the standard plans."[17] With these recommendations in hand, the Roberts government brought in a pilot Medical Services Insurance Program and introduced Bill 163 embodying its proposals, invited comment, and proposed the establishment of a further special committee to conduct public hearings.[18] Ontario's medical insurance was structured as the "first stage – time, experience and the report of the Royal Commission on Health Services will lead to careful, sound progress."[19]

Roberts appointed the medical-services insurance committee on 31 August 1963, naming the president of the University of Waterloo, Gerald Hagey, as its chair. The group, which included medical practitioners and actuaries, was mandated to put flesh on the bones of the earlier recommendation from the health-insurance subcommittees. The Hagey commission's recommendations were to be "consonant with the basic principles, purposes and objectives of Bill 163."[20] When the federal Hall commission released its recommendations, the Ontario commission was still conducting hearings. Although Premier Roberts has been described as "not strongly wedded to the Ontario plan,"[21] there was no escaping the fact that, as had been the case with pensions, the Ontario government had done considerably more investigation into the question of health insurance than had the national Liberals.

Liberals everywhere, both at the federal and the provincial level, watched with interest the activity in those provinces which were in the throes of attempting to implement some form of health insurance. At the time of the doctors' strike, Liberals in Saskatchewan and Ontario agreed that "the bitterness that has been created throughout the general population is another one of the legacies that we can put at Mr. Douglas' doorstep."[22] At their provincial Liberal convention six months later, Ontario Liberal Party members were somewhat surprised to discover the extent of physicians' opposition to "any scheme which provides what they call a monopoly for any carrier even if it is an agency owned and controlled by them."[23] Yet this opposition was misleading. The most important lesson the federal Liberals could take from events in Saskatchewan was that the physicians did not have the power to mount a successful blockade of public health insurance. Any suspicion that Saskatchewan represented merely the doctors' first feeble attempts and that they were dedicated to regrouping and trying again was dismissed in the aftermath of the implementation of the Saskatchewan scheme. Health insurance was so popular that even the originally disenchanted Liberals in Saskatchewan abruptly changed their 1964 election tactics and pledged "not to change the existing Medicare legislation by as much as a comma."[24] Yet, while federal Liberals were quick to heed the lesson that physicians represented little threat to their own health-insurance plans, they remained reluctant to introduce legislation.

Not only had the provincial governments given a great deal of consideration to the question of how best to provide for the medical-care needs of their citizens, their investigations had also fuelled the public's interest in the issues surrounding health insurance. The Hall commission had a similar effect, for as it toured the country investigating the future of health insurance in Canada, public interest was piqued. The commissioners received over three hundred submissions from various individuals and groups. The usual participants in the health-insurance debate presented their opinions – the medical associations, insurance industry, labour unions, and business associations. Because the public inquiry offered a unique forum for discussing health insurance, views were often presented in a more balanced manner than was characteristic of the debate. As the hearings went on through the autumn of 1961 and into the late spring of 1962 in the increasingly tense atmosphere of the impending doctors' strike in Saskatchewan, there was a marked contrast between the judicious inquiry of the Hall commission and the feverish political manipulation occurring in the prairies. This was exactly what the Canadian Medical Association had anticipated when it pressed Diefenbaker to appoint the commission in the first place, stating that it preferred that health insurance be studied rationally, outside "the hectic arena of political events."[25] The context of the Hall commission's hearings made its task all the more difficult: in an overheated political environment, the commissioners were entrusted with the chore of making sense out the hundreds of individual submissions, the information gleaned from the health-insurance experience in other countries, and the investigations of medical and research consultants.

The opinions expressed in the submissions were not particularly surprising in and of themselves. Most organizations' views were widely known to people familiar with the lines that had already been drawn on the question of state-sponsored medical-care insurance. The Canadian Labour Congress argued for a system that was "universal in application and comprehensive in coverage" and one that would "present no economic barrier between the service and those who need it."[26] In accord with its belief in the "freedom of the individual" and its opposition to "the introduction of a 'socialized medicine' scheme in Canada," the executive council of the Canadian Chamber of Commerce recommended that "Canadians place a higher priority on budgeting for health care and in particular avail themselves of an appropriate plan to assist in defraying the costs of medical care."[27] The position outlined by the national organization was repeated by various chambers of commerce across the country.[28] The Canadian Medical Association was not as vehement in its opposition to government funding since the association was, after all, in the business of making sure that its members earned a decent wage. The CMA and its provincial wings all submitted proposals for government subsidies for low-income groups but emphasized the continued use of private-insurance carriers for the remainder of the population.[29] Special-interest groups did not monopolize the submission process – provincial governments and private citizens with a particular interest in the issue also submitted their views to the Hall commission.

Canadians demonstrated their interest in health insurance in the clearest possible manner in the early 1960s. They elected provincial governments committed to taking action, they submitted proposals by the hundreds to the Royal Commission on Health Services, and they anxiously awaited an indication of the lead the federal government was prepared to take. The recommendations of the Hall commission, as representing the collective opinion of all who had made submissions, should not have been unexpected. However, the commissioners themselves had been more strongly influenced by some views than others. Ironically, given the genesis of the inquiry, the CMA position was not one that was particularly persuasive. The first volume of the commission's report, issued on 19 June 1964 and outlining the most important and most fundamental recommendations, began with an umbrella recommendation "that the objectives of the [Health] Charter be achieved

through the development of a comprehensive Health Services Programme universally available to all Canadian regardless of age, condition, place of residence or ability to pay."[30] In the words of the group's
research consultant, the "royal commission had given 'dispassionate
and objective consideration to the future pattern of health care' and
had reached the same conclusion that the [medical] profession feared
would emerge from the 'hectic arena of political controversy.'"[31]

The first volume recommended broad health-insurance coverage for
Canadians, including prescription drugs, children's dental and optical
services, and home-care programs. The commissioners concluded that
"Canada's human resources, men, women and children, are worth the
price that must be paid in taxes in ensuring that all Canadians may
enjoy the best health possible in this era of scientific advancement and
that Canada can afford that price."[32] They believed that a full health-
insurance scheme was well within the financial capacity of the country,
although they recognized that, despite constitutional difficulties,
"financial assistance" from the federal government would be necessary. The commission, therefore, recommended an arrangement similar
to that employed in the Hospital Insurance and Diagnostic Services
Act, whereby the federal government would contribute 50 per cent of
the cost of operating a health-insurance system to all participating
provinces. By involving the national government in the system, the
commissioners expected that the objective of universality would be
more realistic.

The commission had paid careful attention to the provincial studies
of health insurance that were being conducting simultaneously with its
own hearings. One of the most important recommendations, however,
was the rejection of a voluntary system on the ground that it would
not be able to achieve maximum coverage. The commissioners warned
against the adoption of a national program similar to those which
Alberta and Ontario had been discussing. Universality made sense to
them: "in order to spread the risks over the whole population, rather
than only those who chose to insure voluntarily, all Canadians should
be covered by health insurance. This requires both social action and
government participation in the provision of health care."[33] Only one
question remained. Would the Pearson Liberals, exhausted by the
strain of negotiations over the Canada Pension Plan, uncomfortable
with the insecurity of minority government, and barely masking the
divisions in cabinet, be up to the challenge?

Royal commissions are notorious tools of delay, offering the government of the day the luxury of appearing to be interested in a particular

issue while in reality merely waiting through the long process of official study and deliberation. When the Hall commission reported in the summer of 1964, the Liberals did not immediately leap into action: there followed a necessary period when the implications of the Report were weighed and the appropriate course of action considered. In fact, the question of timing was the most important problem facing the Pearson Liberals as they grappled with the implications of the Hall commission's report. The most serious issues revolved around whether to begin negotiations with the provinces over medicare before reaching an agreement on the Canada Pension Plan, and how the next election might affect the future of Liberal social policies. With little other than their experience with pensions to go by, the Liberals were ill-prepared to predict the course that health insurance might follow. Too many things had changed.

While the federal government remained fairly quiet in the months following the publication of the Hall recommendations, other organizations could not afford to delay their response. The medical community, for one, was not in a position to refuse comment on the Hall report. The initial reaction was one of shock, absolute rejection of the recommendations, and ultimately the hope "that the eventual provincial plans will be a compromise between what [Hall] said and what [the physicians] say now."[34] The CMA did not want a repeat of the Saskatchewan health-insurance plan. Minister of National Health and Welfare Judy LaMarsh tried to smooth the physicians' ruffled feathers and assured the Medical Society of Nova Scotia that "the government subscribes fully" to the principle of "autonomous professional organizations" as outlined in the royal commission report.[35] She was not forthcoming, however, on what the Liberal government planned to do about the commission's recommendations, saying only that "very careful consideration must ... be given to all its recommendations before any definite policy proposals are put forward."[36] Through the parliamentary session, however, the Liberal government was kept busy negotiating a final agreement on the Canada Pension Plan and action on health insurance had to wait.

On the surface, it appeared that even the left-wing social-policy planners were divided over how, and when, to approach national health insurance. Interestingly, the opinions on medicare had less to do with the financial capabilities of the federal government than with the timing of the next general election. Their minority government situation dictated that the Pearson Liberals had to constantly be on the alert for the best time to go to the voters for a majority. Although the left-wing politicians and advisers had different views about timing, they were in fundamental agreement on the need to strengthen the progressive forces in Parliament before embarking on health-insurance negotiations.

Walter Gordon, finance minister and chair of the national campaign committee, favoured calling an election in the spring of 1965, and he could count on the support of most of the committee in advancing that view.[37] The group identified a number of reasons for going to the voters in the late spring. Foremost among them was the clear indication that the Conservatives were in disarray. During the final session of Diefenbaker's administration, the Chief's indecisiveness had created divisions in cabinet over the question of nuclear weapons, divisions that were so serious that Defence Minister Douglas Harkness resigned and a cabinet coup was just barely averted. The loss of power did nothing to unite a party already deeply split, and despite Diefenbaker's own powerful parliamentary performances as leader of the Opposition, Conservatives continued to fight among themselves. Most serious was the threatened defection of Leon Balcer, named as Quebec lieutenant at the party's 1964 convention but subsequently all but completely ignored by the Chief. Balcer's patience with Diefenbaker finally ran out over the leader's inability to recognize the importance of Quebec in regaining power; in December 1964 Balcer told the press he was considering resigning and in January the Quebec Conservative caucus requested that party president Dalton Camp call a leadership convention. Balcer complained specifically about Diefenbaker's attacks on many of the Liberal policies – most particularly during the debates over the new national flag and the Canada Pension Plan, when Diefenbaker adopted a generally anti-French line of argument.[38] Liberals watched with glee the machinations of the Opposition, but with the possibility of a new Conservative leader looming, the national campaign committee argued that the best time to hold an election was when Diefenbaker, a shadow of his former self in terms of the support he could muster among his allies, was still at the helm.

In assessing the electoral circumstances that favoured the Liberals, as opposed to those that hampered the Conservatives, the campaign committee pointed out that Canadians had been generally receptive to the new national flag and to the prime minister's performance in the House of Commons, and it predicted that the Liberals would be able to pick up another thirty seats across the country if an election were called soon.[39] This was certainly the view of the committee's chairman. Gordon, who had grown immeasurably more politically astute since his first weeks in Parliament, was still firmly committed to a progressive social-policy platform and was now fighting for his political future. Though he still enjoyed the support of a significant portion of the Ontario caucus, Gordon's political appeal had been steadily deteriorating since the budget debacle in 1963 and he no longer had quite the same access to the prime minister. With strong support from Keith Davey, Gordon advocated an early election in part because it would present the Liberals with an opportunity to start afresh: he was convinced that the present government "is never going to be much good" and hoped that the next election would stack the cards more favourably for the progressive group of Liberals.[40]

An early election was not designed to interfere with the question of health insurance. To the contrary, Gordon hoped to use medicare as a way of securing the quick election call, which would in turn result in a House of Commons filled with Liberals firmly committed to implementing a comprehensive system of national health insurance. Early in 1965, during the Christmas recess, Pearson wrote to the caucus soliciting input on what should be included in the Speech from the Throne. He offered some guidelines, suggesting that he did "not think we can plan to take [medicare] on, at least in any comprehensive way, in 1965."[41] In response, Gordon suggested that since medicare was not an issue that the Liberals could afford to ignore completely, it should at least be mentioned in the Throne Speech.[42] Pearson followed Gordon's advice. Three months later, however, an election still not called, Gordon pressured the prime minister into making a decision, reminding him that "as the Throne Speech made clear, there is a great deal of work to be done – but it will take new elections and a majority government to do most of it."[43] Thus, after having pressed for the inclusion of medicare in the first instance, Gordon used it as an argument for calling an early election. His commitment to health insurance had not wavered since he had first drafted the "Liberal Plan for Health" after the Kingston Conference, but his faith in the commitment of his present colleagues had most certainly been shaken.

Tom Kent did not share Gordon's views on timing or on the unredeemable nature of the present cabinet. In this he was perhaps naive. Kent was opposed to the majority view held by his colleagues on the campaign committee regarding the election, calling it a reflection of "the smart-alec, fix-it-up, let's-think-of-a-gimmick, advertising-salesman view of politics, which is responsible for a good deal of the Liberal party's troubles."[44] He thought the more appropriate course would be to wait until the Liberals had engineered themselves into a position of strength, a position that he believed to be attainable with the existing cast of characters.[45]

Kent based his advice on two things: his 1963 policy agenda, and his conviction that health insurance would have to be dealt with before the next general election. In opposition, Kent had envisaged negotiating a system of national health insurance sometime near the end of a four-year stint in office. Thus 1965 was too soon to begin work on medicare, a view that explains why Kent did not want the subject included in the Speech from the Throne.[46] However, since the Liberals had committed themselves to acting on health insurance as part of their campaign platform in both 1962 and 1963, Kent firmly believed that it would have to be considered before another election was called. He just did not want that to be too soon. Yet, as the pressure for an early election increased, Kent responded with his usual alacrity and began to outline the issues involved in negotiating national health insurance. Characteristically, he advised the government to lay its cards on the table by announcing the type of plan it favoured and then discussing that plan with the provinces. The advantage of such an approach was that "it would give the Federal Government time – the time that it needs to work out with the provinces the approach that should be taken to bringing about the introduction across Canada of new social measures. This time is needed in any event – to permit public digestion of the Canada Pension Plan, and to permit officials of the federal and provincial governments to work on the technical aspects of any proposed medical care scheme."[47] Kent still did not advocate rushing headlong into negotiations over health insurance, but if there was going to be an early election he accepted that the issue had to be addressed.

Regardless of when the Liberals chose to go to the electorate, national health insurance could not be swept under the table: the release of the recommendations of the Hall commission had negated that possibility. The publication of volume 2 of the commission's report in 1965, highlighting the administration of the health program and addressing some of the objections raised against volume 1, placed medicare firmly on the national agenda.[48] In this atmosphere, the government's decision to include a mention of medicare in the Throne Speech of 5 April was insufficient to placate its critics. Tommy Douglas, national leader of the NDP, was quick to criticize the government for failing to endorse the recommendations of the Hall commission and instead contenting "itself with saying that the quality of health services should be improved and made available to all Canadians" without explaining how.[49] Despite commanding few supporters in the House of Commons, Douglas expressed a concern shared by the Canadian Labour Congress and a growing number of Canadians.[50]

The cabinet moved cautiously on medicare. Ignoring Kent's advice to set the national policy first, it began by soliciting the views of the provinces. Judy LaMarsh invited the provincial health ministers to a federal-provincial conference at the end of May 1965 to "discuss the

way in which federal and provincial action can most effectively contribute to programs that will provide health services to Canadians on
a comprehensive basis."[51] Before the actual face-to-face negotiations
occurred, LaMarsh suggested that senior federal officials meet with
their provincial counterparts to determine "the main concepts and
objections which can be expected to influence our discussions at the
forthcoming Federal-Provincial Conference."[52] For most of April and
May 1965, officials jetted around the country trying to establish
where the different provincial governments stood on national health
insurance.

The federal officials discovered that all the provinces agreed with
the "broad principle" outlined by the prime minister. But Pearson had
been purposely vague in his earlier letter, stating little more than that
"the federal government believes that public policy should be directed
to improving the quality of health services," and so general agreement
did not guarantee the future of the sort of program Hall envisaged.
For example, while all provinces endorsed the concept of universality,
the term meant different things in each of the provincial capitals. Half
of the provinces would "probably accept" a system similar to that
used for hospital insurance, which used techniques to ensure that 85
per cent of the population was covered from the outset; two provinces
wanted to begin with compulsory coverage only for the young and
old; and two or three provinces preferred subsidized voluntary programs.[53] Moreover, the provinces "stressed their right to determine the
method to be used for provincial financing" and argued that "provincial organization and administration should be a matter for their primary decision."[54] The federal officials reached the general conclusion
that national health insurance should be structured upon much the
same principles that had guided the hospital-insurance program in the
1950s: Ottawa should set the terms for national participation in provincial schemes and demand that a majority of the provinces accept
the deal before any money was forthcoming. Tom Kent, for one,
thought that traditional joint programs were no longer viable and that
the report on the provinces "was quite out of touch with provincial
views at the points of policy decision."[55]

While departmental officials investigated the options open in the
health-insurance field, their travels around the country were designed
to camouflage the basic federal reluctance to act on medicare. For a
variety of reasons, even the progressive Liberals were hesitant to act
immediately, and their more conservative colleagues were beginning to
emphasize the enormous expense involved. Everyone believed that the
achievement of a system of national medicare would be a Herculean

feat, one demanding either a more stable economy or more progressive Liberals in government, or both. Deputy Minister of Finance Robert Bryce went so far as to describe medicare as one of the "horrors ahead," identifying the likelihood of Quebec opting out, the effects on future tax policy, and the magnitude of the political issue as particular areas for concern.[56] The survey of provincial opinions and the calling of an initial federal-provincial conference all gave the impression of a government merely going through the motions. Ultimately, the federal officials and not a few of the politicians hoped that they would be able to "stall our way through" medicare at the next federal-provincial conference called for July 1965.[57]

The difficulties that Bryce identified for the upcoming year would be less daunting if addressed by a strong Liberal government. The Liberal program of "equalizing economic and social opportunity," argued MP Pauline Jewett, could not be done in "bits and dribbles" but depended on "complete government commitment."[58] For this reason, Gordon continued to press for an early election call – necessary in order to receive a "mandate to implement the program outlined in the Speech from the Throne." Not only would a majority of the population endorse the Liberal social agenda, but Gordon also expected that the election victory would "strengthen the position of the Federal Government vis-à-vis the Provinces ... especially if it included a clear endorsation [sic] by the Province of Quebec."[59] Although Gordon did not expect that much of substance would be accomplished at the July federal-provincial conference, he nevertheless anticipated that it would be "somewhat strenuous" and might have the effect of turning the election into a "contest between the Federal and Provincial Governments."[60] He therefore recommended that Pearson at least issue the election writs prior to convening the first ministers' conference.

The Liberals seemed even more indecisive than usual in the spring of 1965. Although committed to universal health insurance, half of the troops wanted to wait until after the next election before proceeding. The other half wanted to move slowly enough that health insurance would cost the federal government little in the foreseeable future, but quickly enough to avoid the political difficulties associated with yet again relegating the issue to the back burner. The publication of the Hall commission's recommendations forced the Liberals to move in the direction of a national medicare program, but most participants seemed to hope that the cross-country investigative trip taken by the federal bureaucrats and an inconclusive federal-provincial conference would suffice – at least in the short term. The only other alternative seemed to be for the relatively weak, minority government to throw itself into gruelling negotiations that, given the Liberal record in the pension-plan discussions, might cripple its chances of re-election.

In the spring of 1965 the Liberals needed to answer a number of questions that were on everyone's minds: the date of the next election; how the government would fulfil its commitment to implementing social-security legislation; and what would become of the Hall commission's recommendations on medicare. Whatever the solutions to these problems, they were bound to create additional dilemmas, either for the Liberals themselves in Parliament or for the future of federal-provincial relations. But rather than settling any of the existing questions once and for all, the Pearson government spent a considerable amount of time in the spring of 1965 designing, discussing, and debating what had become known as the Canada Assistance Plan,[61] a coordinated welfare program that until then had not even been considered beyond the darkest confines of the backrooms.[62] This new program envisaged the coordination of existing categorical assistance (for blind and disabled persons), shared administrative costs, and the provision of benefits on the basis of need rather than through a means test. Unlike the political dilemmas that confounded agreement over national health insurance, the Canada Assistance Plan had withstood bureaucratic conflict to emerge as a component of Speech from the Throne[63] – a much more impressive victory for the assistance program than for health insurance. Work on the Canada Assistance Plan through the spring of 1965 effectively stalled any further commitments to national medicare. It was a welcome break for politicians cautious about the political effects of another round of federal-provincial social-policy negotiations, as it was for the bureaucrats charged with the responsibility of finding both the funds and the intergovernmental formula for the program. There seemed to be general agreement in Ottawa that health would mirror pensions – all involved in the issue anticipated, and postponed, a difficult series of substantive discussions with the provinces.

In many ways, the Canada Assistance Plan was an anomaly in the social reforms of the Pearson government. It was not really a new program but rather the coordination of existing provincial measures. Its origins are to be found in the bureaucracy, not with the progressive advisers who migrated to the Liberal Party in the late 1950s and early 1960s. But, despite its uniqueness, the Canada Assistance Plan conformed to the standards of national responsibility embraced, if sometimes reluctantly, by the federal Liberals, and it influenced the factors that led to the achievement of the final component in the social net.

Welfare reform bought the government some time for health insurance and made clear the important lessons of pension negotiation. With the Canada Pension Plan, and in part with the Canada Assistance Plan, the Liberals had succeeded in subtly altering the structure of Canadian federalism – not from a centralized to a decentralized system, as critics argue, but from a strictly jurisdictional understanding of the division of powers to a functional division of powers.[64] In attempting to legislate in matters that, constitutionally, were a provincial responsibility, the national government necessarily had to adopt tactics that affected the structure of federalism. In the case of the Canada Pension Plan, after much abortive negotiation at the outset, the federal government ultimately settled on determining the general principles for the pension legislation and leaving their interpretation to provincial discretion. Thus Canadian federalism shifted to a more horizontal configuration: one level of government (the national) was concerned with "the formulation and development stages in the policy process and the other level with implementation and control."[65] The same approach, minus the false starts at the beginning, could be used to reach an agreement on a national health-insurance program.

Not only did the federal government benefit from its previous experience in federal-provincial relations, but the personnel of government had changed slightly but significantly since the initial round of pension negotiations. Al Johnson had been deputy provincial treasurer in Tommy Douglas's CCF government in Saskatchewan, and in that capacity he had played a major role in the provincial medicare debate. He migrated to Ottawa in 1964, having been encouraged by both Robert Bryce and Walter Gordon for several months, and assumed the duties of assistant deputy minister of finance. That Johnson had a realistic idea of what the government could afford, combined with a real progressive zeal, appealed to both his bureaucratic and his political bosses.[66] His recruitment was a considerable coup for the federal government, for Johnson was regarded as "the ablest of all the Saskatchewan mafia."[67] He certainly made a decisive contribution to the achievement of full health insurance.

Thoughts regarding the tactics the federal government should use at the July 1965 federal-provincial conference – at which time medical insurance would be discussed – had not been particularly fruitful. Health officials within the Department of National Health and Welfare offered their proposals, which included a shared-cost medical-service insurance program based on the same principles that had been utilized for hospital insurance, a drug plan, and the inclusion of mental hospitals and tuberculosis sanatoria.[68] Anticipating that these recommendations might be regarded as too sweeping, alternative proposals were presented suggesting a preliminary program of prescription-drug insurance.[69] A broader committee, including representatives of the departments of health and welfare and finance and of the Privy Council Office, examined the report and found it wanting. This second interdepartmental committee recommended a course of action for the federal government:

acknowledge the constitutional jurisdiction of the provinces in this field; firmly state the policy objectives of the federal government and the role which it is prepared to play; express a willingness to consult with the provinces on the principles of medical services insurance and on the best federal-provincial methods of putting these principles into effect, taking into account, in particular, the terms of reference and eventual recommendations of the Tax Structure Committee; establish the necessary machinery for such consultations and call for a report and recommendations in time for the 1966 meeting of the Federal-Provincial Conference.[70]

In other words, the committee counselled continued delay.

The constraints within which the federal government had to work were serious enough to convince the officials that the best course would be to wait for a more opportune time to open up the health-insurance question. Not only had Premier Lesage already stated categorically that Quebec would no longer participate in any shared-cost programs, but medicare threatened to be a costly scheme for a federal treasury already stretched to the limit. Add to the mixture the political volatility of the issue, the general public interest in some sort of health-insurance plan, and the legacy of Liberal promises of action, and the result was a recipe for disaster. Fortunately, the new assistant deputy minister of Finance, Al Johnson, charted a route through the tangled mess of conditions and expectations and produced a health-insurance proposal which Tom Kent has described as "the kind of solution that, once you have heard it, you kick yourself for having failed to think of."[71]

In a long memo to Bryce, Johnson outlined the general features of his plan and explained how the new approach differed from traditional shared-cost programs. Essentially, he proposed that, instead of requiring the provinces to accept legislation devised and announced by the federal government, "they would simply have to enact legislation which established a plan in conformity with the principles enunciated by the Federal Government after, and as a consequence of, consultation with the provinces." Johnson was somewhat less clear on the question of financing. He suggested that compensation to participating provinces take the form either of an equal per-capita payment or a combination of "the reduction of certain federal taxes to enable the provinces to raise their same taxes by an equivalent amount and ... equalization payments. He preferred the latter approach, despite concerns about the size of the growing abatement, since it was "sufficiently dissimilar from present shared cost formulae that Quebec would accept it."[72]

Would Quebec accept? Bryce was the only person aware of the sort of program Johnson was proposing and, while he made a few suggestions and asked a few probing questions, he was not in a position really to evaluate its viability. Yet, given the fact that Bryce was usually cautious about committing the government to expensive social-welfare legislation,[73] his general acceptance of Johnson's plan spoke highly of its merits. It was thus with Bryce's knowledge and blessing that Johnson met with Claude Morin, Quebec's deputy minister of intergovernmental affairs, to discuss the possibilities for federal-provincial agreement on national health insurance. The men met for two hours in the Chateau Laurier bar and agreed to a procedure whereby the national government set the criteria for contributions to provincial health-insurance legislation. In essence, Ottawa demanded that provincial schemes be universal, comprehensive, portable, and publicly administered. Since Lesage had no need to sign an agreement, Morin accepted that this system could not be categorized as a shared-cost program.[74] It was only after and as a result of the meeting with Morin that Johnson knew that the medicare scheme would work.[75] It remained to be seen whether other provinces would agree.

The four principles for federal participation in medicare were immediately submitted to cabinet and approved as the definite national approach at the federal-provincial conferences scheduled for 19–23 July 1965. With its near-foolproof strategy determined, the government now moved quickly. In his opening statement to the conference, Pearson announced the federal medicare proposal and explained that it demanded merely "a general federal-provincial understanding as to the nature of the health programs which will make a federal fiscal contribution appropriate."[76] The criteria, he explained, were that all services provided by physicians be covered (comprehensive), that all provincial residents be covered on uniform terms and conditions (universality), that the provincial scheme be administered either directly by the government or by a provincial government agency (public administration), and that all benefits be fully transferable when people were away from their home provinces (portability). Pearson anticipated "general approval" and suggested that a committee of health ministers be established to express the principles "in language sufficiently precise to prevent misconceptions."[77]

Pearson correctly assumed that there would be relatively little provincial opposition to the criteria. Prior to the opening of the conference, he had informed cabinet that while Ontario and Quebec would likely introduce medicare systems that would conform to the national standards, British Columbia and Alberta, which each already had provincial health-insurance legislation, "would not likely wish to go as far as the plan contemplated by the federal proposal, and they would seek assistance for more limited plans."[78] Pearson was correct about Alberta's reaction: Premier Manning argued that the federal principles violated the rights of a free society, that the Alberta plan was significantly less expensive than that proposed by Ottawa, and that publicly operated universal plans "inevitably invite abuse."[79] Premier Robarts of Ontario also raised some concerns about the course the national government was following, suggesting that the politicians were manipulating medicare for electoral advantage and that their strategy would in the long run have a detrimental effect on the quality of medical care in Canada.[80] Provincial opposition at the conference made little difference, however. Despite the fact that provincial governments had been the first to act on health insurance, and were in many ways more familiar with the requirements of such a program, the national government had seized the initiative at the conference and proposed a scheme that was virtually impossible to turn down – or at least without appearing to have sacrificed the health of citizens by arbitrarily rejecting the offer of federal money.

If the national government was to play any role at all in the provision of social services for Canadians, it was necessary to find and adopt an alternative to encroaching on provincial jurisdiction. Al Johnson later advised the federal government that while its expenditure power should not be abused, "the interest of the national government in establishing new social services on a country-wide basis should also be recognized." He concluded that, for social policy, "this implies that new approaches must be sought to federal or national initiatives, and some substitute must be found for the unilateral federal sanctions which are now a part of most established shared-cost programs. An obvious example of what we should move towards is the 'medicare model'; indeed this new approach was developed with precisely these factors in mind."[81]

Johnson's plan to secure a national health-insurance scheme moved Canada more decisively in the direction of functional federalism than had the debate over the Canada Pension Plan. Based on the experience of the pension negotiations, it seemed realistic to believe that the national government could set basic standards for the health program but that to try to dictate the program's precise nature would be impossible. For medicare, the federal government accepted its responsibility to conceptualize and initiate the program from the outset and did not attempt to dictate anything more to the provinces than the four principles for federal participation. After having delayed the commencement of federal-provincial negotiations for months, desperately trying to avoid a conflict that would hamper their chances for re-election, the Liberals were pleasantly surprised at the speed with which an agreement could be reached when an appropriate strategy was followed. As Pearson acknowledged at the beginning of the federal-provincial conference, "no national policy will succeed without full and genuine respect for" the "large area of [provincial] responsibility and jurisdiction." With this in mind, he asserted that the national government would "proceed on the basis of consultation and co-operation with the Provinces. On that basis we will discharge to the best of our ability the responsibilities of national leadership which must be undertaken from the centre and which require us to use our powers for the good of all Canada."[82]

7 Liberal Party Dynamics and the Achievement of Medicare, 1965–68

The Liberals were much better situated to face the electorate in the summer of 1965 than they had been earlier in the year. The discussions with the provinces over national health insurance had gone well, largely because Ottawa had refused to engage in the detailed negotiations characteristic of its other forays in the sphere of federal-provincial relations. Instead, it had merely enunciated the minimum standards a provincial health-insurance system would have to meet in order to qualify for federal contributions. Having successfully designed this new approach to federal-provincial negotiations, the federal politicians were in the enviable position of being able to present themselves to the electorate as true social reformers, initiators of important pieces of social-welfare legislation, and defenders of national standards. Ironically, then, despite following some important advances in the completion of the Canadian welfare state, the election of 1965 dealt a heavy blow to the progressive wing of the Liberal Party. The voters returned a Liberal government so different in outlook and approach from the idealistic group elected in 1963 that even the future of national health insurance was in question. Two years of government had demonstrated the difficulty of remaining true to principles first conceived in opposition. Although the Liberal commitment to a strategy of progressive social policies had been subtly diminishing since the debacle of the Gordon budget in 1963, it was not until the election of 1965 that the Liberals truly embraced a cautious approach to politics and turned noticeably away from both the people and the policies that had been dominant in the brief reformist interlude.

Approaching their fourth election with Pearson at the helm, the left-leaning Liberals in the party were blissfully unaware that their position within the party was threatened. The success of the federal-provincial discussions over medicare, in marked and delightful contrast to similar negotiations about portable pensions, suggested to many Liberal advisers that the sooner the election was called, the better. Tom Kent, who had originally advised postponing an election, now stressed to Pearson that the fundamental issue in the upcoming election was the need for a mandate to "get on with the job" of national unity and "achieving economic and social progress."[1] Kent and Walter Gordon now agreed on this point. Gordon, who had remained consistent in his support for an early election, was convinced that medicare had only "grown in importance" during the summer months and was an issue the Liberals could use to their advantage.[2] Prime Minister Pearson still opposed calling an election, in much the same way as he avoided making policy decisions, although Gordon believed his failure to act was largely because "he does not want to face up to campaigning."[3] Yet Pearson was eager to restructure the balance of power within the Liberal Party and had confided to a reporter that he would prefer a cabinet of seasoned politicians to one of political neophytes.[4] An election, however difficult to fight, might eliminate the more idealistic of the present crop of cabinet ministers or at least present the opportunity to shift the cabinet positions around.

The prime minister continued to waffle on the question of election timing long past the point when a decision, one way or the other, should have been made. The indecision was so infuriating that Gordon threatened to resign his position as head of the campaign committee if Pearson did not make up his mind during the first week of September.[5] Meanwhile, the key strategists busied themselves preparing guidelines for the campaign, whenever it might begin. Tom Kent outlined the issues, arguing, among other things, that the Liberals should emphasize their strong record in the social-security field and be wary of Conservative attacks on Liberal "political morality."[6] Gordon and Keith Davey designed the campaign's actual structure, which represented a significant break from the past because instead of taking a "Leader's tour" the prime minister would remain in Ottawa throughout most of the campaign, issuing statements of national policy from the nation's capital.[7] The 1962 and 1963 campaigns had been especially draining for Pearson, who was neither comfortable on the hustings nor able to keep up the relentless pace Kent, his chief speechwriter, set for him.[8] The new election tactic would be a bit easier on the prime minister but still would not represent a reversion to the style of campaigns in the St Laurent period, although there were those in the party who argued that that approach would be far the best. Senator J.J. Connolly, for one, urged the Liberals to "try to develop five great regional policies and unveil them at large meetings in each of the regions," but his advice fell on deaf ears.[9] By keeping the prime minister close to Ottawa, the Liberals would be able to emphasize that theirs was a program for all Canadians, capable of being broadcast from the centre without need for regional interpretation. None of this was possible, however, until the prime minister decided to call an election.

The positive nature of the federal-provincial health-insurance discussions in July 1965 had alarmed the Conservatives. Conservative strategists noted that the popularity of recent advances in social security meant that "the bulk of the argument on the welfare state is over"[10] and therefore that medicare should be kept out of the campaign as much as possible, especially since the Conservatives themselves had set up the Hall commission to address the problem of inequity in the delivery of health services. Because the Liberals could hardly be criticized for acting on the recommendations of the royal commission, the government had a virtually unassailable election issue with social security.[11] It appeared that the Conservatives' only hope was for Diefenbaker to be replaced as leader before the next election: and the longer Pearson waffled, the more the Liberal advisers worried that this might occur.[12]

It took an enormous effort to convince Pearson to call an election for the fall of 1965, most particularly on the part of Walter Gordon. As a consistent supporter of a quick election – he argued, in fact, that were one not called, the Liberals would be unable to dissolve Parliament for at least another eighteen months, given the political agenda and the upcoming electoral redistribution – Gordon felt responsible for Pearson's ultimate decision to call the vote for 8 November 1965.[13] He believed that it was a decision the prime minister "did not want to make" and therefore noted, at least to himself, that if the electorate did not return a Liberal majority he would have to resign from government, having "no influence left anyway."[14] Although most, if not all, of the other cabinet ministers agreed with Gordon that an early election was desirable, it was he alone who accepted the responsibility for the decision, and he alone who would bear the consequences.

The election machinery had been in place for weeks prior to the call. As national campaign director, Keith Davey had only to emphasize that the goal was to "stress the same points [and] say the same things in all parts of the country" and issue the strategy paper outlining the main points in "building the new Canada."[15] Medicare, and social security in general, were prominent subjects of discussion in the campaign. The federal government accepted 1 July 1967 as a "realistic target date" for starting a national health-insurance scheme, and discussions with provincial representatives during the election campaign did nothing to alter that view.[16] Representatives of the Canadian Medical Association who attended the conference as members of provincial delegations gave no indication that the medical profession presented a threat to national health insurance.[17] The central campaign strategists confidently outlined the history of the federal-provincial negotiations over medicare, stressing the popularity of the federal position and the almost universal agreement that "federal leadership is essential to all Canadians having medicare."[18]

The national organizers did not expect many provincial governments to commit themselves to the federal plan prior to the election, but they firmly believed that "everyone knows that the federal proposal is just what was needed to achieve medicare."[19] Alberta represented the only real problem, but this was not surprising since Premier Ernest Manning's objections to national health insurance were characteristic of his political style. He charged that the prime minister had been "convinced by socialistic advisors" to introduce an arbitrarily universal scheme that, by limiting freedom of choice, "violates a fundamental principle of free society." He also questioned the federal government's cost estimates and the long-range impact of medicare on medical standards. In a nationally televised broadcast, which Manning maintained was necessary in order "to bring to the attention of the Canadian people what I regard as a serious objection to the present proposal," the Social Credit premier suggested that Ottawa implement a scheme along the same lines as the voluntary, privately sponsored plan in existence in Alberta.[20] The national address had little impact on Pearson, who merely reminded the Alberta voters that "a medicare system which means that everyone can get medical care when he needs it ... clearly makes people more free, not less free."[21] Other provincial delegations, even those from provinces uncertain of the benefits of the national health-insurance plan, were less hostile than Manning. Representing Ontario, Colin Brown and C.A. Naylor were both impressed that Tom Kent would take a couple of hours out of orchestrating the national campaign to discuss medicare with them, giving them the impression "that the Federal Government is taking a very relaxed and flexible position on Medicare, and giving the provinces considerable freedom to work out the details of their plan."[22]

To the disappointment of many observers, social policies – or indeed policy issues of any kind – did not play a major role in the outcome of the 1965 election. Of much greater significance were the scandals that had plagued the Liberals since gaining office, most particularly the question of Guy Favreau's involvement in accepting illegal campaign contributions and the government's knowledge of Soviet spy George Spencer. The Winnipeg *Free Press* declared the election "an insult to public intelligence. Candidates on all sides are not arguing the nation's actual problems and proposing alternative solutions. Most of them are either talking tittle-tattle, spreading innuendo with a leer, striking moral attitudes, or making unlimited promises with no regard to their cost."[23] This was despite the earnest efforts of the campaign committee to ensure a positive campaign with an emphasis on Liberal policies for prosperity, social security, and equal opportunity and a national leadership style designed "to make federalism work, for the benefit of all of Canada."[24] Although the Liberals made some gains, the electorate refused to heed Pearson's call for a majority government, apparently agreeing with the Toronto *Star's* Ron Haggart that "what Canada needs is a fighting Liberal *minority* government, one which must constantly win the consent of Parliament."[25] The new House of Commons boasted two more Liberals than before, but it was still two seats shy of a majority government.[26]

As usual in the aftermath of an election, many were willing to identify the weaknesses of the Liberal effort. Senator T.A. Crerar pointed to Pearson's poor television performances and an unwillingness on the part of English voters to support a party widely perceived to be too responsive to Quebec interests.[27] Others suggested that more efficient provincial organization "would have made all the difference on November 8th."[28] Tom Kent believed that the basic problems of disorganization and lack of commitment evident in 1963 were still very much apparent in 1965.[29] Only Walter Gordon, however, was willing to take the blame for the failure to achieve a majority government. The day after the election he wrote to the prime minister: "As Chairman of the Liberal Party's National Campaign Committee I believed that if you conducted a good campaign we would obtain a comfortable majority. Your campaign was superb in every way. You could not have done any better or any more than you did. The conclusion is quite clear. I gave you bad advice, both as a minister and as campaign chairman. I accept the full responsibility for this and therefore submit my resignation from the cabinet."[30] Although Pearson could "not accept [Gordon's] assumption of responsibility for the decision to hold the recent election," he felt he had "no choice but accept [the] resignation."[31]

Gordon's was not the only departure. Even Pearson himself had apparently toyed with the idea of resigning immediately after the election and allowing the party to begin its search for another leader.[32] Others, however, did more than contemplate their resignations. Shortly after the election Keith Davey resigned as national director and Kent moved from his senior advisory position in the Prime Minister's Office to the civil service as deputy minister of the newly created Department of Manpower and Immigration.[33] A massive cabinet shuffle before Christmas resulted in even more changes to the complexion of the Liberal government: Judy LaMarsh was demoted from National Health and Welfare to the office of Secretary of State; Mitchell Sharp replaced Gordon in Finance; and Allan MacEachen was brought in to complete the program of national health insurance. The senior progressive Liberals, politicians and advisers alike, seemed to slip noiselessly away in the aftermath of defeat in 1965. Gordon was not alone in fretting about the apparent "move to the right." He feared that the party was about to repeat "what happened in the late fifties when Mr. St Laurent was ill, and after Brooke Claxton left the government. If the same thing should happen again, it might very well mean the Liberal party will break up."[34] Gordon was understandably gloomy about the prospects of Liberalism in Canada, but the Toronto *Star* posed a more serious question: "Mr. Gordon's resignation has left the Pearson Cabinet without a Liberal rudder. The man Prime Minister Pearson chooses to fill the key post of Minister of Finance will largely determine whether the country's economic resources will continue to be directed towards social reform and economic independence."[35] Sharp's appointment cast some serious doubts over the future of medicare.

Early indications, however, suggested that there would be few changes in the way the new cabinet dealt with medicare. The civil service remained unchanged, and the relevant bureaucrats were unwavering in their support for the approach the federal government had adopted towards the provinces. The medicare arrangement seemed to represent a turning point in social-policy tactics and objectives. Deputy Minister of Finance Robert Bryce noted that while "the cumulative intervention of the Federal Government in continuing social programmes under provincial jurisdiction seems undesirable," Ottawa still had an important role in "initiating new nation-wide programmes" and in safeguarding "certain major national interests." He advised adopting the medicare approach for all future joint programs in the social-policy field.[36] One of the most appealing features of the federal strategy was that it circumvented the unpleasant possibility of contracting-out, which many in the civil service seemed to believe "would lead to an associate state." At the same time, however, it allowed a high degree of provincial variation and offered "Quebec the special status she seems to want, for symbolic reasons" without denying similar status to the other provinces.[37]

The new cabinet ministers also seemed to find little wrong with the medicare arrangements as they had been left by Judy LaMarsh in Health and Welfare and Walter Gordon in Finance. Allan MacEachen outlined the four principles of portability, universality, accessibility, and public administration and sought cabinet agreement on the federal position. He suggested only one minor change to the position that had been adopted at the federal-provincial conference in the summer of 1965. The start-up date had previously been set for 1 July 1967, a realistic goal in 1965 and one that was designed to take advantage of the sense of national pride anticipated for the centennial celebrations. However, MacEachen suggested that "since provinces have not stated their intentions and since July 1st, 1967 is approaching, consideration of a more positive federal approach may be necessary." He advised that the federal government state that it "would be prepared to commence contributions to a province which has a programme incorporating the four principles in operation at that date" as a means to hurry the recalcitrant provinces into a decision.[38] In the subsequent cabinet discussion, the ministers agreed that this was an appropriate tactic but that no announcement be made until it was more clear when the provinces "expected to be in a position consistent with the Federal criteria." Of utmost importance, however, was "to avoid any impression ... that the Federal Government had changed its view about going ahead by July 1st, 1967."[39] For the time being at least, the cabinet was firm in its commitment to proceed with medicare in exactly the same fashion as those who had laid the groundwork. By the middle of May, cabinet had agreed to proceed with the preparation of the legislation.[40]

The continuity between the cabinets of the first and the second Pearson administrations was artificial, however. At the first sign of difficulties with the provinces, the differences between the two groups of people and the priority they assigned to social policies became readily apparent. The old divisions between the left and the right of the Liberal Party, never quite reconciled but usually hidden behind a façade of unanimity, began to have as significant an impact on the implementation of social programs in Canada as the same debates had had on the adoption of these policies in the opposition period. Pearson had never been eager to be associated too closely with either wing of his party, although he was usually considered progressive. But in 1966 his leadership was severely weakened by a series of unanswered attacks in the press from Senator Crerar and Saskatchewan premier Ross Thatcher.[41] Moreover, there seemed to be a general sense that, as one observer noted, "the leadership of Mr. Pearson is now in its final stages of disintegration."⁴² Even had he wished to do so, Pearson was in no position to lend his support to the left wing of either his party or his cabinet.

The first signs of federal hesitation in going ahead with the medicare plan became apparent in the spring and summer of 1966. The failure of any province to announce its intention to legislate on full health insurance suggested to certain cabinet ministers that there were fundamental flaws in the design of the medicare criteria that had been presented to the premiers a year earlier. Some ministers buckled under criticism of the public-administration component and "expressed support for the suggestion that private insurance companies be allowed to participate in the administration of provincial medical care plans provided they could satisfy the other criteria approved by the government."⁴³ While Sharp was not one of the hesitant ministers, he was beginning to have doubts about the timing of the federal medicare bill.

Quebec's recalcitrance was not unexpected, but with Premier Jean Lesage defeated on 5 June 1966 by the less well-known Daniel Johnson of the Union Nationale, it was less well understood. Al Johnson informed his superior, Robert Bryce, that Maurice Sauvé believed the federal government should continue with its medicare plans regardless of whether Quebec participated. He added that journalist Peter Newman "says that Daniel Johnson told him firmly that he was not going to be pushed by Ottawa on medicare, and that he didn't like Ottawa trying to jiggle provincial priorities on matters within provincial jurisdiction."⁴⁴ Publicly, Daniel Johnson had already announced his intention to examine Quebec's financial situation before he made a decision on whether his province would accept the federal terms for medicare contributions. For his part, Al Johnson had advised his minister that since neither Ontario nor Quebec had given any firm indication of their intentions, "it might be quite unwise for the Minister to make the Bill effective on July 1st."⁴⁵ Johnson indicated that the most effective tactic would be to telephone the new Quebec premier and "offer to withhold the Bill for two or three weeks to enable the Premier-designate to examine his financial situation and to discuss the medicare plans with the Federal Government, informally."⁴⁶

Quebec was by no means the only problem. By mid-summer 1966 the premiers were collectively complaining that "the priority accorded to medicare is wrong" and that "the federal government proceeded without consulting the provinces [and therefore] should not deny compensation to provinces which refuse to conform with the conditions." On the basis of these concerns, the premiers argued that a federal-provincial conference devoted to the discussion of the medicare bill should be called. Al Johnson disagreed but suggested that the government "announce that medicare will be deferred for an unspecified time" because, despite considerable consultation with the provinces, only Newfoundland, New Brunswick, and Saskatchewan favoured universal medical care.[47] Sharp himself was concerned about the government's financial capabilities, and he was especially worried that the promise of federal funds to cover 50 per cent of the cost of provincial health-insurance schemes had been made prematurely.[48] Armed with advice from his officials to delay the medicare legislation, Sharp announced that the starting date would be pushed back one year to 1 July 1968.

Al Johnson had seen in Saskatchewan the effects of implementing a universal health-insurance program, and he had been lured to Ottawa as assistant deputy minister of finance with the promise that his primary responsibility would be for federal-provincial relations. In advising his minister to delay the introduction of medicare legislation, he understood the need to have a "demonstration of a greater consensus of public opinion in favour of medicare in the provinces whose government oppose it." This was by no means an indication of any wavering commitment on Johnson's part; he was merely recognizing political realities. Moreover, for Johnson, a delay in legislation was far better than having the provinces "chip away the criteria so as to defeat universal medical care while getting federal money for their existing partial plans."[49] Sharp had not demonstrated the same concern for ensuring the success of the medicare program as the federal government had originally proposed it, and so his acceptance of the delay was perhaps more a function of his conservative approach to fiscal matters than was the case with Johnson.[50]

The senior federal bureaucrats had advised the delay in order to give the provinces a chance to come on board prior to the commencement date. The civil servants, and Johnson in particular, had also considered the consequences of calling a further federal-provincial conference and dismissed the proposal as most likely to encourage a diminution of the original criteria. The tactic of delay, therefore, was designed to persuade the reluctant provinces to join without jeopardizing any of the federal conditions. Ironically, although not surprisingly, Sharp's announcement that the federal government would not initiate universal medicare until 1 July 1968 had little impact in the provincial capitals. Manitoba's Duff Roblin was the most vocal in his demands that federal health-insurance legislation provide provinces the "widest possible latitude," but none of the reluctant provinces gave any indication that it was prepared to accept the terms of the federal contribution.[51]

If the announced delay had little impact on the premiers, it had enormous implications for the balance of power within the Liberal

Party. The structure of the post-1965 cabinet had obviously been an indication of the rising importance of the right wing of the party, of which the finance minister was generally considered a major component.[52] Delaying medicare ironically demonstrated that the party's left wing still had some life in it. Andy Thompson, leader of the Ontario Liberal Party, led the attacks on the federal Liberals for postponing the implementation of national health insurance. He was roundly chastised for his "public expression of contradictory views" on medicare, and rebuked for giving "the general public the impression of confusion, indecision and conflict within our ranks."[53] But in recalling Walter Gordon's contribution to the initial stages of medicare development, Thompson ensured that the old left of the Liberal Party was not completely forgotten.

Gordon was no longer as powerful as he had been during the party's years in opposition, and most of his supporters were outside the inner circles of power. However, calls continued both for Gordon's return to cabinet and for a more progressive approach to government. The quick implementation of universal medicare would be a good indication that left-wing Liberalism still mattered. Maurice Lamontagne, whose own future with the Liberals was uncertain, identified the problems with the party at the close of 1966:

Two solitudes are developing within the Liberal Party. The back-benchers, especially in Ontario, are worried by the present situation of the Party. They know that we will suffer substantial losses, unless something is done fairly soon ... [C]omplacency and a business-as-usual attitude seem to characterize the more conservative members of the cabinet who are, for the time being, the most influential. They do not appear to be interested in reform and they resent those who regard change as inevitable. The orientation of the policy is left to the managerial group in the Cabinet, which uses its influence to paralyze and even to eliminate the more dynamic elements of the Party.[54]

Lamontagne encouraged the preparation of a new party platform along the lines of that which he recalled emanating from the Kingston Conference and the Liberal Rally, and he suggested the appointment of Walter Gordon "to organize the preparation of the new platform and to set up the federal organization in Ontario."[55]

Enough people supported Gordon's return to cabinet that Prime Minister Pearson began to ask his colleagues for their opinions on the matter. Mitchell Sharp's support for Gordon's return convinced Pearson that it was the appropriate thing to do – his resignation had been both offered and accepted in the first place for rather dubious reasons.[56] Whether Gordon would agree to return to cabinet was another matter altogether. He believed that the "Government is becoming conservative and bureaucratic in its attitudes and is out of touch with public opinion, especially in Ontario and with the younger generation everywhere in the country." As a result, he wanted to "get out" and would only agree to return to cabinet if the position was "sufficiently senior to satisfy the press and the public that I could do a proper job."[57] No promises were made at the meeting Pearson had called with Gordon and Sharp to discuss the former's cabinet future, but in January 1967 Gordon became president of the Privy Council with primary responsibility for overseeing the task force on foreign ownership and the structure of Canadian industry.[58] Although Gordon's main concern was economic nationalism and ensuring that Canadian interests were not threatened by foreign ownership, his return to cabinet marked a minor victory for the much weakened left wing of the Liberal Party.

Yet Gordon's entry into the cabinet had no effect on the government's approach to medicare. Although the initial decision to delay medicare had led to acrimonious debates in cabinet, generally pitting such left-leaning Liberals as Jean Marchand against the stalwarts of the right, Gordon did not provide enough new weight to the progressive side to succeed in changing the government's mind. Allan MacEachen continued to speak of 1 July 1968 as the starting date, dismissing opponents of the delay as viewing "with Olympian disdain ... the battle of politics" and failing to understand the necessity of "balance between what a country needs and what its taxpayers can afford."[59] The opposition parties in the House of Commons, who bore the brunt of MacEachen's criticisms, were not alone in complaining about the delay. Voluntary associations such as the Canadian Welfare Council also voiced concern about the fact that medical insurance was "still many months away from becoming operative."[60]

On the other side of the debate, the provincial premiers still pressed for further delay, frequently adopting the approach of calling for renewed federal-provincial consultation on "public priorities."[61] It was an old tactic, but the provincial governments were becoming increasingly sophisticated in their use of such strategies. Pearson learned that Duff Roblin of Manitoba was spearheading a drive to have each provincial minister write to his or her federal counterpart "on some problem of common interest and [suggest] that it could best be dealt with in the context of ... a conference [on] public priorities." Pearson suspected the provinces of attempting "to take advantage of any lack of co-ordination which may exist between federal departments and agencies on this issue to force the government into a position where it would have to modify its policy" of no public discussion of priorities.[62] The federal government had obviously demonstrated a distinct lack of unity on this issue, and the provincial premiers intended to take full advantage of the resulting chaos. Although the Department of National Health and Welfare was firmly opposed to opening discussions with the provinces for fear that medicare would be jeopardized, other departments might view a debate on public priorities as beneficial. The Pandora's box of "priorities" could not be opened without threatening the future of a national health-insurance plan as originally conceived.

With little progress made towards national medicare, premiers from all of the delinquent provinces except British Columbia officially requested the federal government to reduce its criteria for receipt of a national contribution to provincial health-insurance schemes.[63] The provincial demands were made just as Sharp was contemplating "a way to give to residents of provinces where there is no qualifying medical care programme a tax reduction roughly equal to the amount which would have been contributed by the federal government."[64] The provincial hesitation about enacting acceptable health-insurance legislation had led Sharp to search for a means to assist the non-participating provinces, despite the fact that any benefits received from the federal coffers would make it even more unlikely for the provinces to implement state-sponsored medical insurance. For this reason, Al Johnson argued to Bryce that "to provide tax refunds or tax credits to the taxpayers of non-participating provinces would be to introduce a substantial deterrent to the future of the federal spending power, and to provide a significant brake upon the introduction of universal medical care in Canada."[65]

The provincial reluctance to commit to medicare did not substantially weaken the federal position: the four criteria remained in place and key members of the civil service remained committed to the original conception of national health insurance. However, provincial intransigence weakened federal resolve and illuminated the deep divisions in the cabinet and, according to Walter Gordon, also "in caucus and throughout the Party."[66] Gordon was seriously worried about the direction in which the Liberals seemed to be headed, a sentiment only exacerbated by the continued delays on the medicare question and Sharp's inability to understand the significance of the program as it was originally designed. He was also concerned that the Liberal Party's growing conservatism threatened its electoral prospects, especially now that Diefenbaker had been replaced by Robert Stanfield as Conservative leader: "the Liberal Government has given the impression of becoming increasingly conservative in attitude. In the process, we have given the public a confused impression of what we stand for. The more conservative elements in the cabinet, both because of their numbers and the portfolios they hold, exert a dominating influence, one that tends to be deadening and unimaginative. And yet, left to themselves, the individuals in question would have no chance against Stanfield in an election."[67] Gordon suggested that Pearson make a public statement to the effect that he was going to continue to serve as prime minister for another year, thereby disabusing everyone of the notion of an immediate leadership convention. This would give the Liberals a chance to clarify their own stance on particular issues.[68] It might also give the left-wing members of the caucus and cabinet an opportunity once again to shift the intraparty balance of power in their favour.

There were new obstacles on the horizon, however. New Brunswick Premier Louis Robichaud, writing in his capacity as chair of the Inter-Provincial Conference, demanded that a federal-provincial conference be called to discuss health insurance. Al Johnson had earlier warned Sharp not to proceed in this direction. By the autumn of 1967, however, Sharp was enough concerned about the "substantive federal-provincial problems inherent in a decision to proceed with Medicare" that he was leaning towards agreeing to Robichaud's request. Other cabinet ministers opposed the idea, and all that they could agree on was to send the premier a "non-committal [reply], merely indicating that the matter was still under consideration."[69] But putting off making a decision did not lessen the troubles confronting the federal government. Within the Department of Finance there was a general anxiety about how best to "restore the credibility of the Government and to reassure the markets that the Government has the financial situation firmly under control."[70] One civil servant suggested that the most important challenge confronting the Pearson government was reducing the deficit, which at the time stood at about $750 million. He pointed to the necessity of "delaying or dropping a number of important significant programs" and included medicare in this category. Pearson noted his approval of this suggestion in the margin of the memorandum.[71]

In the face of further retrenchment, Gordon again attempted to redirect the debate. He argued before a divided cabinet that the important issue was "to distinguish between the alleged crisis in the fields of finance and economics and the real crisis, or rather, the growing lack of confidence in the government itself."[72] Gordon then went on to outline the areas of Liberal inconsistency between public statement and private objective, and the means by which the 1968 budget could be balanced without jeopardizing the future of social programs. When he finished speaking, Gordon reported that Sharp "summed up by saying that he was terribly disappointed that his colleagues were apparently unwilling to face up to the crisis which faces us ... He was obviously angry."[73] Indeed, he was so angry that Gordon suspected him of leaking information about the cabinet meeting to the press. The following day the *Globe and Mail* reported that cabinet was leaning towards postponing medicare in order to reduce current spending by about $175 million and "give a lead to the provinces, labor and management in the battle against inflation." Bucking this trend, however, were Gordon and MacEachen, who reportedly insisted "that there can be no further delay in medicare."[74] Prior to the appearance of the article Gordon had been willing to "discuss the subject objectively and with an open mind," but he had been put "in an entirely different position" as a result of the story.[75] Instead of arguing with cabinet as a whole, Gordon increasingly worked with smaller groups of sympathetic politicians to ensure that a reformist Liberal was chosen to replace Pearson as leader, an amazing turnaround given that it was Gordon who was largely responsible for securing the Liberal leadership for Pearson in the first place.[76]

The longer the provinces waited to join the national health-insurance program, the more volatile the issue became politically. Thus, in addition to considering further delays of the inauguration date, the cabinet also toyed with the idea of somehow forcing the provinces to pass provincial legislation. In order to meet its goal of reducing federal expenditures, the government intended to raise taxes to cover some of the costs of medicare. Maurice Sauvé "expressed concern" about this "and suggested that any tax increases should be explained as having the purpose of meeting the needs of the entire budget." While many ministers cautioned against adopting a stance that would essentially force the provinces into health insurance and perpetuate inflation, Paul Martin "forcibly objected to the implication that the implementation of medical care was necessarily inflationary, and reminded the Cabinet that this program had been a policy of the government party for a great many years ... [It] would be inexcusable for the government to postpone yet again the implementation of the program."[77]

In mid-November Sharp met with his provincial counterparts to discuss national solutions to the problem of inflation. Medicare was an important topic of discussion, but the meeting served more to affirm existing views about the future of national health insurance than to convince the advocates of postponement that such a tactic was unnecessary. Most of the finance ministers complained about the costs involved in setting up provincial health-insurance schemes and seemed to welcome the possibility of a further delay in the federal legislation. Newfoundland was the only province that had "deeply committed itself to the federal plan"[78]; even Saskatchewan and New Brunswick, both publicly committed to establishing provincial plans, admitted that it was an expensive proposition. Since Saskatchewan already had a provincial health-insurance plan in operation, but was in need of the federal contribution, Premier Ross Thatcher suggested that in order to deal with inflationary circumstances, "the Federal Government would be well advised to postpone medicare care and, at the same time, compensate Saskatchewan for its financial loss by postponing the decline in its equalization grants." It was unlikely to be a proposal seriously entertained by the federal contingent.

Of greater concern were the objections put forward by the largest provinces. W.A.C. Bennett of British Columbia expected "the Federal Government to live up to its commitment" but also recognized the need "to act responsibly in the face of inflation." He advised Ottawa to decrease the share of its contribution to a flat per-capita amount which, if set at $10, he anticipated would save the federal government $300 million in the first year of operation.[79] The Quebec government was in somewhat of a quandary over health insurance: while Premier Johnson and his finance minister considered it too expensive an undertaking, the provincially sponsored Castonguay commission had recently recommended a full medicare plan. By mid-November "the Quebec Government had not decided on the commission's recommendations but might favour gradual implementation."[80] Regardless, it questioned the constitutionality of the federal government setting such rigid requirements and pushed for a provincial share of any national taxation necessary to finance the system. These were doubts echoed by Ontario. In addition to expressing concern about jurisdiction, Finance Minister Charles MacNaughton reminded the audience that if a number of provinces entered the federal plan, Ontario would be forced to participate because Ontario citizens paid approximately half of federal taxes.[81]

The meeting of finance ministers essentially served as a forum on medicare in place of the federal-provincial conference that the premiers had requested. If possible, Sharp became even more sceptical about the 1 July 1968 goal for implementing national legislation. He reported to the press that medicare would cost $1 billion – a not improbable figure considering both federal and provincial contributions, but one that NDP leader Tommy Douglas felt was designed "to frighten the provincial governments into postponing the implementation of medicare" and shift the blame for failure off the federal government's shoulders.[82] While there was no immediate indication that the future of national health insurance was in jeopardy, Sharp began to lay the groundwork for alternate sources of funding medicare. In his mini-budget of 30 November 1967 the finance minister indicated that additional tax revenues would be needed when medicare finally got under way, although he did not mention any further postponement on the part of the federal government.[83]

The question of delay was still not resolved, however, and the debate in cabinet became acrimonious. Fuelling the fire was Pearson's 14 December 1967 announcement of his intention to resign.[84] As one commentator described the cabinet crisis in January 1968, some ministers, "girding for the battle to be [Pearson's] successor, were faced with the delicate problem of maintaining cabinet solidarity and supporting existing law, and risking the loss of support from those provinces which wanted postponement."[85] Pearson informed the press that although there was no question of reviewing the desirability of national health insurance, the cabinet was still considering the best time to begin payments as outlined in the Medical Care Insurance Act of 1966. This apparent "review" of timing, and "the recent developments" regarding the split in cabinet, opened the door for the Canadian Medical Association once again to question "the insistence on universality" and to recommend "the implementation of a medical insurance program for the low and marginal income groups in the country."[86] Pearson's statement, designed to settle the disputes among his own cabinet ministers, instead only bought the government a few days in which to come to some sort of decision on medicare and further raised public expectations that some significant changes would be made.

The cabinet meetings continued to be volatile. Having met again with the provincial finance ministers, Sharp warmed to the possibility, put forward by Quebec, of implementing national health insurance "gradually." He argued that there was "a very serious problem of a direct confrontation with the provinces which could do great damage in many fields, including the constitutional area" and that for Ottawa to remain committed to its criteria "would reflect an unwillingness to discuss with the provinces a matter of prime importance to them."[87] Other cabinet ministers debated all sides of the question, including the damage further postponement would cause the Liberal Party of Ontario, the damage to national unity if medicare was implemented in the face of Quebec opposition, and the proposition that "while the delay in Medicare might split the Party, the implementation of it might split the country."[88] All that the group could ultimately agree on was to make no public statements regarding the status of cabinet discussions on medicare.[89] At a press conference the next day, Pearson was true to the cabinet decision. He said little more than that premiers had requested a review of the timing of health insurance legislation, and "when provincial governments ask to make a request of this kind, you accept it."[90]

But if Pearson revealed little, there was a press leak somewhere, and the newspapers were full of reports of the attitudes expressed in cabinet by the various ministers. This made even more difficult the attempts to reach a solution to the question of timing. To complicate matters further, Pearson was conducting his own examination of the possibility of phasing-in national health insurance, and in doing so he confirmed suspicions that he himself was in favour of deferring the legislation.[91] Within a week, Pearson informed the cabinet about the results of his inquiries. To go ahead with the 1 July starting date would result in only a few provinces participating, which meant that the federal government would face substantially lower costs than anticipated for universal health insurance. At the same time, "such limited participation would point up the fact that the plan was not initially national in scope."[92] If the ministers agreed that "the initial participation of all the provinces were considered to be of primary importance," Pearson suggested the possibility of "phasing-in the program, over a period possibly of three years, with emphasis on early coverage of the more needy categories."[93] The familiar points regarding national unity, the future of the Liberal Party, and the importance of following through on promises already made were raised in the meeting, but cabinet failed to reach a decision.

Well aware of the impasse in the cabinet, Robarts took the opportunity to issue a statement on his government's intentions regarding health insurance. He stated that Ontario would not participate in the national medicare plan "as presently enacted" because "under present economic conditions Canada cannot afford the 'universal' scheme" and because his government was philosophically opposed to the idea of a compulsory plan.[94] Other opponents of the scheme were impressed with Robarts's argument that educational services, transportation, urban redevelopment, and increases to electrical-power capacity all needed to be taken into consideration in determining provincial spending priorities.[95] Robarts's most interesting argument was that the proposed method of financing national health insurance "would work counter to the whole principle of equalization." He argued that if all provinces except the Maritimes participated in the program, the fact that additional federal taxes would be nation-wide would mean that "the citizens of those three Provinces would pay an additional 8 1/2% income tax for a service in the other and wealthier parts of the country" and Ontario would receive about $2 million more than if all the provinces participated.[96] More to the point, but not mentioned, was the fact that if Ontario did participate, it would be financing the health insurance of much poorer areas of the country. Despite questionable logic and motivation, Robarts's statement was designed to encourage the federal cabinet to agree to delay the implementation of national health insurance.

But it was impossible for that particular cabinet to reach a unanimous agreement on the future of medicare. Mitchell Sharp was opposed to early implementation and gave the impression of being opposed to many of the features of the national plan. Minister of National Health and Welfare Allan MacEachen supported his department's proposals, but he was a junior minister and did not carry much clout in cabinet. Walter Gordon was an active participant in the cabinet debates, but he, too, suffered from diminished power. When, on 31 January 1968, the cabinet finally decided to go ahead with medicare for 1 July 1968, it was obvious that not all ministers were pleased with decision. Nor was Pearson pleased with the behaviour of his ministers, and he felt obliged to remind them of cabinet solidarity the next day. While Pearson noted "that all members of the government would be expected to support the government's position unequivocally, and that all members of Caucus should support the government's position, [he] expressed regret at the failure of some Ministers to be more flexible with regard to a formula for phasing-in the Medicare program, or for otherwise obtaining more provincial participation."[97]

It is impossible to offer a definitive explanation for why that final Pearson cabinet did not vote to delay the implementation of medicare. The prime minister, apparently, believed that all of the provinces should have been brought in at once, even at the expense of some of the previously stated national criteria; it was the weakened and the junior ministers who supported the initial deadline. Jean Marchand, minister of manpower and immigration, voted in favour of the July 1968 deadline and his support was probably key in swinging the balance in favour of early implementation. Although his department was not especially powerful, his position as a senior Quebec minister in an administration that had had difficulty maintaining a strong French presence and was facing more challenges from Quebec nationalists was significant.[98] It was in spite of the prime minister's personal opinion, therefore, that the cabinet agreed to let the health-insurance deadline stand.

Pearson's final, rather inconsequential, contribution to the passage of the federal Medical Services Act of 1968 is characteristic of his role in social-security legislation throughout his whole tenure as leader of the Liberal Party. While an examination of social policy reveals a great deal about the Liberal Party in opposition and in power between 1957 and 1968, it does not reveal much about the strengths of the party leader, since these great accomplishments occurred in spite of, not because of, Pearson. The Liberals who banded together during the early years of opposition had not been handpicked by the leader; he did not surround himself with them. Rather, they came and developed both a new structure and new policies because they believed Pearson to be a progressive reformer. After years of alternately advising and cajoling their leader, many became sorely disappointed with his refusal to take their side in public and cabinet debates. Lester Pearson was at best and at most a diplomat. The social programs implemented during his tenure of office did not come into being because of lengthy and conciliatory negotiation. They came into being because there were other people in the Liberal Party who fundamentally believed in principles – the principle of national programs, the principle of national standards, the principle of social progress – that even the leader's chronic indecisiveness and inability to state his own principles failed to derail the campaign for these new social programs.

Epilogue

By the early spring of 1968, Pearson's government was finished with national health insurance, despite continued pressure to reconsider the question of timing. A federal-provincial conference on the constitution provided the occasion for eight of the premiers to raise with the prime minister "the question of Medicare in vigorous terms." Pearson seemed to take some satisfaction in reporting to cabinet that some premiers argued "Ottawa had no right to force the pace of Medicare" but he did not attempt to reopen the question.[1] For the most part, medicare shifted to the background as the Liberal Party prepared to select a new leader at the convention set for the first week of April.

Social policy was not a major issue in determining the new leader of the Liberal Party of Canada and next prime minister. Of the serious candidates who emerged to seek the leadership, Paul Martin, Pierre Trudeau, and Allan MacEachen were considered on the left of the party, while Mitchell Sharp, Robert Winters, and Paul Hellyer were further to the right. Martin, who had been campaigning informally for some time and who was regarded as the early favourite, was by far the most knowledgeable about social issues and considered himself the father of national hospital insurance. Sharp, on the other had, had to combat his reputation for caring little about the social needs of the voting public. To this end, he chose the former head of the Canadian Welfare Council, Neil Morrison, as his chief policy adviser. Morrison was responsible for carefully outlining Sharp's proposal for a complete overview of existing social-security programs in order to eliminate "the pockets of poverty which persist in the midst of plenty."[2] The fiscally and socially conservative Winters, however, gave scant regard to polishing his image on social policy. He advocated a more decentralized approach and pledged not "to force a programme of Federal design upon the provinces."³ Ultimately, however, neither social policy in general, nor the particular future of medicare, played much of a role in the outcome of the leadership race: the constitution, French-English relations, and the entrancing presence of Pierre Elliott Trudeau were more than enough to keep both the candidates and the delegates occupied.⁴

Shortly after posting a narrow third ballot victory at the Liberal leadership convention, Prime Minister Trudeau called a federal election for 25 June 1968. The Conservatives under Robert Stanfield made medicare an important component of their election platform, vowing to "get together with the provinces and try to work out a medicare plan that the provinces can implement and put into effect."⁵ The Liberals campaigned much more on the new Trudeau approach to Quebec, however, than they did on the unfinished social-policy agenda of the Pearson government. The tactic was successful, and on 25 June 1968 the Liberals registered their first majority victory since 1953, winning 155 seats to the Conservatives' 72. Armed with a mandate of its own, the Trudeau government turned its attention to finishing the business of medicare.

By August 1968, more than one month after the starting date for federal contributions to provincial health-insurance schemes, only Saskatchewan and British Columbia had introduced programs that met Ottawa's four criteria. Except Quebec, all other provinces had taken "concrete steps towards developing qualifying programs" but nothing was complete.⁶ Noting the slow movement towards a national health-insurance program, officials in the Department of Finance urged cabinet to consider alternative methods of encouraging provincial participation. The approach generally favoured in the civil service was for the federal government to make "contributions to those provinces with qualifying medical care plans and grants ... of roughly equivalent amounts to those provinces not participating." The advantages of this proposal included the fact that it would "take some of the fiscal 'pressure' off non-participating provinces; would provide a form of 'phasing-in' of medicare; and would provide the provinces with revenues which might partially offset the problems of high and rising provincial (health) costs."⁷ Unfortunately, it would also almost certainly discourage non-participating provinces from ever joining the national scheme.

The Trudeau government seemed notably more decisive than its predecessor. The system of federal financial participation in provincial

health-insurance plans had been designed during the Pearson administration, and there is no evidence to suggest that the new government
wanted to back away from that commitment. On the contrary, it
seemed only to want to fulfil the commitment in as prompt a fashion
as possible; medicare was not something that it wished to have hang-
ing over its head. In his first budget, in the fall of 1968, Finance
Minister Edgar Benson introduced a 2 per cent social-development tax
on income to a maximum of $120 per year which was designed to
assist the federal government in financing medicare.[8] Unlike the proposal from the officials in the Department of Finance, this tax was to
be levied on all Canadians regardless of whether they lived in a province that had accepted Ottawa's health-insurance offer. The social-
development tax was also in contrast to the additional taxes contemplated by the previous government, since the Trudeau administration
made perfectly clear that this was a tax levied in order to pay for
medicare. Premier Robarts immediately denounced it as "medicare by
coercion."[9] He described the social-development tax as a "Machiavel-
lian scheme that is in my humble opinion one of the greatest political
frauds that has been perpetrated on the people of this country."[10]
Robarts's complaints fell on deaf ears, for he was no longer dealing
with a government that wasted time reviewing decisions once made.
Moreover, the Trudeau ministers demonstrated a firmer ideological
commitment to national health insurance. As Benson explained to a
businessmen's association in Toronto: "The cost-sharing formula for
Medicare naturally underpays the wealthier provinces with the highest
costs and overpays the less wealthy which have lower costs. These are
the prices and benefits of Confederation, a confederation which has
benefited the province of Ontario, for instance, by making it a key
centre for commerce, industry, transportation – all of which bring the
province great revenues. This also involves taxing all Canadians for
Medicare whether the province in which an individual Canadian
resides is a participant or not. The Federal Government taxes only
Canadians without regard to where they live."[11]

And so it took the decisiveness of a new administration to complete
the social-policy agenda of the Pearson government. Plagued by
chronic battles between competing interest within the party and a
wavering commitment to the social goals they had once held so dear,
the Pearson Liberals were not in a position to see a national health-
insurance plan to completion. A new leader, even one who presided
over a cabinet that included many of the old faces, was finally able to
put the finishing touches on a truly national health-insurance system.
By the end of its first year, the Trudeau government had secured commitments from all provinces except Quebec to implement provincial

health-insurance schemes in accordance with the federal criteria. Quebec's plan was in operation by 1972, making state-sponsored health
insurance a reality from coast to coast.

The completion of the social-security net in Canada was accomplished
amidst such profound political debate, most conspicuously within the
Liberal Party itself and between the two levels of government, that the
success of the legislation was at no point guaranteed. It is best to
understand the process by which the Canada Pension Plan and state-
sponsored medical insurance came into being in two parts. The initial
design of the programs occurred largely during the period in which
the Liberals were in opposition, and thus the shape of the proposed
legislation was affected by a variety of factors which were quite distinct from those that influenced the second, governmental, period of
implementation. Examining both of these periods makes it easier to
assess the effects of social pressure, federal-provincial relations, and
intraparty dynamics than would be the case if one focused solely on
the years when Pearson was in power.

The social policies enacted in the 1960s were sketched out in a
general way between 1957 and 1963. Two important factors shaped
the Liberal approach to policy design in this period. Clearly, the Liberals were driven by the need to regain power, and the policies they
began to articulate in opposition reflected that desire. On the one
hand, the public was receptive to an extension of the social-security
net into broader protection against the exigencies of old age and ill
health. While there was little in the way of organized pressure for the
adoption of new programs, there was equally little opposition, and
thus the environment was a conducive one for the development of new
social policies. The same could not be said for the 1920s, or for the
1990s. The relative economic security of the 1950s and 1960s combined with an acceptance of government intervention secured a positive atmosphere within which the Liberals could begin to think about
their role in the provision of social services. Social policies were likely
to be popular and therefore a useful strategy for achieving electoral
victory.

On another level, the need to get back into power also affected the
type of social programs the Liberals proposed. Unable to campaign
regionally in the tradition of the Liberal Party during the post-war
period, the Liberals in opposition needed to design policies with a
universal, national appeal. That would allow the party to centralize
the process of policy formulation, an absolute necessity after the electoral defeat of St Laurent's regional cabinet bosses and the isolation

of the Liberals from the bureaucracy. Social programs in general served as a means to attract enough support to get back into power, and universal programs were not only possible to design under the constraints of opposition but would also serve to reorient the Liberals away from their adherence to regional ministers.

The second major factor that influenced the design of social programs in opposition was the arrival of a new group of Liberals who pushed and cajoled the party into adopting a program that was in contrast to the traditional Liberal platform of the King and St Laurent period. The effects of these individuals cannot be underestimated. Had a group of people committed to a government role in social betterment not migrated towards the Liberal Party, quite different strategies for regaining power might have been adopted. One need only remember the advice of the dominant politicians in the St Laurent administration to recognize that the formulation of a contributory pension plan and a universal health-insurance program depended heavily on the existence of people such as Tom Kent, Walter Gordon, and Maurice Lamontagne within the renewed Liberal Party.

The second stage in the process of the completion of the national social-security system was that of implementation, which began virtually the day the Liberals returned to power in 1963 and was not finished until well into the Trudeau administration. Again, two factors appear most significant in affecting the way in which pensions and medicare were introduced. The political actors, both those in the House of Commons and those in the backrooms, remained key and had as determinative an effect on the legislative success of the programs as they had had on their design. Within the context of a Liberal Party increasingly uncertain about the wisdom of introducing costly social programs, those who remained firm in their commitment were instrumental in keeping the party on its previously conceived track. In fact, the governmental and bureaucratic commitment to pensions and health became even more firm in the face of the most serious obstacle to the achievement of national social policy.

This obstacle, the second factor affecting the implementation of the Canada Pension Plan and medicare, was the structural impediment of federalism. Social services in general fall within the constitutional jurisdiction of the provinces. The experience of pension negotiations, during which the federal government was forced to rethink the proposals the Liberals had designed in opposition, served to steel the commitment of the social-policy proponents in Ottawa. The result was a somewhat different pension plan than had been conceived earlier but one with an even greater commitment to the ideals of universality or national coverage and state as opposed to private administration. These ideals then formed the core of the national Liberal health-insurance scheme. Federal constraints had forced a distillation of Liberal policy down to its very basic components, thus indicating that pension negotiations influenced health strategy, and key governmental actors ensured that the central commitment to those ideals remained firm.

In the implementation process, factors outside the structure and personnel of government had minimal effect. Without the pressing need to appeal to the public in order to regain power, the Liberals paid little heed to outside opinions on the details of either the pension plan or health insurance. Still, the assumption remained that once the programs were successfully in place, they would be regarded positively by all concerned – the public that benefited from them, employers that were forced to contribute to them, and insurance companies that were circumvented by them. Interestingly, in recent years, the Canadian social-security net has undergone a number of transformations both at the governmental level and within the public perception. The government cutbacks, while much reviled, have not been surprising given the neo-conservative environment and deficit-reduction hysteria of much of the 1980s. More intriguing has been the relatively sudden appearance of social security, perhaps most particularly the Canadian system of state-sponsored health insurance, as a symbol of what makes Canada unique. A recent Angus Reid poll indicated that fully 95 per cent of Canadians believed our social-welfare system in general and our health-care system specifically to be the best in the world; similarly, a *Maclean's* poll found that Canadians identified medicare as one of the defining features of what it is to be Canadian.[12] Successive governments in the 1980s and 1990s have been forced to heed the public popularity of the social-security legislation implemented in the 1960s. The 1996 Speech from the Throne included a commitment to sustaining a national social-security net; the motion to accept the Speech noted that "perhaps nothing unites us as a national like our belief in the need to preserve the fabric of the Canadian social safety net."[13] Thus, what began as largely state-generated pieces of legislation have now come full circle and are being used by the public to wrest from the state promises of continued commitment to full social-security coverage. While it is yet to be seen whether this will be successful, the current public popularity of social welfare in Canada attests to the correctness of the assumptions planners and politicians in the 1950s and 1960s made about the necessity and desirablity of social-security legislation.

Notes

INTRODUCTION

1 In his seminal article "The National Policy – Old and New," Vernon Fowke used the "perspective of the national policy concept" to explain both economic development and the role of the federal government (278). He argued that following the completion of John A. Macdonald's National Policy in the 1930s, the Canadian state needed to turn to other areas of activity, one of which was the provision of social security. Other scholars since Fowke have also commented on the evolutionary nature of the federal government's "national policies." See Craven and Traves, "The Class Politics of the National Policy, 1872–1933"; Eden and Molot, "Canada's National Policies: Reflections on 125 Years."

2 For an overview of the American theoretical frameworks, see Abramovitz, *Regulating the Lives of Women*, chapter 1; Gordon, "The New Feminist Scholarship on the Welfare State" and "What Does Welfare Regulate?"; Skocpol, "State Formation and Social Policy in the United States" and *Protecting Soldiers and Mothers*, chapter 1; Struthers, *Limits of Affluence*, 5–16.

3 See Wilensky and Lebeaux, *Industrial Society and Social Welfare* and *The Welfare State and Equality*.

4 See, for example, Rimlinger, *Welfare Policy and Industrialization in Europe and America*.

5 See, for example, Berkowitz and McQuaid, *Creating the Welfare State*; Quadagno, "Welfare Capitalism and the Social Security Act of 1935."

6 See, for example, Esping-Andersen, *Politics Against Markets*; Korpi,
   The Democratic Class Struggle; Piven and Cloward, *Regulating the
   Poor* and *Poor People's Movements*.

7 The key figure in this school is unquestionably Theda Skocpol – see her
   edited collections *The Politics of Social Policy in the United States*
   (with Margaret Weir and Ann Shola Orloff) and *Bringing the State
   Back In* (with Peter Evans and Dietrich Rueschemeyer). More recently,
   she has acknowledged the importance of extra-state actors in achieving
   social-security legislation, but she continues to argue that "politicians
   and administrators must be taken seriously. Not merely agents of other
   social interests, they are actors in their own right, enabled and con-
   strained by the political organizations within which they operate. Political officials can therefore make independent contributions to the
   development of a nation's social policy." See Skocpol, *Protecting Soldiers and Mothers*, 41–2.

8 See ibid. as well as Abramovitz, *Regulating the Lives of Women*, and
   Gordon, *Pitied but Not Entitled*.

9 Exceptions to this generalization include Swartz, "The Politics of
   Reform: Conflict and Accommodation in Canadian Health Policy";
   Finkel, "Origins of the Welfare State in Canada"; and Moscovitch and
   Drover, "Social Expenditures and the Welfare State." All these scholars
   work within the Marxist framework. For feminist perspectives on
   welfare-state developments, see Jane Ursel, "The State and the Maintenance of Patriarchy: A Case Study of Family, Labour and Welfare Legislation in Canada," and Cynthia Comacchio, *Nations Are Built of Babies*.

10 Gray, *Federalism and Health Policy*; Gray and White, "Federalism and
   the Evolution of Public Hospital and Medical Care Coverage"; Mahler,
   New Dimensions in Canadian Federalism. Studies that focus on Canadian federalism and its impact on social policy are also common. See,
   for example, Simeon, *Federal-Provincial Diplomacy*; Ismael, ed., *Canadian Social Welfare Policy*; Banting, *The Welfare State and Canadian
   Federalism*.

11 See Bryden, *Old Age Pensions and Policy-Making in Canada*; Taylor,
   Health Insurance and Canadian Public Policy, 2nd ed.; Haddow, *Poverty Reform in Canada, 1958–1978*. Dennis Guest stands out among
   scholars in the field of social policy in that he has provided an overview of all of the major developments in twentieth-century Canada. See
   Guest, *The Emergence of Social Security in Canada*.

12 An exchange over the roots of unemployment insurance is the clearest
   example of the two sides of the debate. See Pal, "Relative Autonomy
   Revisited: The Origins of Canadian Unemployment Insurance," and
   Cuneo, "Comment: Restoring Class to State Unemployment Insurance."
   The society-centred approach can trace its intellectual ancestry to the

earlier Marxist argument that the welfare state developed in Canada because of the desire on the part of the capitalist class to dissipate class conflict and protect its interests by offering tidbits of social security.

13　See English, *The Worldly Years: The Life of Lester Pearson, 1949–1972, Volume II*; Granatstein, *Canada, 1957–1967*.

14　In the effort to sort out the important events of this period in Canadian history, social policies have frequently been virtually disregarded. J.L. Granatstein, who has written most explicitly about these years in *Canada, 1957–1967*, examines the battle in Saskatchewan for provincial health insurance but devotes only a few sentences to the parallel battles in Ottawa. In John English's biography of Lester Pearson, external affairs are examined in much greater detail than domestic policy. See *The Worldly Years*.

15　Although Peter H. Russell does not pinpoint social programs, he does identify the mid-1960s as a transition to "mega constitutional politics" which "address the very nature of the political community upon which the constitution is based." See *Constitutional Odyssey*, 72.

CHAPTER ONE

1　John Meisel, "After June 10," *Canadian Forum*, July 1957; Brennan, *Reporting the Nation's Business*, 164–7.

2　Hutchison Papers, Power to Hutchison, 17 June 1957.

3　Royal Commission on Dominion Provincial Relations, *Final Report*, vol. 2: 33–43.

4　Davidson, "Improving the Social Services," 77.

5　Special Committee on Social Security, *Health Insurance: Report of the Advisory Committee on Health Insurance Appointed by Order in Council P.C. 836 Dated February 5, 1942*, pt. 1; Canadian Medical Association, *A Submission by the Canadian Medical Association to the Royal Commission on Dominion-Provincial Relations*, 14–16.

6　Naylor, *Public Practice, Private Payment*, chapter 5; Bothwell and English, "Pragmatic Physicians," 486–90; Bothwell, "The Health of the Common People," 206–8.

7　See Frank R. Breul, "The Genesis of Family Allowances in Canada." Leonard Marsh first raised the idea of children's allowances, but Prime Minister Mackenzie King adopted it as policy only after being convinced by office staff member J.W. Pickersgill that perhaps "three-quarters of labour's real grievances on the score of wages could be removed by the immediate establishment of children's allowances paid by the State." See Marsh, *Report on Social Security for Canada*, 196–208, and Pickersgill as quoted in Granatstein, *Canada's War*, 267. Also, see Owram, *The Government Generation*, 310–15.

8 Martin Papers, vol. 41, file: Old Age Security, Correspondence, Martin to St Laurent, 21 Nov. 1950.
9 Thomson, "The Political Ideas of Louis St Laurent," 153.
10 *Federal-Provincial Conference, 1955: Preliminary Meeting,* 19.
11 See Taylor, *Health Insurance and Canadian Public Policy,* 69–104, 167–9.
12 Quoted in Thomas H. McLeod, "Federal-Provincial Relations, 1958," 9.
13 Department of National Health and Welfare Papers, vol. 1,372, file 1–1, memo, "Health Insurance and Ontario," Davidson to Martin, 5 Aug. 1955.
14 Ibid., "Informal Discussion Concerning Health Insurance," no author, 25 Aug. 1955. George Gathercole had previously indicated that Ontario was considering a proposal that would require the patient to cover 50 per cent of the cost of hospitalization and medical expenses, a figure that Davidson thought excessive. See ibid., memo, "Health Insurance and Ontario," Davidson to Martin, 5 Aug. 1955.
15 *Proceeding of the Federal-Provincial Conference, 1955,* 9.
16 Department of National Health and Welfare Papers, vol. 1,372, file 1–1. memo, George Davidson to Dr Jackson, 20 Sept. 1955.
17 *Proceedings of the Federal-Provincial Conference, 1955,* 10–11. See also Department of National Health and Welfare Papers, vol. 1,372, file 1–1. RBB, JJD, and GFD [R.B. Bryce, J.J. Deutsch, and George Davidson], "Memorandum Re: Health Insurance Policy," 20 Jan. 1956.
18 Taylor, *Health Insurance and Canadian Public Policy,* 131.
19 Press communiqué, 6 Oct. 1955, reproduced in *Proceedings of the Federal-Provincial Conference, 1955,* 127.
20 Ibid., 24.
21 See Progressive Conservative Party Papers, vol. 430, file: Research Reports, 87–93, Report #88, "Comparison of the Federal Government's Hospital Insurance Legislation with the Plan Proposed by the Government of Ontario," 5 July 1957.
22 Department of National Health and Welfare Papers, vol. 1,372, file 1–1, Statement by Paul Martin before the Committee on Estimates of the Department of National Health and Welfare, 16 March 1956.
23 Kent Papers, vol. 1, file: Correspondence, Sept.–Dec. 1960, "Ideas developed during a conversation with Dr J.A. Hannah, managing director of Associated Medical Services, Tuesday, January 8, 1957," no author, no date.
24 A.D.K., "Health Insurance," *Canadian Medical Association Journal,* vol. 71, 1 May 1956. In the end, physicians found that they were generally able to work effectively under the plan, experiencing only minor discomfiture with the decline of home care, the new need for professional hospital administrators, and the differences between covered and

non-covered hospital care. See "Symposium on Hospital Insurance," *Canadian Medical Association Journal*, vol. 78, no. 10 (15 May 1958).

25 Canadian Labour Congress Papers, vol. 268, file: Canadian Welfare Council–Health Services Commission, pt. 1, 1953–54, Speech, W.M. Anderson, at North American Life Assurance Company annual meeting, 1 Feb. 1954.

26 Department of Insurance Papers, file 2–C–6, vol. 1, "Statement to the Health Committee of the Ontario Legislature by the Canadian Life Insurance Officers Association re: Proposed Ontario Hospitalization Plan," 22 March 1956.

27 Martin Papers, vol. 29, file: Health Insurance Memos, Davidson to Martin, 12 March 1956.

28 Ibid., vol. 30, file: Health Insurance Statements (5). "Notes for an Address by the Rt. Hon. Louis St Laurent to the Canadian Labour Congress," 24 April 1956.

29 Ibid., vol. 29, file: Health Insurance Memos, Davidson to Martin, 12 March 1956.

30 Diefenbaker Papers, vol. 24, file 618 (1956), reel M–5,558, "The Canadian Life Insurance Officers Association, Memorandum re: The Financing of Hospital Care, 9 Oct. 1956."

31 Department of National Health and Welfare Papers, vol. 1,074, file 502–3–5, pt. 1. Frost to St Laurent, 11 Dec. 1956.

32 Ibid., file 502–3–5, pt. 2, St Laurent to Frost, 22 Jan. 1957.

33 Ibid., Frost to St Laurent, 24 Jan. 1957.

34 Ibid., St Laurent to Frost, 28 Jan. 1957.

35 Ibid., Frost to St Laurent, 30 Jan. 1957.

36 Diefenbaker Papers, vol. 24, file 618 (1956), reel M–5,558. D.R.C. Bedson to Duff Roblin, 12 Feb. 1957.

37 Martin Papers, vol. 29, file Health Insurance, Provincial Proposals, Martin to Dana Porter, 12 March 1957.

38 Ibid., Martin to Porter, 19 March 1957.

39 For example, Alberta authorities encountered some difficulty in getting Ottawa to accept their draft legislation. One of the reasons was that the federal government defined an "insured service as one to which a resident is entitled under provincial law but not including service to which a resident is entitled under an Act of the Parliament of Canada" (Department of National Health and Welfare Papers, vol. 1,082, file 502–3–8, pt. 2, R.E. Curran, Legal Advisor, to G.D.W. Cameron, Deputy Minister of National Health, 23 April 1958). Alberta's proposed hospital plan excluded those who were covered by the federal government and was thus unacceptable in Ottawa. But this and other such concerns were not as significant as those in Ontario and so did not represent a major rift between the two levels of government.

40 Hastings, "Federal-Provincial Insurance for Hospital and Physician's Care in Canada," 408; see also Roth, "Hospital Care Insurance in Canada: Background to Developments."
41 P.W.F., "Election Myths," *Canadian Forum*, May 1957.
42 Norrie and Owram, *A History of the Canadian Economy*, 549–51, 569–71.
43 Bryce Papers, vol. 10, file 11, Bryce to St Laurent, 9 March 1957.
44 House of Commons, *Debates*, 14 March 1957, 2,221; Thomson, *Louis St Laurent*, 501.
45 Campbell, *Grand Illusions*, 115.
46 E.P. Neufeld, "A Bland Budget," *Canadian Forum*, April 1957.
47 Thomson, *Louis St Laurent*, 502.
48 House of Commons, *Debates*, 2 April 1957, 2,970. Paul Martin had earlier pointed out that one of the problems that the Liberals had with tying social welfare increases to rises in the GNP was that there would ultimately be calls for decreases in assistance. See ibid., 22 March 1957, 2,610.
49 Ibid., 28 March 1957, 2,783.
50 Diefenbaker Papers, reel M–5,555, vol. 17, file 339.4, Jan.–June 1957, D.R.C. Bedson to Diefenbaker, 16 April 1957; reel M–5,550, file 304–1957, Jan.–April 1957, Norman Dunn to Diefenbaker, 25 April 1957.
51 Bryce Papers, vol. 10, file 11, Bryce to St Laurent, 9 March 1957.
52 Pearson Papers, MG 26 N2, vol. 127, file: K. Kersell, Kent to Pearson, 13 June 1960, quoting from an earlier letter to Jo Grimond, British Liberal leader, on the Canadian political situation.
53 Guest, "The Development of Income Maintenance Programmes in Canada, 1945–1967," 165–6.
54 Diefenbaker Papers, reel M–5,558, vol. 25, file 632, Dec. 1956–Jan. 1957, George Edwards to Martin, 26 Jan. 1957.
55 House of Commons, *Debates*, 22 March 1957, 2,612.
56 Beck, *Pendulum of Power*, 292.
57 Thomas, "The Role of the National Party Caucus," 86.
58 St Laurent Papers, vol. 293, file: Election Campaign–First National Broadcast, Draft, 22 April 1957.
59 Ibid., vol. 294, file: Election Campaign, London Speech, 16 May 1957.
60 Ibid.
61 Ibid., file: Election Campaign, Speech, Halifax, 22 May 1957.
62 Ibid., vol. 292, file: Election Address, "Draft Outline for the Prime Minister's Western Tour," 16 April 1957.
63 Ibid., vol. 293, file: Election Campaign, Speech, Edmonton, 30 April 1957.
64 Ibid., file: Election Campaign, French Broadcast, 30 April 1957.
65 Whitaker, *The Government Party*, 179–85.

66 See Ward, "The Politics of Patronage: James Gardiner and Federal Appointments in the West, 1935–57"; Smith, "Cabinet and Commons in the Era of James G. Gardiner"; Ward and Smith, *Jimmy Gardiner*; Martin, *A Very Public Life, II: So Many Worlds*; Bothwell and Kilbourn, *C.D. Howe*.

67 See Smith, *The Regional Decline of a National Party*, 46.

68 Whitaker, *The Government Party*, 207.

69 Diefenbaker Papers, reel M–5,557, vol. 22, Menzies to Diefenbaker, 12 April 1957.

70 House of Commons, *Debates*, 25 Oct. 1957, 411.

71 Diefenbaker Papers, reel M–5,557, vol. 22, Menzies to Diefenbaker, "National Policy," 6 April 1957.

72 Ibid., Menzies to Diefenbaker, 10 April 1957.

73 See Meisel, *The Canadian General Election of 1957*, 42–3, for a concise analysis of Merril Menzies's "New National Policy."

74 Diefenbaker Papers, reel M–5,557, vol. 22, file 391.8, Menzies to Diefenbaker, 28 March 1957.

75 Ibid., reel M–5,555, vol. 18, file 391, Jan.–May 1957, Deanne Finlayson to Alvin Hamilton, 10 Jan. 1957.

76 Diefenbaker Papers, reel M–5,557, vol. 21, file 391.8, Menzies to Diefenbaker, 14 May 1957.

77 From "A New National Policy" (Ottawa: The Progressive Conservative Party of Canada 1957).

78 See Young, *The Anatomy of a Party*, 313–17.

79 Kidd Papers, vol. 5, file 17, Maxwell Cohen to Duncan MacTavish, 26 April 1957.

80 See Meisel, *The General Election of 1957*, 44–62, and especially 52–4.

CHAPTER TWO

1 Howe Papers, vol. 108, file: Politics–General (5), Howe to W.A. Fraser, 20 June 1957.

2 Smith, *The Regional Decline of a National Party*, 52. For a thorough examination of Liberal "ministerialism," see Whitaker, *The Government Party*.

3 J.E. Hodgetts, "The Liberal and the Bureaucrat," *Queen's Quarterly*, vol. 62 (summer 1955), 183. It is interesting to note that throughout his tenure as prime minister, Diefenbaker continued to look at the senior civil servants as tools of the Liberal Party and distrusted them accordingly. See also Granatstein, *The Ottawa Men*, 271.

4 Smith, *The Regional Decline of a National Party*, 52.

5 Meisel, "The Formation of Liberal and Conservative Programmes in the 1957 Canadian General Election," 573.

6 Only 38.5 per cent of the popular vote went to Diefenbaker. However, voter turnout was at a high of 75 per cent (compared to 68 per cent in 1953). The public's interest in the evangelical fervour of Diefenbaker's speeches, and his ability to prod apathetic voters to action, doubtlessly contributed to the increase in voter turnout and ensured that the new voters were casting their ballots for the Conservative Party. See Meisel, *The Canadian General Election of 1957*, 271–3.

7 Whitaker, *The Government Party*, 22–37, 41–3; Granatstein, *The Politics of Survival: The Conservative Party of Canada, 1939–1945*, 157–8, 128–36.

8 Claxton Papers, vol. 83, file: Political Comments, "The Political Situation," Aug. 1957.

9 Interview, Tom Kent, 22 March 1993.

10 National Liberal Federation Papers, vol. 876, file: J.J. Connolly, Dunning to Connolly, 13 Nov. 1957.

11 Ibid. Mackintosh to Connolly, 28 Nov. 1957.

12 Ibid. Garson to Connolly, 14 Nov. 1957.

13 See Brennan, *Reporting the Nation's Business*, 145, 172.

14 National Liberal Federation Papers, vol. 876, file: J.J. Connolly, Hutchison to Connolly, 4 Dec. 1957.

15 Claxton Papers, vol. 83, file: Political Comments, Duncan MacTavish, "Some After-Thoughts on June 11, 1957."

16 National Liberal Federation Papers, vol. 724, file: Election Reports–1965–Post Election, "Memorandum Concerning the Liberal Party in Canada after June 10th 1957," no author, no date (attributed to Gordon Dryden by Joseph Wearing, *The L-Shaped Party: The Liberal Party of Canada, 1958–1980*, 17n.1).

17 Claxton Papers, vol. 83, file: Political Comments, Kidd to Claxton, 5 Nov. 1957. Given the comments Claxton scribbled in the margins of the letter, he apparently thought this assessment was "nonsense."

18 Ibid., vol. 79, file: Liberal Association, "A Note on Organization," no author, no date (pre-convention, Jan. 1958).

19 "A Rival for Uncle Louis," *Economist*, 8 June 1957.

20 National Liberal Federation Papers, vol. 875, file: Duncan MacTavish (1), Draft, "Some observations on how to improve the present position of the Liberal party," 21 Sept. 1957. Emphasis in the original.

21 Ibid., vol. 724, file: Election Reports–1965–Post Election, "Memorandum Concerning the Liberal Party in Canada after June 10th 1957," no author, no date.

22 Brennan, *Reporting the Nation's Business*, 172.

23 See, for example, Kent Papers, vol. 1, file: Correspondence, 1956, Kent to Dexter, 19 May 1956.

24 Kent, "Liberalism and Canada's Future," *Canadian Liberal*, vol. 9 no. 4 (last quarter, 1957), reprint of address given by Kent to the Manitoba Young Liberal Convention, 19 Oct. 1957.
25 Claxton Papers, vol. 83, file: Political Comments, Gordon to Claxton, "Draft Memorandum for Discussion," 4 Dec. 1957.
26 Power, *A Party Politician: The Memoirs of Chubby Power*, 371–2.
27 Smiley, "The National Party Leadership Convention in Canada: A Preliminary Analysis."
28 National Liberal Federation Papers, vol. 880, file: Social Security Resolutions, Marler to Martin, 18 Nov. 1957.
29 Howe Papers, vol. 185, file: Family and Personal Correspondence, June–Dec. 1957, Crerar to Howe, 26 Nov. 1957.
30 National Liberal Federation Papers, vol. 881, file 1958, Convention News Releases, press release, 14 Jan. 1958.
31 Ibid., vol. 876, file: J.J. Connolly, Kent to Connolly, 4 Dec. 1957; to be fair, it was Kent's views of free trade and the global economy that were most evident in this stage of his association with the national Liberal Party.
32 By some accounts, Kent's ultimate departure from the *Free Press* was as a result of the degree of journalistic support newspaperman Grant Dexter believed *he* had given Duff Roblin's Conservative forces in the Manitoba election of 1958 (interview, J.W. Pickersgill, 10 April 1991).
33 By the conclusion of the convention, the gradual evolution of a free-trade agreement with Britain had become a major plank in the new platform, and it seemed to generate a considerable degree of support among those present. The resolution was presented by Saskatchewan Liberal leader Ross Thatcher, not the most popular of Liberals. See *Globe and Mail*, 16 Jan. 1958.
34 Kent Papers, vol. 1, file: Correspondence, Jan.–Feb. 1958, draft memo on Liberal principles, no date.
35 Pearson Papers, MG 26 N2, vol. 127, file: K. Kersell, Kent to Pearson, quoting letter to British Liberal leader Jo Grimond, 13 June 1960.
36 National Liberal Federation Papers, vol. 877, file: Platform Speeches, Croll, "The Liberal Party Social Goals." 16 Jan. 1958.
37 Montreal *Gazette*, 16 Jan. 1958.
38 National Liberal Federation Papers, vol. 877, file: Platform Speeches, Croll, "The Liberal Party Social Goals." 16 Jan. 1958.
39 Ibid., vol. 876, file: J.J. Connolly, Harris to Connolly, 20 Nov. 1957.
40 Kent Papers, vol. 1, file: Correspondence, Jan.–Feb. 1958, Kilgour to Kent, 10 Jan. 1958.
41 Interview, Malcolm Taylor, 5 Feb. 1991.

42 Kent Papers, vol. 1, file: Correspondence, Jan.–Feb. 1958, Kilgour to Kent, 10 Jan. 1958. Emphasis added.

43 Ward, "The Liberals in Convention."

44 *Globe and Mail* (13 Jan. 1958) editorialized about the prospect of Harris running, although it noted that his past position in the party was a serious handicap in the light of the mood of the convention. "The money Mr. Martin gleefully showered upon people, Mr. Harris grimly extracted from them ... The voters see him as the man who not only took a large part of their earnings, but took far more than he needed." Harris's fiscal conservatism was not representative of the feelings of the majority of people at the convention.

45 Interview, Senator Keith Davey, 13 April 1992; Gordon, *A Political Memoir*, 72.

46 Claxton Papers, vol. 83, file: Political Comments, Gordon to Claxton, "Draft Memorandum for Discussion," 4 Dec. 1957.

47 Interview, Senator Keith Davey, 12 March 1992; Walter Gordon suggested that it would be important "for Pearson to stay in character" and that he should say "his only real interest [in the leadership] is in trying to bring about world peace." Claxton Papers, vol. 83, file: Political Comments, Gordon to Claxton, "Draft Memorandum for Discussion," 4 Dec. 1957.

48 "Future of the Liberal Party," Toronto *Telegram*, 13 Jan. 1958.

49 "The Liberal Role for Liberty-Minded Canada," Toronto *Daily Star*, 11 Jan. 1958.

50 National Liberal Federation Papers, vol. 881, file 1958, Convention News Releases, press release, 14 Jan. 1958. According to other sources, the number of resolutions received by the resolutions committee was around 360. See, for example, "New Spirit Needed," Halifax *Chronicle-Herald*, 14 Jan. 1958.

51 National Liberal Federation Papers, vol. 881, file 1958, Convention News Releases, press release, 14 Jan. 1958.

52 Ward, "The Liberals in Convention."

53 National Liberal Federation Papers, vol. 877, file: Convention, 1958, Speeches, address by Jimmy Gardiner, 15 Jan. 1958.

54 P.F.W., "Liberals Convene, But Can They Convince?" *Canadian Forum*, Feb. 1958.

55 Quoted in "Lester Pearson, Politician," *Globe and Mail*, 18 Jan. 1958.

56 Paul Martin charged that the party leaders were trying to force Pearson into power: "If the brass feel that the party can survive only through their dictates as a closed corporation telling delegates how they should think, then the time has come for new leadership" (Martin, quoted in Toronto *Telegram*, 15 Jan. 1958). A Winnipeg youth delegate moved that more time be allotted to policy discussions and less to formal

speeches, and the defeat of this motion led to widespread, albeit quiet, protest that the rank and file was being gagged (see "The 'Brass' – And the 'Grass,'" *Globe and Mail*, 16 Jan. 1958; J.A. Hume, Ottawa *Citizen*, 15 Jan. 1958). Most important was the reminder that "too much self righteousness, too much disdain for the 'common people' (and their rights and their opinions), too much power clutched tightly in too few hands – these were the things that toppled the Liberal Government seven months ago" ("The 'Brass' – And the 'Grass'").

57 David MacDonald, "Who Will Lead the Liberals into the Campaigning to Come?" *Globe Magazine*, 4 Jan. 1958.

58 National Liberal Federation Papers, vol. 877, file: Platform Speeches, Pearson nomination address, 15 Jan. 1958.

59 Ibid., Martin nomination address, 15 Jan. 1958.

60 "Day of Decision," Toronto *Daily Star*, 16 Jan. 1958.

61 Vancouver *Sun*, 17 Jan. 1958.

62 Quoted in Frank Swanson, "It Was Pearson All the Way," Ottawa *Citizen*, 17 Jan. 1958.

63 Ward, "The Liberals in Convention."

64 Pearson Papers, MG 26 N2, vol. 114, file: Health Insurance c. 1957, draft statement, no date.

65 National Liberal Federation Papers, vol. 875, file: Duncan MacTavish (3), 4th National Liberal Convention, L.B. Pearson acceptance speech, 16 Jan. 1958.

66 Progressive Conservative Party Papers, vol. 415, file: Liberal Party Convention, 1958, "New Statements of Liberal Policy–1958," 25 Jan. 1958. Emphasis added.

67 Blair Fraser, "Liberal dilemma: hang on or topple the Tories?" *Maclean's*, 1 Feb. 1958.

68 Forsey Papers, vol. 9, file: letters to the editor, 1952–59, Eugene Forsey to Norman Smith (vice-president of the Ottawa *Journal*), 29 Jan. 1958; Claxton Papers, vol. 76, file: R.M. Fowler, Fowler to Gordon, 2 Feb. 1958.

69 Beck, *Pendulum of Power*, 311–28; Granatstein, *Canada, 1957–1967*, 35–9; Wrong, "Parties and Voting in Canada: A Backward and Forward Glance in the Light of the Last Election"; Regenstreif, "The Canadian General Election of 1958"; Smith, *Rogue Tory*, 279–83.

70 Progressive Conservative Party Papers, vol. 164, file: Liberal Policy, 1958, "The Pearson Plan."

71 Kent Papers, vol. 1, file: Correspondence, April–December 1958, Kent to Col. Ted Leslie, 12 April 1958.

72 See John A. Stevenson, "Votes vs. Principles," *Saturday Night*, 29 March 1958.

73 Beck, "Quebec and the Canadian Elections of 1958."

74 John Meisel, "After the Deluge–What?" *Canadian Forum*, May 1958.

75 Kent Papers, vol. 1, file: Correspondence, April–December 1958, Kent to Col. Ted Leslie, 12 April 1958.

76 Ibid., Kent to Pearson, 1 April 1958.

77 *One Canada: Memoirs of the Right Honourable John G. Diefenbaker*, vol. 1: 277.

78 Grosart Papers, vol. 8, file 14, Camp to Grosart, 14 April 1958.

79 Howe Papers, vol. 109, file: Politics–General (8), Harris to Howe, 2 May 1958.

80 Ibid.

81 Ibid., Howe to Harris, 5 May 1958 (misdated 5 April 1958).

82 Ibid.

83 Ibid., vol. 107, file: Political–General, Howe to Gardiner, 24 May 1958.

84 Ibid., file: Politics–General, 1958, Gardiner to Howe, 11 Dec. 1958.

85 Hutchison Papers, Hutchison to Dexter, April 1958.

86 Howe Papers, vol. 108, file: Political–General (5), letter, no author, no date.

87 Ibid., vol. 107, file: Political–General, W.A. Fraser to Duncan Mac-Tavish, 16 May 1958.

88 Lamontagne Papers, vol. 7, file 3, Lamontagne to Pearson, "The Organization of the Party," 1 Oct. 1959.

89 Ibid.

90 Ibid.

91 Pearson Papers, MG 26 N2, vol. 127, file: K. Kersell, Tom Kent, "Reply to Questions about the N.L.F. Constitution, September 1960."

92 Howe Papers, vol. 109, file: Politics–General (8), Howe to Harris, 5 May 1958 (misdated 5 April 1958).

93 Private collection, Walter Gordon Papers, Gordon to Pearson, 8 July 1960.

94 Interview, Senator Keith Davey, 13 April 1992.

95 Kidd Papers, vol. 3, files 1953, 1955, 1957–63. Kidd to MacTavish, 22 April 1960.

96 Howe Papers, vol. 109, file: Political–General (7), Howe to Fraser, 30 Jan. 1959.

97 Claxton Papers, vol. 79, file: H.E. Kidd, Claxton to Matthews, 30 Nov. 1959.

98 Kidd Papers, vol. 3, files 1953, 1955, 1957–63, H.E. Kidd, "Memorandum of conversation with Mr. Pearson in his office, 9:00 a.m., April 13th, 1960," 22 April 1960.

99 Ibid., Kidd to MacTavish, 22 April 1960.

100 Gordon, *A Political Memoir*, 79–85; Kent Papers, vol. 1, file: Correspondence, 1959, Kent to George Davidson, 24 June 1959. The deputy

minister of welfare "could probably say that, to the extent of about 80 per cent, I agree entirely with what you say in your paper; and that as far as the rest is concerned, while it is in some degree arguable, it is almost at no point in direct conflict with my own general point of view." It was important to Kent that officials in the Department of National Health and Welfare agree in principle to the social policies he advocated and hoped would form the basis of the new Liberal platform; Howe Papers, vol. 107, file: Political–General, Jean Lesage Speech, 4 Dec. 1958.

101 On the Conservative position, see Progressive Conservative Party Papers, vol. 385, file: Elections, 1962–Policy, Waldo Monteith, in "New National Policy in Action," no. 1 (November 1959); Lamontagne Papers, vol. 7, file 3, Maurice Lamontagne, "Conservative Social Justice," 4 Dec. 1959. On the CCF, see in the same collection Maurice Lamontagne, "The New Party: Its Origin," 23 Nov. 1959.

102 Private collection, Walter Gordon Papers, Gordon to Pearson, 8 July 1960.

CHAPTER THREE

1 Kent, *A Public Purpose*, 77–8.

2 J.R. Stirrett, a member of the board of the *Canadian Liberal*, actively pushed for a conference of Liberals to stir up enthusiasm among the electorate and provide "very real inspiration to the hundreds of Liberal intellectuals who would attend." Pearson Papers, MG 26 N2, vol. 108, file: Study Conference on National Problems (3), Stirrett to Pearson, 2 Oct. 1959.

3 Stursberg Papers, vol. 37, file: Sharp, 26–7–76, Stursberg interview with Mitchell Sharp, 26 July 1976.

4 Kidd Papers, vol. 3, file: Correspondence, A. Bruce Matthews, Kidd to Matthews, 17 July 1960.

5 Ibid., 2nd draft, "Report of the President," 15 Nov. 1959.

6 Pearson Papers, MG 26 N2, vol. 107, file: Liberal Party Study Conference on National Problems, 1960, John Payne to Pearson, 15 June 1960; ibid., vol. 108, file: Study Conference on National Problems (3), Pearson to Fowler, 17 June 1960.

7 Private collection, Kent Papers, Kent to Sifton, 1 Jan. 1959; interview, Tom Kent, 2 Aug. 1995.

8 Kent Papers, vol. 6, file: Study Conference, September 1960, Sharp to Kent, 17 June 1960.

9 Pearson Papers, MG 26 N2, vol. 108, file: Study Conference on National Problems (3), Gordon to Pearson, 22 April 1960.

10 See, for example, ibid., Kent to Pearson, 5 Aug. 1960. Kent's interest in Pearson's opinion on his paper seems more a result of personal respect than because of Pearson's position as leader of the party.

11 Martin, *A Very Public Life Volume II*, 344; Stursberg Papers, vol. 34, file: Martin, 1976; interview, Paul Martin, 20 November 1990.

12 "New lead for Liberals," Toronto *Daily Star*, 7 Sept. 1960; "Looking for new ideas," *Globe and Mail*, 8 Sept. 1960.

13 Gordon Papers, file 3, Summary, Monteath Douglas, "Old Age Security," Kingston Conference, 6–10 Sept. 1960.

14 Chevrier Papers, vol. 12, file: Study Conference on National Problems (1), J. Wendell Macleod, "Basic Issues in Hospital and Medical Care Insurance."

15 CCF–NDP Papers, vol. 494, file: Liberal Party, T.W. Kent, "Towards a Philosophy of Social Security," July 1960.

16 *Globe and Mail*, 9 Sept. 1960; ibid., 10 Sept. 1960; "Who isn't a Liberal, anyhow?" *Canadian Forum*, November 1960.

17 Newman, *Renegade in Power*, 427.

18 Toronto *Daily Star*, 10 Sept. 1960; Martin, *A Very Public Life*, 344.

19 J.W. Pickersgill, as quoted in Stursberg, *Lester Pearson and the Dream of Unity*, 64; Pickersgill, *The Road Back by a Liberal in Opposition*, 98.

20 Stursberg, *Lester Pearson and the Dream of Unity*, 64; Martin, *A Very Public Life*, 344. On the pressure to remove the "radicals," see Maurice Lamontagne as quoted in Stursberg, *Lester Pearson and the Dream of Unity*, 63; Gordon, *A Political Memoir*, 86.

21 See Martin, *A Very Public Life*, 344.

22 National Liberal Federation Papers, vol. 886, file: Rally–Announcement, "Possible Questions–Press Conference," 15 June 1960; "Report on Kingston," *Canadian Liberal*, vol. 9, no. 5 (October 1960).

23 Walter Gordon, unpublished memoirs, vol. 5: 16, quoted in Smith, *Gentle Patriot*, 70.

24 Private collection, Gordon Papers, Gordon to Pearson, 8 July 1960.

25 Kent Papers, vol. 1, file: Correspondence, Sept.–Dec. 1960, Gordon to Kent, 4 Oct. 1960; Kent, *A Public Purpose*, 90.

26 Reported in Saywell, ed., *The Canadian Annual Review for 1961*, 70.

27 Kent Papers, vol. 1, file: Correspondence, Sept.–Dec. 1960. Kent to Gordon, 6 Oct. 1960.

28 National Liberal Federation Papers, vol. 888, file: Misc. Views from National Organizations, A.D. Kelly, general secretary of the CMA to Paul Laford, secretary of the Rally organization committee, 7 Nov. 1960.

29 Interview, Robert MacIntosh, 29 March 1992; Kent Papers, vol. 1, file: Correspondence, Sept.–Dec. 1960, Gordon to Kent, 11 Nov. 1960.

30 National Liberal Federation Papers, vol. 889, file: Health Insurance, "Plan for Health" statement for Rally, Jan. 1961.

31 Toronto *Daily Star*, 6 and 7 Jan. 1961.

32 Reported in the Toronto *Telegram*, 9 Jan. 1961

33 Ibid., 10 Jan. 1961; Kidd Papers, vol. 7, file 3, press release, Jan. 1961.

34 Kent Papers, vol. 1, file: Correspondence, Jan.–April 1961, "The Health Plan of the Liberal Party" as approved 10 Jan. 1961.

35 Kent, *A Public Purpose*, 92.

36 Kent Papers, vol. 6, file: National Liberal Rally, Gordon to Kent, 16 Jan. 1961.

37 Pearson Papers, MG 26 N6, vol. 107, file: Liberal Party Policy–J.J. Connolly, Fowler to Gordon, 2 March 1961; Kent Papers, vol. 6, file: National Liberal Rally, Gordon to Kent, 14 March 1961.

38 Pearson Papers, MG 26 N6, vol. 107, file: Liberal Party Policy–J.J. Connolly, Fowler to Gordon, 2 March 1961; Gordon, *A Political Memoir*, 91.

39 Kent Papers, vol. 1, file: Correspondence, Jan.–April 1961, Joe O'Sullivan to Pearson, 14 Jan. 1961.

40 Saywell, ed., *Canadian Annual Review for 1961*, 61; Sauvé Papers, vol. 124, file: Parti Libéral du Canada, remarks by Tom Kent, Manitoba Liberal Convention, 21 April 1961.

41 Kidd Papers, vol. 25, file: Second Preliminary Report on a National Opinion Study, 1961; Kent Papers, vol. 7, file: Opinion Survey, Sept.–Oct. 1961, "National Opinion Study." Keith Davey, the newly appointed national director of the party, found a number of flaws with the study and was disturbed by what he regarded as an "effort to take over as the federal Liberal party's principle advertising agency" in the wake of the dismissal of Cockfield Brown. He ultimately went to American pollster Lou Harris for assistance in the next election. See Davey, *The Rainmaker*, 45.

42 Kent Papers, vol. 1, file: Correspondence, Jan.–April 1961, Kent to Gordon, 21 March 1961.

43 Pearson Papers, MG 26 N2, vol. 27, file: National Rally, Upper to Gordon, 30 March 1961.

44 House of Commons, *Debates*, 21 Dec. 1960, 1,023–5; Gruedning, *Emmett Hall*, 85.

45 Progressive Conservative Party Papers, vol. 334, file: Diefenbaker, Rt. Hon. John–General, 1960 (Oct.–Dec.), W.D. Butt, MD, to Diefenbaker, 26 Dec. 1960.

46 Department of National Health and Welfare Papers, vol. 1,107, file 504–1–2, pt. 1, notes for Diefenbaker speech at opening of the headquarters for the College of Physicians and Surgeons, 19 Jan. 1961.

47 Progressive Conservative Party Papers, vol. 346, file: Monteith, J. Waldo, Monteith to Grosart, 2 March 1961; Fisher Papers, Series B–1, MU 4,209, file: National Development, draft speech for Alvin Hamilton, Sept. 1961.

48 Latimer Papers, MU 4,543, "Minutes of the Ontario Progressive Conservative Leadership Convention, 23–25 Oct. 1961," address by John Diefenbaker.

49 Monteith Papers, vol. 2, file: Oct.–Nov. 1961, "Second Report of the Interdepartmental Committee on Social Security," 19 Oct. 1961; Bryce Papers, vol. 8, file 19, "Social Security–Views Expressed by Individual Cabinet Ministers at Cabinet Meetings October 10th, 12th and 26th 1961," 27 Oct. 1961.

50 See Young, *The Anatomy of a Party*, 313–17.

51 Saywell, ed., *The Canadian Annual Review for 1961*, 81–2.

52 Ibid., 83.

53 Paul Fox, "Three Views of the New Party Convention: Democracy at the Convention," *Canadian Forum*, September 1961; Ramsay Cook, "Moderation Wins Down the Line in NDP," *Saturday Night*, 2 Sept. 1961, and "Three Views of the New Party Convention: A Calculated Risk," *Canadian Forum*, September 1961.

54 Chevrier Papers, vol. 12, file 5, "A MacDuff Ottawa Report: Toil and Trouble," 7 Aug. 1961.

55 Kent Papers, vol. 1, file: Correspondence, Jan.–April 1961, Kent to Gordon, 21 March 1961.

56 Interviews, James Coutts, 16 Dec. 1994, and Richard O'Hagan, 13 Dec. 1994. Pearson has been described by some, including that consummate politician Paul Martin, as more of a politician than anyone really recognized (interview, Keith Davey, 13 April 1992).

57 It is Pearson's official biographer who somewhat unsatisfactorily explains his chronic indecisiveness as evidence of an all-inclusive, nonpartisan approach to politics. See English, *The Worldly Years*, 162–3.

58 Kent Papers, vol. 1, file: Correspondence, Jan.–April 1961, Pearson to Kent, 7 March 1961.

59 Ibid., Kent to Pearson, 21 March 1961.

60 Pearson Papers, MG 26 N2, vol. 115, file: Old Age Security (2), address by L.B. Pearson on "The Nation's Business," 4 Oct. 1961.

61 Kent Papers, vol. 1, file: Correspondence, Nov. 1961, Pearson speech, 27 Nov. 1961.

62 Peter C. Newman, "Yes, there is a new Mike Pearson; now he *wants* to be Prime Minister," *Maclean's*, 26 Aug. 1961; National Liberal Federation Papers, vol. 685, file: Weekly Reports, 1961, "Pre-campaign Strategy," 10 Aug. 1961.

63 See Bakvis, *Regional Ministers*, 72–3.

64 Kent Papers, vol. 1, file: Correspondence, Jan. 1962, Kent to Joe O'Sullivan, 5 Jan. 1962.
65 Martin Papers, vol. 209, file: Pension Plan (2), "Extract from Speech by Hon. Paul Martin Delivered in Ottawa, January 30, 1962."
66 Lamontagne Papers, vol. 7, file 12, "The Liberal Party and Federal-Provincial Programmes," 5 Jan. 1962.
67 House of Commons, *Debates*, 18 Jan. 1962, 2–3. Diefenbaker's explanation for the necessity of a constitutional amendment was that the amendment authorized in 1951 permitted the federal government to devise a scheme for old age pensions only, and in writing his report on pensions for the Conservative government Robert Clark had received a legal opinion "that the addition of survivors' and disabled persons' benefits would not be covered by the 1952 amendment unless the beneficiaries themselves were aged persons" (Saywell, ed., *The Canadian Annual Review for 1962*, 322). The Liberals' legal opinion suggested that while "a constitutional amendment would eliminate every doubt," nevertheless a "beginning could be made under existing law" (Martin Papers, vol. 209, file: Pension Policy Papers, 1962, Gordon Blair to Martin, 22 Jan. 1962). Pearson pointed out that "people who dwell on alleged constitutional difficulties about a contributory pension plan are really trying to avoid the issue," and Martin charged that it was "an obvious ruse designed to conceal the government's neglect of this vital issue for almost five years" (Kent Papers, vol. 1, file: Correspondence, Jan. 1962 (1), memo, Kent to Pearson, "Pensions: Possible Questions and Answers at Press Conference," 8 Jan. 1962; House of Commons, *Debates*, 5 Feb. 1962, 543). The provincial premiers had not been enthusiastic about agreeing to an amendment to the constitution without being clear about its possible repercussions, a sentiment that Diefenbaker and his cabinet ought to have anticipated. Moreover, they were unable to answer the requests for more information on the type of legislation envisaged. Premier Lesage of Quebec was particularly concerned about the constitutional ramifications, which served only to raise the ire of National Health and Welfare Minister Waldo Monteith. In a draft reply to the premier, Monteith argued: "You say you would not place before the Legislature a proposal to amend the constitution without explicit details of the proposed legislation to be enacted by parliament after the constitutional amendment is made ... As a question of constitutional principle, I believe that a Provincial Legislature does not need to take responsibility for the explicit details of the way in which Parliament would use the powers we are proposing it should have; indeed, the whole purpose of the proposal is to enable Parliament to take that responsibility itself." See Monteith Papers, vol. 2, file: Department of National Health and Welfare–Social Security, Jan.–Aug. 1962, draft reply to letter from Premier Lesage, no date.

68 Martin Papers, vol. 209, file: Pension Plan (2), "Extract from Speech by Hon. Paul Martin Delivered in Ottawa, January 30, 1962."

69 Kent Papers, vol. 1, file: Correspondence, Jan. 1962 (1), David Stanley to Pearson, 19 Jan. 1962.

70 Chevrier Papers, vol. 11, file 6, "Health Care as Needed," 27 March 1962.

71 Ibid., vol. 8, file 16, "Campaign Strategy," Feb. 1962.

72 Pearson Papers, MG 26 N2, vol. 82, file: Elections, pt. 2, "Pre-campaign Strategy," no date.

73 See Peter Newman, "How to win votes and avoid the election issues," *Maclean's*, 16 June 1962; Kenneth McNaught, "Lose the issues, win the election," *Saturday Night*, 23 June 1962.

74 Interview, Richard O'Hagan, 13 Dec. 1994

75 *Globe and Mail*, 1 June 1962. Diefenbaker used the idea of a brains trust to his own electoral advantage. It was a system the Conservatives had nothing but contempt for, suggesting that the "hand-picked elite of the Liberal bureaucratic hierarchy ... represents a movement to de-democratize Canadian politics to return to the 'Board of Directors' concept of government where academic considerations out-weigh human considerations, where Parliament again becomes an instrument of a corporate directorate rather than the instrument of the national will" (Progressive Conservative Party Papers, vol. 387, file: Campaign Strategy–Memoranda, 1962, "Election 1962," no date). Other Conservatives, such as former Ontario premier Leslie Frost, argued that Diefenbaker himself needed to appoint a group of advisers who were experts in fields in which national programs were being designed. The Chief ignored all such counsel. See Robarts Papers, MU 7,997, file: Diefenbaker, John, 1962, Frost to Diefenbaker, 19 Feb. 1962.

76 Pearson Papers, MG 26 N5, vol. 45, file: Memoirs, vol. 3, chapter 10, 1963–71, L.B. Pearson to Geoffrey Pearson, 26 June 1962.

77 Kent Papers, vol. 2, file: Correspondence, July 1962, Kent to Pearson, Gordon, Davey, and O'Hagan, "Memorandum on Machinery," 9 July 1962.

78 Kent Papers, vol. 2, file: Correspondence, July 1962, Kent, "Strategy: The 'Left' and 'Right' Aspects," 16 July 1962.

79 National Liberal Federation Papers, vol. 685, file: Weekly Reports, 1962, weekly report from Keith Davey, 30 Aug. 1962; Smith, *The Regional Decline of a National Party*, passim.

80 Kent Papers, vol. 2, file: Correspondence, Nov. 1962, "Summary of the Meeting on Health," memo from Harry Harley, 6 Nov. 1962.

81 Pearson Papers, MG 26 N2, vol. 14, file 612, "Health Care as Needed," Health Committee Approved Draft, 5 Dec. 1962.

82 Ibid.

83 Kent Papers, vol. 2, file: Correspondence, Nov. 1962, speech by David Kilgour to the American Life Convention, Chicago, 10 Oct. 1962.

84 Ibid.

85 Chevrier Papers, vol. 12, file 16, John B. Frosst to Chevrier, 13 April 1962.

86 Ibid.

87 Pearson Papers, MG 26 N2, vol. 41, file 618.1–Medicare, Kent to Pearson, 29 Nov. 1962.

88 Ibid.

89 For details on the cabinet crisis, see Saywell, ed., *Canadian Annual Review for 1963*, 5–16.

90 Department of National Health and Welfare Papers, Acc. 88–89/012, vol. 4, file 2,101–5–2 pt. 2, "Memorandum on Alternatives to Old Age, Survivors and Disability Insurance and Portable Pensions," January 1963. Later in the spring, the Conservative set up a committee to examine the question of health insurance, although virtually no progress had been made prior to the dissolution of Parliament preparatory to the federal election. See ibid., vol. 1,129, file 504–4–15, pt. 1, Departmental Group to Study Health Insurance, 1 February 1963.

91 Ibid., Acc. 88–89/012, vol. 4, file 2,101–5–2, pt. 2, "Interdepartment Committee on Social Security," 18 April 1963. Members of the committee were informed of both the pros and the cons of the Ontario proposals. On the one hand, "it seemed undesirable to depart from the principle followed in the case of unemployment insurance and family allowance where coverage was on a national basis," and, "from the point of view of total economy, it seemed more sensible to adopt a single national scheme, even though it might take time to get if fully operational." However, the benefits of a provincial scheme were that "it would result in a diversity that could take into account regional needs," would allow for the continuation of private pension plans, and would ultimately "remove political pressures that are on the Federal government to provide a national scheme having fairly generous terms." Ibid.

92 The best contemporary account of the last days of the Conservative government is found in Saywell, ed., *The Canadian Annual Review for 1963*, 1–16. Also, see Granatstein, *Canada, 1957–1967*, 127–33.

93 Ottawa *Citizen*, 23 March 1963, quoted in Beck, *Pendulum of Power*, 354.

94 Kent Papers, vol. 8, file: Election, March–April 1963, Fraser to Kent, 29 March 1963.

CHAPTER FOUR

1 Munro and Inglis, eds., *Mike, Volume 3: 1957–1968*, 84.

2 Ibid., 84–5; interview, Tom Kent, 22 March 1991; Davey, *The Rainmaker*, 75.
3 Quoted in Saywell, ed., *The Canadian Annual Review for 1963*, 48.
4 Gordon, *A Political Memoir*, 131.
5 Ottawa *Citizen*, 23 April 1963.
6 Davey, *The Rainmaker*, 79.
7 John T. McLeod, "Living in a House of Minorities," *Canadian Forum*, June 1963.
8 See LaMarsh, *Memoirs of a Bird in a Gilded Cage*, 46; English, *The Worldly Years*, 266–7; interview, Tom Kent, 22 March 1991.
9 Interview, Tom Kent, 22 March 1991.
10 Interview, Gordon Robertson, 20 Dec. 1995.
11 Dexter Papers, box 1/5, file: 1961, Dexter to Malone, 7 Sept. 1961.
12 Hellyer Papers, vol. 422, "Major Urgent Problems for Consideration and Decision during the Next Thirty Days," 20 April 1963. Of thirty-three pressing concerns, the Canada Pension Plan ranked eleventh and included "decisions on details of plan; securing of Provincial agreement to revision of B.N.A. Act; Parliamentary action on Address to Queen; instructions to prepare legislation."
13 Pearson Papers, MG 26 N5, vol. 45, file: Memoirs, vol. 3, chapter 10, 1963–71, Pearson to Geoffrey and Landon Pearson, 26 May 1963.
14 Department of National Health and Welfare Papers, RG 29 88–89/012, vol. 4, file 2101–5–2, pt. 2, "Interim Report of Task Force on Old Age, Survivor and Disability Insurance," May 1963.
15 Privy Council Office Papers, Cabinet Minutes, 9 May 1963, 7–8. Unfortunately, the identity of the dissenting ministers is rarely clear in these records. Other evidence suggests that Hellyer, Sharp, Pickersgill, and Chevrier were likely candidates.
16 See LaMarsh, *Memoirs*, 78–83. LaMarsh reports: "I saw the pamphlets which we distributed about the pension scheme during the 1963 election, but I was not even remotely familiar with its details, only its general principle" (78).
17 LaMarsh Papers, vol. 5, file 5–4, Gordon to John A. Tuck, managing director of the Canadian Life Insurance Officers Association, 16 May 1963; ibid., Gordon to LaMarsh, 16 May 1963.
18 Gordon Papers, vol. 4, file 6, Robert Reid to Pearson, 29 May 1963.
19 See LaMarsh, *Memoirs*, 78, and Kent, *A Public Purpose*, 92.
20 Health insurance is dealt with more fully in chapter 6.
21 See, for example, Peon, *Harry S. Truman versus the Medical Lobby*.
22 Stursberg Papers, vol. 15, file: LaMarsh, Judy, interview 28 May 1975.
23 Kent Papers, vol. 2, file: Correspondence, June 1963 (1), Kent to Pearson, 6 June 1963. Kent advised that the conference be called for September, pointing out that the "reason for the urgency on our side is to have the conference precede the Ontario election campaign."

24 Kent, *A Public Purpose*, 236.
25 Purvis and Smith, "Fiscal Policy in Canada," 14.
26 Gordon Papers, vol. 3, file 1, Michael Mackenzie to Walter Gordon, 21 June 1963.
27 Ibid., Ian Wahn Grant, radio broadcast transcript, CFRB, 18 June 1963.
28 CCF/NDP Papers, vol. 389, file 389–14, Convention Correspondence, Walter Young to Terence Grier, 8 July 1963. The rumours of despondency and fear among the left came through Laurier Lapierre, "who seems to be in fairly close touch with Sauvé, Lamontagne and Turner."
29 Interview, Mitchell Sharp, 14 Aug. 1991.
30 Memories differ on when the resignation was offered. Gordon contends that it occurred prior to the withdrawal of the withholding-tax proposal on 19 June 1963 (Gordon, *A Political Memoir*, 149). Kent recalls discussing it with Gordon at about the same time (Kent, *A Public Purpose*, 233). Pearson, on the other hand, places the timing of the offer of resignation at a meeting of cabinet at Harrington Lake, 4 July 1963 (*Mike*, 107–8). Since Pearson seems to be the only one placing the timing in July, one must assume that the earlier date is correct.
31 English, *The Worldly Years*, 274.
32 Interview, Robert MacIntosh, 29 April 1992; MacIntosh, *Different Drummers*, 139.
33 Stursberg Papers, vol. 15, file: LaMarsh, Judy, interview, 28 May 1975.
34 Russell B. Irvine, "Ottawa: The First Session," *Canadian Forum*, July 1963.
35 Crerar Papers, vol. 131, file: Pearson, 1958–64, Crerar to Pearson, 3 July 1963.
36 Ibid., Pearson to Crerar, 9 July 1963.
37 Kent Papers, vol. 2, file: Correspondence, July 1–15 1963 (1), memorandum to the Prime Minister *et al.* from Kent, 1 July 1963.
38 Ibid., vol. 3, file: December 1963, Tom (?) to Tom Kent, 24 June 1963.
39 Bryce Papers, vol. 11, telephone notes, mid-July 1963.
40 Gathercole Papers, MU 5,330, file: Source Papers, Charles E. Hendry to Gathercole, 25 Feb. 1960.
41 Ibid., Walter E. Duffett, Dominion statistician, to Gathercole, 28 June 1960.
42 Ibid., file: Committee Documents, 1960–63. "A Summary Report of the Ontario Committee on Portable Pensions," Feb. 1961.
43 Ibid., "Proceedings of the Meeting of the Canadian Pension Conference in the Royal York Hotel, 6 December 1961."
44 Ibid., MU 5,332, file: Portable Pension Submissions, "Main Points Made in Submissions to Committee at September Hearings," Sept. 1962.
45 See ibid., file: Portable Pensions Correspondence, W.J. Adams to John Roberts, 1 Nov. 1962; George Gathercole to W.J. Adams, 5 Nov. 1962; George Gathercole to Oakley Dalgleish, 13 Dec. 1962. In the last of

these pieces of correspondence, Gathercole reassured the editor of the
Globe and Mail: "Another virtue is that while it does legislate the adoption of a certain minimum patter of pensions, it channels no money
through public hands by way of taxation ... It leaves the actual business of income related pensions to private enterprise and private institutions, and as such embodies a great deal more flexibility than is likely
to be possible under ... the American Social Security Plan."

46 Kent Papers, vol. 2, file: Correspondence, June 1963, Robarts to Pearson, 6 Feb. 1962 (copy).

47 See Gathercole Papers, MU 5,332, file: Portable Pension Submissions,
memo to committee on portable pensions from the Life Underwriters
Association of Canada, 20 July 1962; memorandum with respect to the
proposed Pension Benefit Act, 1961–62 from the Canadian Bankers
Association, Sept. 1962; memo, Canadian Life Insurance Officers Association to chairman and members of the Ontario committee on portable pensions, 18 Sept. 1962.

48 The president of the Ontario Chamber of Commerce urged the federal
government to follow the Ontario example and "encourage the prov-
inces to foster free enterprise contributory employer-employee pension
plans." Similarly, the Chartered Trust Company predicted that the
Ontario legislation "should have far reaching social significance not
only in this province but all across Canada" (Department of National
Health and Welfare, vol. 1,278, file 30–6–2, pt. 1, "Presidential
Address Delivered by W.J. Adams at the Annual Meeting of the
Ontario Chamber of Commerce Held in Toronto, May 29 1963"; *The
Counsellor*, published by Chartered Trust, May 1963).

49 Gathercole Papers, MU 5,332, file: Portable Pension Correspondence,
Gathercole to Connolly, 1 May 1963.

50 Ibid., file: Portable Pension Correspondence, 1963, George Gathercole
to John Robarts, 8 May 1963.

51 LaMarsh Papers, vol. 5, file 5–4, Robert Clark to Judy LaMarsh,
4 June 1963.

52 Gathercole Papers, MU 5,332, file: Portable Pensions Correspondence,
Gathercole to Oakley Dalgleish, 13 Dec. 1962. There were some federal Liberals who had been made aware of activity in Quebec, but the
knowledge did not seem widespread. For example, Gathercole
informed Senator J.J. Connolly that Premier Lesage had expressed interest in Ontario's commission at the Charlottetown Inter-Provincial Conference of 1961, and that more recently that Lesage was intending to
implement legislation modelled after the Ontario Pension Benefits Act
at the next session. See ibid., George Gathercole to J.J. Connolly,
1 May 1963.

53 Hutchison Papers, Crerar to Hutchison, 12 July 1963.

54 Sauvé Papers, vol. 124, file: Parti Libéral du Canada, Sauvé to Kent, 10 July 1963.
55 J.M.L.[Jean-Marc Léger], "Cooperative Federalism or the New Face of Centralization," *Canadian Forum*, October 1963, reprinted from *Le Devoir*, 3 Sept. 1963.
56 Morin, *Quebec versus Ottawa*, 8.
57 Thomson, *Jean Lesage and the Quiet Revolution*, 186–7.
58 Interview, Paul Hellyer, 26 March 1993; Hellyer, *Damn the Torpedoes*, 29–31.
59 Pearson Papers, MG 26 N6, vol. 44, file: CPP, 1963–65, Pearson to premiers, 20 June 1963.
60 Department of National Health and Welfare Papers, vol. 2,114, file 23–3–4, Splane to deputy minister of welfare, 9 July 1963.
61 John S. Morgan, "Welfare," in Saywell, ed., *The Canadian Annual Review for 1963*, 398–9; Kent Papers, vol. 2, file: Correspondence, June 1963 (2), Laurence Coward, president of Canadian Pension Conference, to Pearson, 21 June 1963; ibid., draft letter, Pearson to Canadian Pension Conference, 25 June 1963.
62 Privy Council Office Papers, Cabinet Minutes, 11 July 1963, 12–13.
63 Robarts Papers, vol. 478, file: Federal Government, Canada Pension Plan, 1963, Norman G. Kirkland, vice-president of Alexander and Alexander Services, consulting actuaries and employee-benefit-plan consultants, to LaMarsh, 12 July 1963.
64 Gathercole Papers, MU 5,332, file: Portable Pension Submissions, "Translation of the Letter the Hon. Jean Lesage Wrote to the Prime Minister of Canada on June 27th, 1963."
65 Kent, *A Public Purpose*, 229.
66 Stursberg Papers, vol. 33, file: Kent, Tom, interview 1977.
67 Privy Council Office Papers, Cabinet Minutes, 16 July 1963, 4; ibid., 18 July 1963, 6.
68 Herridge Papers, vol. 57, file 57–31, #1, "Statement by the Minister of National Health and Welfare, the Honourable Judy LaMarsh, Respecting the Canada Pension Plan, July 18, 1963."
69 Gathercole Papers, MU 5,333, file: Portable Pensions, 1963, July to December, Frank Dimock to George Gathercole, 24 July 1963; Peter Stursberg, "Judy's Punch with the pensions," *Saturday Night*, September 1963.
70 Robarts Papers, vol. 478, file: Federal Government, Canada Pension Plan, 1963, press release from Alexander and Alexander Services, "Canada Pension Plan: Panacea or Pitfall for Canada?" 25 July 1963.
71 "Pensions: Federal or Provincial," *Canadian Life Insurance Current Topics*, no. 75 (20 August 1963).

72 Progressive Conservative Party Papers, vol. 423, file: Parliament, 25th, "Candid Comments from the Commons," by Walter Dinsdale, 26 July 1963.

73 Ibid., vol. 420, file: NDP, 1966, policy statements adopted at the second federal convention of the New Democratic Party, Regina, August 1963.

74 Privy Council Office Papers, Cabinet Minutes, 30 July 1963, 3.

75 Pearson Papers, MG 26 N6, vol. 44, file: Canada Pension Plan, 1963–65, L.B. Pearson to premiers, 5 Aug. 1963.

76 Privy Council Office Papers, Cabinet Minutes, 28 Aug. 1963, 15–16; Department of National Health and Welfare Papers, vol. 1,278, file 30–6–2, pt. 2, Judy LaMarsh to L.B. Pearson, 28 Aug. 1963.

77 "Reconsider the Pension Race," Montreal *Gazette*, 19 Aug. 1963.

78 Gordon Papers, vol. 16, file 10, memorandum to Pearson, 8 Aug. 1963.

79 Privy Council Office Papers, Cabinet Minutes, 28 Aug. 1963, 15.

80 S. Peter Regenstreif, "The pulse of the province," Toronto *Daily Star*, 19 Sept. 1963.

81 Kent Papers, vol. 2, file: Correspondence, August 21–30 1963, "Pensions for the September 9th Conference," 30 Aug. 1963.

82 Gordon Papers, vol. 16, file 10, Gordon to Pearson, 4 Sept. 1963, re: conversation with Louis Rasminsky, 27 Aug. 1963; Department of National Health and Welfare Papers, vol. 2,431, file 5,004–2, pt. 1, memorandum to cabinet from minister of national health and welfare, 3 Sept. 1963.

83 Kent Papers, vol. 7, file: Federal Provincial Conference on Pensions, November 12–25 1963, pension strategy, 4 Sept. 1963.

84 Privy Council Office Papers, Cabinet Minutes, 5 Sept. 1963, 2.

85 Ibid., 3.

86 Kent Papers, vol. 7, file: Federal Provincial Conference on Pensions, November 12–25 1963, pension strategy, 4 Sept. 1963. LaMarsh, in her memoirs, describes it as "the first (and because of its outcome, the only) such gesture of co-operation I ever saw between federal and provincial politicians" (LaMarsh, *Memoirs*, 84).

87 McDougall, *John P. Robarts*, 106.

88 Pearson Papers, MG 26 N6, vol. 44, file: Canada Pension Plan, 1963–1965, "Statement by the Prime Minister Regarding the Objectives of the Federal-Provincial Conference on Pensions," 9 Sept. 1963.

89 Department of National Health and Welfare Papers, vol. 2,431, file 5004–2, pt. 1, "Minutes of the Federal-Provincial Conference on the Canada Pension Plan September 9 and 10, 1963."

90 LaMarsh, *Memoirs*, 85.

91 Bill Rudd worked for the London Life Insurance Company, a fact that "to LaMarsh and Wintermeyer confirmed their suspicion that London

Life was lurking prominently in John Robarts' political world." McDougall, *Robarts*, 108.

92 Privy Council Office Papers, Cabinet Minutes, 12 Sept. 1963, 2.
93 Department of National Health and Welfare Papers, vol. 2,431, file 5,004–2, pt. 1, "Minutes of the Federal-Provincial Conference on the Canada Pension Plan September 9 and 10, 1963."
94 Ibid.
95 Privy Council Office Papers, Cabinet Minutes, 12 Sept. 1963, 3.
96 Ibid., 4.
97 *Le Devoir*, 3 Sept. 1963.
98 Department of National Health and Welfare Papers, vol. 2,431, file 5,004–2, pt. 1, "Minutes of the Federal-Provincial Conference on the Canada Pension Plan September 9 and 10, 1963."
99 Ibid.
100 Privy Council Office Papers, Cabinet Minutes, 12 Sept. 1963, 3. Also, see LaMarsh, *Memoirs*, 85.
101 Quoted in McDougall, *Robarts*, 108. His officials also believed that the Ontario position had been made "crystal clear," although they felt that there were still a number or questions which needed to be answered regarding integration, portability, and financing before they would be "stampeded into making any decision" (Gathercole Papers, MU 5,337, file: Portable Pensions, July–December 1963, "Notes on Pension Conference–September 9th and 10th 1963").
102 Privy Council Office Papers, Cabinet Minutes, 12 Sept. 1963, 2.
103 Bryce Papers, vol. 9, file 18, Johnson to Bryce, 25 Sept. 1963. Johnson wrote to Bryce that he had previously been under the impression that his services were more desired in terms of "taxation *qua* taxation – in the legal chartered accountant sense," which was something he found "rather less than appealing." The option of working towards the implementation of national social policies was much more interesting.
104 Gordon Papers, vol. 4, file 6, Gordon to J.D. Mingay, Consumers Gas, 13 Sept. 1963; "Pension muddle," Calgary *Herald*, 10 Sept. 1963.
105 Privy Council Office Papers, Cabinet Minutes, 26 Sept. 1963, 2.

CHAPTER FIVE

1 "Delay in Pension Legislation," Ottawa *Citizen*, 18 Oct. 1963.
2 Kent Papers, vol. 3, file: Correspondence, Oct. 1963, Johnson to Kent, 6 Oct. 1963.
3 Privy Council Office Papers, Cabinet Minutes, 10 Oct. 1963, 7.
4 Robarts Papers, MU 8,005, Pearson to Robarts, 4 Oct. 1963, and Robarts to Pearson, 9 Oct. 1963; Laurence Coward, head of the

Canadian Pension Conference, also believed that it was necessary to have some sort of agreement at the elite level before the technical committees could make any headway (Toronto *Star*, 17 Oct. 1963).

5 Kent Papers, vol. 3, file: Correspondence, Oct. 1963, "Pensions–Some Basic Notes," 16 Oct. 1963.

6 Robarts Papers, RG 3, Series A–13–1, vol. 478, file: Federal Government, Canada Pension Plan, 1963, "To Mr. W.M. McIntyre," no date.

7 Kent Papers, vol. 3, file: Oct. 1963, Pearson to Robarts.

8 Kent Papers, vol. 3, file: Correspondence, Oct. 1963, "Draft House Statement," 25 Oct. 1963; Simeon, *Federal-Provincial Diplomacy*, 50.

9 Kent Papers, vol. 3, file: Correspondence, Oct. 1963, "Notes on Meeting of the Canada and Ontario Representatives to Discuss the Canada Pension Plan," 31 Oct. 1963; Toronto *Star*, 2 Nov. 1963.

10 Kent Papers, vol. 3, file: Correspondence, November 1–11, 1963, "Ontario's Suggestions," 1 Nov. 1963.

11 Ibid., J. Albert Blais to chairman of task force, Canada Pension Plan, 8 Nov. 1963.

12 Ibid., vol. 7, file: Federal-Provincial Conference on Pensions, Nov. 12–25, 1963, deputy minister of welfare to minister, 12 Nov. 1963.

13 Ibid., vol. 3, file: Correspondence, November 1–11, 1963, J. Albert Blais to chairman of task force, Canada Pension Plan, 8 Nov. 1963.

14 Herridge Papers, vol. 57, file 57–31, #1, draft of article for publication in local 480 Mine Mill newspaper "Commentator," 1963. See also Milling, "Labour's Interest in Pension Planning," 190.

15 Gathercole Papers, MU 5,333, file: Portable Pensions, 1963, July to December, speech to Kiwanis Club delivered by Cecil G. White, 25 Oct. 1963; ibid., W.B.C. Burgoyne to Robarts, 29 Oct. 1963.

16 Kent Papers, vol. 7, file: Federal-Provincial Conference on Pensions, Nov. 12–25, 1963, deputy minister of welfare to minister, 12 Nov. 1963.

17 Ibid., vol. 3, file: Correspondence, Oct. 1963, L.B. Pearson speech, Tom Kent draft, 28 Oct. 1963.

18 This discussion is based on John S. Morgan, "Welfare," in Saywell, ed., *Canadian Annual Review for 1963*, 396–401.

19 Ibid., vol. 7, file: Federal-Provincial Conference on Pensions, Nov. 12–25, 1963, Tom Kent to the prime minister, 25 Nov. 1963.

20 Ibid., vol. 3, file: Correspondence, Nov. 1–11, 1963. Tom Kent, "Position Paper Draft: Pensions," 11 Nov. 1963, final version: Herridge Papers, vol. 35, file 35–8, Federal-Provincial Conference, Opening Statement by the Prime Minister, 26 Nov. 1963.

21 See Simeon, *Federal-Provincial Diplomacy*, 51–3.

22 Most people, both inside and outside the halls of power, complained that the Canada Pension Plan as it had been explained was unnecessarily complex. Ian Drummond, writing in *Canadian Forum* ("Lifeboat for

LaMarsh," December 1963) was one of the few commentators who actually identified the plan as "impressively simple and straightforward."
23 Simeon, *Federal-Provincial Diplomacy*, 52.
24 Kent Papers, vol. 7, file: Federal-Provincial Conference on Pensions, Nov. 26–30, 1963, "Notes on the Discussion in Committee I on the Canada Pension Plan."
25 Ibid.
26 Monteith Papers, vol. 14, file: Notes and Clippings, 1960, 1963, Knowles to constituents, December 1963.
27 Douglas Papers, vol. 12, file: Politics, Merger with Liberals, draft statement for T.C. Douglas, written by Terence Grier, 8 Jan. 1963.
28 See for example, Russell B. Irvine, "Commons Comment," *Canadian Forum*, December 1963.
29 Progressive Conservative Party Papers, vol. 406, file: Campagne, Paul (Research), transcript, preview commentary by Norman Campbell, 5 Dec. 1963.
30 "George Hogan's Contemporary Conservatism," *Canada's Young Conservatives*, vol. 1, no. 4, January–February 1964.
31 Kent Papers, vol. 3, file: Correspondence, Oct. 1963, Tom Kent to prime minister, Oct. 1963.
32 Gordon Papers, vol. 16, file 10, memorandum to Mr Pearson, 26 Oct. 1963.
33 Kent Papers, vol. 3, file: Correspondence, Oct. 1963, Tom Kent to J.W. Pickersgill, 4 Oct. 1963.
34 CCF/NDP Papers, vol. 390, file 390-10, "Resolutions Adopted, 23 October 1963"; Progressive Conservative Party Papers, vol. 436, file: Social Welfare Legislation, "Social Welfare Legislation: How Far Should It Go?" 10 Oct. 1963.
35 Kent Papers, vol. 3, file: Correspondence, Dec. 1963, memorandum to the prime minister, 19 Dec. 1963.
36 National Liberal Federation Papers, vol. 742, file: Payne, John deB.–Correspondence, Payne to Davey, 30 Dec. 1963.
37 Saywell, ed., *Canadian Annual Review for 1964*, 4–5.
38 National Liberal Federation Papers, vol. 744, file: PMO, L.B. Pearson, 1963, L.B. Pearson to W.A. Macdonald, 19 Dec. 1963.
39 Progressive Conservative Party Papers, vol. 423, file: Pearson, 1955–65, transcript, "Conversation with the Prime Minister," broadcast on CBC radio and television, 5 Jan. 1964.
40 Kent Papers, vol. 3, file: January 1–20, 1964, Pearson to cabinet ministers, 9 Jan. 1964.
41 Bakvis, *Regional Ministers*, 69–76.
42 Privy Council Office Papers, Cabinet Minutes, 11 Dec. 1963, 3 and 17 Dec. 1963, 2.

43 Kent Papers, vol. 3, file: Correspondence, January 1–20, 1964, memorandum to cabinet, "Pensions for People Aged 65–69," 3 Jan. 1964;
   ibid., deputy minister of welfare to the minister, 6 Jan. 1964.
44 Ibid., file: Correspondence, Dec. 1963, "Draft Memorandum from the
   Prime Minister to the Provincial Premiers," 27 Dec. 1963.
45 Privy Council Office Papers, Cabinet Minutes, 7 Jan. 1964 (dissenting
   ministers are unidentified); Kent Papers, vol. 8, file: Federal-Provincial
   Conference, Quebec, March 31, 1964, "Memorandum from the Prime
   Minister of Canada to Provincial Premiers," 10 Jan. 1964.
46 Robarts Papers, RG 3 Series A–13–1, vol. 478, file: Federal Government, Canada Pension Plan, 1964, #2, Gathercole to Robarts, 6 Jan.
   1964.
47 Kent Papers, vol. 3, file: Correspondence, January 1–20, 1964,
   W.S. Lloyd to L.B. Pearson, 17 Jan. 1964.
48 Robarts Papers, RG 3 Series A–13–1, vol. 478, file: Federal Government, Canada Pension Plan, 1964, #2, "The New Federal Pension
   Plan," prepared by George Gathercole, 24 Jan. 1964.
49 Ibid., "New Pension Proposals," prepared by George Gathercole,
   24 Jan. 1964.
50 Kent Papers, vol. 3, file: Correspondence, January 1–20, 1964, Duff
   Roblin to L.B. Pearson, 18 Jan. 1964.
51 Ibid., file: Correspondence, February 19–28, 1964, deputy minister of
   welfare to the minister, 19 Feb. 1964.
52 Doern, "The Role of Royal Commissions in the General Policy Process
   and in Federal-Provincial Relations," 420.
53 Montreal Star, 18 Jan. 1964.
54 Ontario Premier John Robarts has frequently been attacked for pandering to the interests of the insurance companies based in his home town
   of London. Even his biographer, and friend, notes that during the negotiations on the Canada Pension Plan, Robarts "seemed particularly solic-
   itous of the interests of powerful private insurance companies."
   McDougall, John P. Robarts, 184.
55 Robarts Papers, RG 3 Series A–13–1, vol. 478, file: Federal Government, Canada Pension Plan, 1964, #2, J.W. Tuck to Robarts, 29 Jan.
   1964, and ibid., "Memorandum re: the modified Canada Pension
   Plan," 27 Jan. 1964.
56 Gordon Papers, vol. 4, file: Canada Pension Plan, 1964–1967, press
   release, "Comments on Canada Pension Plan by David Kilgour," 4 Feb.
   1967. Gordon, who was a business friend of Kilgour's, chastised him
   for misrepresenting the details of the federal pension proposals and
   refused to be swayed by the hyperbole of the insurance magnate (Gordon Papers, vol. 4, file: Canada Pension Plan, 1964–1967, Gordon to
   Kilgour, 10 Feb. 1964). Tom Kent also dismissed Kilgour as one of the

"men who come to lunch" and minimized his impact on public policy (interview, Tom Kent, 22 March 1991).

57 Banting, "The Decision Rules: Federalism and Pension Reform," 194. See also Banting, "Institutional Conservatism: Federalism and Pension Reform."

58 Kent Papers, vol. 3, file: Correspondence, February 1–18, 1964, memorandum, deputy minister of welfare to the minister, 18 Feb. 1964; interview, Paul Hellyer, 26 March 1993.

59 Progressive Conservative Party Papers, vol. 435, file: Research Department, 1957–1964, memo to all Progressive Conservative Members of Parliament, from PC Research, 8 March 1964. The MPs were informed of the results of a McDonald Research poll conducted on 1 March. Seventy-two percent of those polled favoured a public plan, as opposed to 25 per cent in favour of privately administered pension schemes; more than 72 per cent favoured a federal plan compared to 24 per cent for provincial schemes. There was a majority in favour of a national, public pension plan in all areas of the country, including Kitchener-Waterloo, which had the highest concentration of insurance-company head offices.

60 Privy Council Office Papers, Cabinet Minutes, 9 March 1964, 4.

61 Kent Papers, vol. 3, file: Correspondence, March 1–15, 1964, Kent to the prime minister, 12 March 1964.

62 Robarts Papers, Series A–13–1, vol. 478, file: Federal Government, Canada Pension Plan, General, 1964–65, Hogan to Robarts, 3 March 1964.

63 Privy Council Office Papers, Cabinet Minutes, 9 March 1964, 3.

64 Kent Papers, vol. 3, file: Correspondence, March 1–15, 1964, Tom Kent to the prime minister, 12 March 1964.

65 Ibid., file: Correspondence, March 16–30, 1964, "Economic Implications of the Canada Pension Plan," no date.

66 Ibid., J.W. Willard to Tom Kent, 18 March 1964; ibid., vol. 8, file: Federal-Provincial Conference, Quebec, March 31, 1964, "White Paper Canada Pension Plan," no date.

67 Ibid., "Canada Pension Plan: Discussions at Quebec," March 1964.

68 Kent, *A Public Purpose*, 272, 273.

69 The federal position was to allow the continuation of short-term capital projects, with the possibility of opting-out of long-term programs. Ontario recoiled at the thought of opting-out provinces being accused of "breaking up Confederation"; the Maritime premiers complained that the tax-abatement system would not equal the federal contribution towards programs in poorer provinces; the prairie premiers accepted the system; British Columbia's Bennett called for an extension of shared-cost programs; and Lesage wanted to withdraw from all shared-cost

programs of a continuing nature and sought federal payment for the shared-cost programs Quebec had refused to participate in during the Duplessis era (Department of National Health and Welfare Papers, vol. 2,114, file 23–3–6, "Federal-Provincial Conference, 31 March 1964–Conditional Grants and Shared-Cost Programs–Opening Statement by the Prime Minister of Canada"; ibid., "Statement by Louis Robichaud at Federal-Provincial Conference, 31 March 1964; Saywell, ed., *The Canadian Annual Review for 1964*, 64–8).

70 Robarts Papers, vol. 478, file: Federal Government, Canada Pension Plan, General, 1964–65, Hogan, "Notes on Federal-Provincial Conference, Quebec City, on Wednesday, April 1, 1964. The Canada Pension Plan."

71 Department of National Health and Welfare Papers, vol. 2,114, file 23–3–6, draft minutes, "Canada Pension Plan, Federal Provincial Conference, Quebec, April 1, 1964," 2–3.

72 Stursberg Papers, vol. 33, file: Judy LaMarsh, 1976, interview.

73 Department of National Health and Welfare Papers, vol. 2,114, file 23–3–6, draft minutes, "Canada Pension Plan, Federal Provincial Conference, Quebec, April 1, 1964," 3–4.

74 Ibid., 4.

75 Stursberg Papers, vol. 33, file: Kent, Tom, 1977, interview.

76 See Simeon, *Federal-Provincial Diplomacy*, 54–5. Simeon claims that the decision to strike a committee during the discussions on shared-cost programs occurred on the first day of the conference and that no one from the Department of Finance was involved. However, Kent's more detailed version of the conference (and one not based on the confidential memories of unnamed officials) puts it on the night of 1–2 April 1964 (Kent, *A Public Purpose*, 275–6). Moreover, Kent claims that he, Robert Bryce, and Gordon Robertson were the people responsible for the idea, in which case Simeon seems wrong about the lack of input from the Department of Finance since Bryce was the deputy minister.

77 *Evening Telegram* (St John's), 3 April 1964. It was Smallwood, apparently, "who first found the word 'revolutionary' to describe it. After that, various other premiers used the word 'revolutionary' and even Prime Minister Pearson himself."

78 Kent, *A Public Purpose*, 276. Interestingly, Lesage's own comments addressed to the opening session of the conference indicated a desire to have a review of fiscal arrangements undertaken (*Globe and Mail*, 1 April 1964).

79 Montreal *Gazette*, 2 April 1964.

80 Department of National Health and Welfare Papers, vol. 2,114, file 23–3–6, Transcripts of Press Conferences Following Closing Session of Federal-Provincial Conference, Quebec City, 2 April 1964.

81 Charles Lynch, "Mr. Lesage begins to talk like Duplessis," *The Province*, 4 April 1964.

82 Kent, *A Public Purpose*, 275; LaMarsh, *Memoirs of a Bird in a Gilded Cage*, 127.

83 Kent Papers, vol. 3, file: Correspondence, April 1964, Gordon Robertson, "Memorandum for the Prime Minister," 6 April 1964. This account differs somewhat from that in John English's recent biography of Pearson, where the Robertson memo is inaccurately attributed to Kent. See English, *The Worldly Years*, 286 and n.77.

84 Kent Papers, vol. 3, file: Correspondence, April 1964, Gordon Robertson, "Memorandum for the Prime Minister," 6 April 1964. He also recommended that the administration of the student-loan scheme be turned over to any provinces that already had comparable plans, and that the same be done with family allowances, both issues which had troubled Quebec.

85 Kent Papers, vol. 3, file: Correspondence, April 1964, Tom Kent to the prime minister, "The State of the Government after Quebec," 7 April 1964.

86 Kent, *A Public Purpose*, 279–80.

87 Kent Papers, vol. 3, file: Correspondence, April 1964, Tom Kent, "Suggested Procedure re: Quebec," 9 April 1964.

88 Pearson had perhaps neglected to inform her, or ask her, about any of these events because of his discomfort in dealing with women (interview, Tom Kent, 22 March 1991). It was an oversight that enraged LaMarsh, whose anger was only barely quieted by Kent and Gordon, both of whom agreed that she had been badly treated by the prime minister. See LaMarsh, *Memoirs of a Bird in a Gilded Cage*, 91; Kent, *A Public Purpose*, 283.

89 Gordon, *A Political Memoir*, 186.

90 Kent Papers, vol. 3, file: Correspondence, April 1964, Tom Kent, "Pension Discussion with Quebec, 11 April 1964."

91 National Liberal Federation Papers, vol. 744, file: Prime Minister's Office, L.B. Pearson, 1964, Davey to Pearson, 9 April 1964; Kent Papers, vol. 3, file: Correspondence, April 1964, Tom Kent, "Pension Discussion with Quebec, 11 April 1964."

92 Ibid., Kent, "Timing: General Considerations," 15 April 1964.

93 Gordon Papers, vol. 16, file 10, Gordon to Pearson, "Re: Tom's Note on Timing," 15 April 1964.

94 Hunt, "The Federal-Provincial Conference of First Ministers, 1960–1976," Hunt's interview with Gordon, 28 March 1978.

95 Kent Papers, vol. 3, file: Correspondence, April 1964, telegram to Robarts, 15 April 1964. The telegram stated, in part, "This is to confirm our telephone conversations referred to in your statement in your Legislature today."

96 Ibid., Pearson to the premiers, 16 April 1964. The existing provisions for tax abatement were at levels of 1 per cent each year.

97 Ibid., Bennett to Pearson, 17 April 1964; Roblin to Pearson, 17 April 1964.
98 Gathercole Papers, MU 5,334, file: Pensions, 1964, Gathercole to Bassett, 17 April 1964.
99 McDougall, *John P. Robarts*, 133; Hunt, "The Federal-Provincial Conference of First Ministers, 1960–1976," Hunt's interview with Robarts, 25 Sept. 1978. See also Pollard, *Managing the Interface*, 11.
100 Kent Papers, vol. 3, file: Correspondence, May 1964, "Pensions: Ontario and 'Opting Out,'" no author, 24 May 1964.
101 Privy Council Office Papers, Cabinet Minutes, 25 May 1964, 7.
102 Kent Papers, vol. 3, file: Correspondence, May 1964, Kent to Louis-Philippe Pigeon, 29 May 1964; Robarts Papers, vol. 478, file: Federal Government, Canada Pension Plan, General, 1964–65, Kent to Coward, 2 June 1964.
103 Ibid.
104 Ibid., file: Correspondence, June 1–17, 1964, "Pensions Bill: Safeguards for Provinces," from the prime minister, no date. A "major amendment" was defined as one that would alter the level of contributions or benefits. An "amendment of substance" was one that affected either the payment of the contributions or benefits or the management of pension funds.
105 Keith Banting describes as "one of the most fascinating anomalies in Canadian federalism" the fact that even as a non-member in the Canada Pension Plan arrangement Quebec is included in the two-thirds ruling governing its changes. See Banting, "The Decision Rules," 194–5.
106 Privy Council Office Papers, Cabinet Minutes, 25 June 1964, 6.
107 Kent Papers, vol. 3, file: Correspondence, July 1964, "Canada Pension Bill: Safeguards for Provinces," 6 July 1964.
108 See Simeon, *Federal-Provincial Diplomacy*, 60–5.
109 This centralized-decentralized approach, or the tight-loose configuration, is borrowed from administrative theory and has recently been suggested as an appropriate model on which to base a new organization of the administration of the national government. See Aucoin and Bakvis, *The Centralization-Decentralization Conundrum*.
110 National Liberal Federation Papers, vol. 685, file: Weekly Reports 1964, "Weekly Report from Keith Davey," 26 March 1964.

CHAPTER SIX

1 Kent Papers, vol. 4, file: Correspondence, March 20–31, 1965, "Task Force Blues," no author, no date.
2 See, for example, Department of National Health and Welfare Papers, vol. 1,131, file 504–5–1, pt. 3, "Draft Minutes of the Meeting of the Health Committee held on Friday, November 29, 1963." At the close

of the meeting between Judy LaMarsh and representatives of the provincial departments of health, the minister "explained that since assuming her office she had been almost fully engaged with the pressing work of the Welfare Branch of the Department" and that, in regard to the other branch of the department, "the federation government is deferring its health plans until the receipt of the Report of the Royal Commission on Health Services."

3 The literature on the Saskatchewan health-insurance system is extensive. See Taylor, *Health Insurance and Canadian Public Policy*, chapter 5; Naylor, *Private Practice, Public Payment*, chapter 7; Granatstein, *Canada, 1957–1967*, chapter 7; Badgley and Wolfe, *Doctors' Strike*; Tollefson, *Bitter Medicine*; Thompson, *Medical Care: Programs and Issues*; Shillington, *The Road to Medicare in Canada*.

4 Granatstein, *Canada, 1957–1967*, 176.

5 Canadian Labour Congress Papers, vol. 274, file: Medical Care, Saskatchewan Federation of Labour brief, pt. 2, Ted Goldberg to Andy Andras, 15 July 1960.

6 Complaining that the majority proposals would result in a state monopoly, the representatives from the SCPS filed a dissenting minority report.

7 Coldwell Papers, vol. 43, file: Saskatchewan Medicare, W.S. Lloyd, "Progress Report on Medical Care," radio and television address, 9 May 1962.

8 Mott Papers, vol. 33, file 33–8, F.D. Mott to personal file, 10 July 1962.

9 Ibid., Les Falk to W.S. Lloyd; CCF/NDP Papers, vol. 500, file: Saskatchewan Medicare, General, A.E. Blakeney, "Press Coverage of Medicare," presentation, 20 Feb. 1963; ibid., file: Saskatchewan Medicare, CPA press release, 13 July 1962.

10 Mott Papers, vol. 18, file 18–18, statement, W.S. Lloyd, 24 July 1962.

11 Coldwell Papers, vol. 43, file: Saskatchewan Medicare, Coldwell to Lloyd, 25 July 1962.

12 "Medicare: snail's pace since Saskatchewan," Toronto *Daily Star*, 9 Nov. 1963.

13 F.B. Roth, "Health," in Saywell, ed., *The Canadian Annual Review for 1963*, 391.

14 CCF/NDP Papers, vol. 500, file: Saskatchewan–Medicare–General, 1960, A.E. Blakeney, "Alberta's Medical Care Plan," 4 July 1963.

15 See, for example, ibid., file: Medicare, Reports, Press Releases, #1, press releases, R.M. Strachan, 31 May 1963, 29 June 1963, 9 Oct. 1964.

16 Hagey Papers, "Combined Recommendations re: Proposals to made Voluntary Medical Services Insurance Available to Every Citizen in Ontario through the Private Carriers," no date. Representatives came from the

College of Physicians and Surgeons of Ontario, the Ontario Medical Association, the Canadian Health Insurance Association, Physicians' Services Incorporated, Associated Medical Services, Windsor Medical Services, and CUMBA Cooperative Health Services.

17 Ibid.

18 McDougall, *John P. Robarts*, 97; Robarts Papers, Series A–13–1, vol. 139, file: Medicare–Health, 1963, Davie Fulton to John Robarts, 1 May 1963.

19 Ibid., MU 8,004, "The Robarts' Record–Medical Services Insurance," 1963.

20 Robarts Papers, Series A–13–1, box 139, file: Medicare, Health, April–Dec. 1963, Robarts press release, 31 Aug. 1963.

21 McDougall, *John P. Robarts*, 161–2.

22 Blair Papers, vol. 24, file: General Correspondence, 1960–1962, Frederick Hill to Gordon Blair, 14 July 1962.

23 Ibid., vol. 29, file: Policy Conference, 1962–63, Gordon Blair to John Wintermeyer, 31 Jan. 1963.

24 National Liberal Federation Papers, vol. 747, file: Saskatchewan Provincial Election, 1965, "Saskatchewan Provincial General Election–tips," no date.

25 "Political Trends and the Future of Canadian Medicine," *Canadian Medical Association Journal*, vol. 84, no. 116 (14 Jan. 1961), quoted in Naylor, *Private Practice, Public Payment*, 221.

26 Canadian Labour Congress Papers, vol. 307, file: Royal Commission on Health Services, CLC submission, May 1962.

27 Royal Commissions/Health Services Papers, vol. 14, file 188, submission of the Canadian Chamber of Commerce, no date.

28 See, for example, ibid., vol. 9, file 66, submission of the Winnipeg Chamber of Commerce, 18 Jan. 1962. The Winnipeg members argued, like their national counterparts, that "government resources should be devoted exclusively to areas of *need* only and with the great majority of citizens left free to meet their health needs in a competitive free economy without assistance or subsidy."

29 See Naylor, *Private Practice, Public Payment*, 216–17.

30 Royal Commissions/Health Services Papers, vol. 27, file 2–8–2–vol. iii, "Press Release Issued by the Royal Commission on Health Services on the Release of Volume I of its Report," 19 June 1964, 1.

31 Taylor, *Health Insurance and Canadian Public Policy*, 347.

32 Royal Commissions/Health Services Papers, vol. 27, file 2–8–2–vol. iii, "Press Release Issued by the Royal Commission on Health Services on the Release of Volume I of its Report," 19 June 1964, 2.

33 Ibid., 8.

34 Ibid., vol. 39, file c–14–a, A.D. Kelly, general secretary of the cma, to Hall, 3 July 1964.
35 Judy LaMarsh, speech to Medical Society of Nova Scotia, 14 Sept. 1964, reprinted as "Minister Looks at Hall," *Canadian Medical Association Bulletin*, October 1964.
36 Ibid.
37 Gordon Papers, vol. 16, file 11, Gordon to Pearson, 5 Jan. 1965.
38 Progressive Conservative Party Papers, vol. 297, file: Executive Meeting, 1965, Balcer to Camp, 15 Jan. 1965; Stursburg, *Diefenbaker: Leadership Lost, 1962–67*, 112–21; Newman, *Distemper of our Times*, 110–20.
39 Gordon Papers, vol. 16, file 11, Gordon to Pearson, 5 Jan. 1965; Kent Papers, vol. 4, file: Correspondence, January 1965, minutes of meeting, national campaign committee, 5 Jan. 1965.
40 Ibid., Tom Kent, memo for file, 15 Jan. 1965.
41 Private collection, Gordon Papers, Pearson to caucus, 27 Jan. 1965. Kent drafted this letter for the prime minister (Kent, *A Public Purpose*, 365).
42 Gordon Papers, vol. 16, file 11, Gordon to Pearson, 28 Jan. 1965.
43 Ibid., Gordon to Pearson, 31 March 1965.
44 Kent Papers, vol. 4, file: Correspondence, January 1965, Tom Kent, memo for file, 15 Jan. 1965.
45 Ibid.
46 Kent, *A Public Purpose*, 364–5.
47 Kent Papers, vol. 4, file: Correspondence, March 1–14, 1965, Kent, "Outline of Issues Involved in any Discussion of the Merits of Introducing Some Kind of Public Medical Care Scheme," 10 March 1965.
48 Royal Commissions/Health Services Papers, vol. 11, file 2–8–2, "Press Release Issued by the Royal Commission on Health Services on the release of Volume II of its Report," no date; F.B. Roth, "Health," in Saywell, ed., *Canadian Annual Review for 1965*, 432.
49 Douglas Papers, vol. 70, file 5–2, Douglas to constituents, 15 April 1965.
50 Herridge Papers, vol. 50, file 50–13, Donald MacDonald to all Canadian Labour Congress chartered and affiliated organizations, 3 Feb. 1965. In declaring that the theme for Citizenship Month would be "A Health Charter for Canadians," MacDonald said: "Much more will have to be done if we are to beat back the attack launched against the recommendations of the Commission by the medical profession, private insurance companies and others."
51 Department of National Health and Welfare Papers, vol. 1,058, file 500–1–12, pt. 3, LaMarsh to provincial ministers of health, 9 April 1965.

52 Ibid.

53 Department of Finance Papers, Acc. 87–88/011, vol. 26, file 5,935–01, vol. 1, "Consolidated Report of Views Expressed by the Provinces on Health Services," 26 May 1965. The identity of each of the provinces was not revealed in the report, although it would seem safe to assume that Ontario, Alberta, and British Columbia preferred the voluntary program since that was what the provincial legislatures had either already implemented or were working towards.

54 Ibid.

55 Kent, A Public Purpose, 365–6. Basically, Kent did not respect the opinions of the civil servants in the health branch of the Department of National Health and Welfare nearly to the extent that he did the welfare branch (interview, Tom Kent, 22 March 1991). It was characteristic, therefore, that they advised following the same course as had been taken for the Hospital Insurance and Diagnostic Services Act.

56 Gordon Papers, vol. 16, file 11, Bryce to the minister, 25 June 1965.

57 Ibid.

58 National Liberal Federation Papers, vol. 736, file: Manitoba Liberal Association, Manitoba Liberal Association, Keynote, vol. 1, no. 5 (15 May 1965).

59 Pearson Papers, MG 26 N5, vol. 45, file: Memoirs, vol. 3, chapter 8, Gordon to Pearson, 30 June 1965 (reference courtesy of John English).

60 Ibid.

61 In January Kent proposed a program designed to "improve the opportunities of people who are not earning adequate incomes; and for those who cannot take advantage even of improved opportunities, it will furnish improved assistance to raise them and their families above the line of abject poverty." He suggested that it be called the "Canada Opportunity Plan," to take advantage of the similarity with the Canada Pension Plan as well as the association with American President Johnson's "War on Poverty." Within three weeks, the "Canada Assistance Plan" was chosen as the title of the program, presumably for the same reason (Kent Papers, vol. 4, file: Correspondence, January 1965, Tom Kent, "Canada Opportunity Plan: A Proposal," 26 Jan. 1965).

62 A recent book on poverty legislation in Canada makes clear that officials in the welfare branch of the Department of National Health and Welfare had been active in the Public Welfare Division of the Canadian Welfare Council (CWC), which provided the impetus to coordinate welfare programs. The CWC's 1958 statement called for the full integration of assistance acts and the extension of coverage to include provincial mothers' allowances, argued for a differential cost-sharing formula for the poorer provinces, and implicitly encouraged the continuation of cost-sharing in the assistance field. The Canada Assistance Plan was the

first federal recognition of these principles. See Haddow, *Poverty Reform in Canada*, chapter 2.

63 See ibid., 50–60. Also on the Canada Assistance Plan, see Hum, *Federalism and the Poor* and "The Working Poor, the Canada Assistance Plan, and Provincial Responses to Income Supplementation"; Bella, "The Canada Assistance Plan" and "The Provincial Role in the Canadian Welfare State: The Influence of Provincial Social Policy Initiatives on the Design of the Canada Assistance Plan"; Dyck, "Poverty and Policy-Making in the 1960s: The Canada Assistance Plan," and "The Canada Assistance Plan: The Ultimate in Cooperative Federalism."

64 For an evaluation of functional and jurisdictional federalism, see Chandler, "Federalism and Political Parties," in Bakvis and Chandler, eds., *Federalism and the Role of the State*. While this discussion is informed by Chandler's model, my conclusion on where Canada falls on the jurisdictional-functional continuum differs considerably.

65 Chandler, "Federalism and Political Parties," 157.

66 Interview, Robert Bryce, 15 Aug. 1991.

67 Kent, *A Public Purpose*, 366.

68 Kent Papers, vol. 4, file: Correspondence, July 1–31, 1965, "Proposals for the Extension of Federal Participation in the Development and Maintenance of Health Services," no date.

69 Ibid., "Alternative Proposals for the Extension of Federal Action in the Development and Maintenance of Health Services," 21 June 1965.

70 Department of Finance Papers, vol. 26, file 5935–01, vol. 1, J.E.G. Hardy, secretary, interdepartmental committee of senior officials on federal-provincial relations, "Extension of Federal Participation in the Development and Maintenance of Health Services," 28 June 1965.

71 Kent, *A Public Purpose*, 366.

72 Department of Finance Papers, vol. 4,854, file 5508–02, vol. 1, A.W. Johnson to Robert Bryce, 16 July 1965.

73 Interview, A.W. Johnson, 21 Nov. 1991. Bryce was also cautious in regard to the coordination of the categorical programs in the Canada Assistance Plan. See Haddow, *Poverty Reform in Canada*, 50–60.

74 Interview, A.W. Johnson, 23 Aug. 1991.

75 Ibid.

76 Department of National Health and Welfare Papers, Acc. 85–86/343, vol. 59, file 3,401–2–2/65–1, Federal-Provincial Conference, "Opening Statement by the Prime Minister of Canada," 19 July 1965.

77 Ibid.

78 Privy Council Office Papers, Cabinet Minutes, 19 July 1965.

79 Kent Papers, vol. 8, file: Federal-Provincial Conference, 19–23 July 1965, notes on possible responses to Manning's criticisms of the federal medicare proposals, July 1965.

80 Kent, *Public Purpose*, 369.
81 NAC, Gordon Papers, vol. 8, file 9, A.W. Johnson, "An Approach to Federal-Provincial Relations in the Fields of Fiscal and Economic Policy," 8 Nov. 1965.
82 Department of National Health and Welfare Papers, Acc. 85–86/343, vol. 59, file 3,401-2-2/65-1, Federal-Provincial Conference, "Opening Statement by the Prime Minister of Canada," 19 July 1965.

CHAPTER SEVEN

1 Kent Papers, vol. 5, file: Correspondence, April 19–31, 1965, Kent to Pearson, 25 Aug. 1965.
2 Private collection, Gordon Papers, Gordon to Pearson, 31 Aug. 1965.
3 Gordon Papers, vol. 16, file 11, Gordon, "Note of conversation with Mike Pearson this morning," 31 Aug. 1965.
4 Hutchison Papers, "A conversation with the Prime Minister," 11 Feb. 1965. The author, who is unknown but is not Hutchison, interviewed Pearson and later wrote this "rough distillation of our exchange."
5 Gordon Papers, vol. 16, file 11, Gordon, "Note of conversation with Mike Pearson this morning," 31 Aug. 1965.
6 National Liberal Federation Papers, vol. 748, file: Strategy–Election, 1965, Kent, "Strategy: Building the New Canada," Sept. 1965; Pearson Papers, MG 26 N5, vol. 45, file: Memoirs, vol. 3, chapter 8, Kent draft, "Strategy," 3 Sept. 1965.
7 Kent Papers, vol. 5, file: Correspondence, 19–31 August 1965, Gordon to Pearson, 27 Aug. 1965.
8 Interview, Keith Davey, 13 April 1992.
9 National Liberal Federation Papers, vol. 723, file: Connolly, J.J., Correspondence, Connolly to Davey, 8 Sept. 1965.
10 Progressive Conservative Party Papers, vol. 344, file: Johnson, James, James Johnson to Diefenbaker, 6 Aug. 1965.
11 Monteith Papers, vol. 1, file: Diefenbaker, John G., Correspondence, 1963–1978, Monteith to Diefenbaker, 31 Aug. 1965.
12 Pearson Papers, MG 26 N5, vol. 45, file: Memoirs, vol. 3, chapter 8, "The points we have to meet," 2 Sept. 1965.
13 Ibid. On the extent of Gordon's cajoling, see Smith, *Gentle Patriot*, 242–57.
14 Gordon Papers, vol. 16, file 11, Gordon, "Memo of discussion with Mike re: the election issue," 12 Sept. 1965.
15 Private collection, Gordon Papers, Davey to all candidates and campaign chairmen, 23 Sept. 1965.
16 Kent Papers, vol. 5, file: Correspondence, 17–30 September 1965, federal-provincial conference of ministers of health, 23 and 24 Sept. 1965.

17 Robarts Papers, Series A–13–1, vol. 138, file: Medical Services Insurance Council, 1961–1965, LaMarsh to R.O. Jones, president of the Canadian Medical Association, 1 Oct. 1965.

18 Kent Papers, vol. 5, file: Correspondence, 13–31 October 1965, position paper 27, "Medicare," October 1965.

19 Ibid.

20 Kent Papers, vol. 4, file: Correspondence, 1–16 September 1965, E.C. Manning, "National Medicare – Let's Look Before We Leap," 8 Sept. 1965; Pearson Papers, MG 26 N3, vol. 214, file 618.4, Manning to Pearson, 8 Sept. 1965.

21 Kent Papers, vol. 5, file: Correspondence, 13–31 October 1965, Kent draft, "Medicare," 18 Oct. 1965.

22 Robarts Papers, RG 3, Series A–13–1, vol. 138, file: Medical Services Insurance Council, 1961–1965, "Report of Meeting of Colin Brown and C.A. Naylor with Mr. Tom Kent in Ottawa on 13 October 1965," 18 Oct. 1965.

23 Quoted in Saywell, ed., *The Canadian Annual Review for 1965*, 83–4.

24 Private Collection, Gordon Papers, Davey to all candidates and campaign chairmen, 23 Sept. 1965.

25 Quoted in Saywell, ed., *The Canadian Annual Review for 1965*, 84.

26 The election results: Liberals, 131; Conservatives, 97; NDP, 21; Créditistes, 9; Social Credit, 5; Independents, 2. See Saywell, ed., *The Canadian Annual Review for 1965*, 110.

27 Crerar Papers, vol. 173, file: Liberal Party (federal), "November 8th 1965: Reasons given by voters for not supporting Liberal candidates," no date.

28 National Liberal Federation Papers, vol. 724, file: Election Reports–1965–Post-election, "Notes made in the course of preparation of a memorandum concerning the Liberal Party in Canada after November 8th, 1965," no author, no date.

29 Pearson Papers, MG 26 N5, vol. 45, file: Memoirs, vol. 3, chapter 8, Kent to Pearson, 12 Nov. 1965.

30 Gordon Papers, vol. 16, file 11, Gordon to Pearson, 9 Nov. 1965.

31 Ibid., Pearson to Gordon, 11 Nov. 1965.

32 Pearson Papers, MG 26 N5, vol. 45, file: Memoirs, vol. 3, chapter 8, Pearson to Geoffrey Pearson, 15 Nov. 1965; interview, Tom Kent, 1995 (?)

33 Davey, *The Rainmaker*, 107–8; Kent, *A Public Purpose*, 392. Kent believed that "it was clear that the work of the PMO would now be almost entirely firefighting; in the post-election government there would be little policy development to be undertaken in the name of the Prime Minister" (392). He offered his official resignation in December. See Kent Papers, vol. 5, file: Correspondence, December 1965, Kent to Pearson, 29 Dec. 1965, and Pearson to Kent, 30 Dec. 1965.

34 Gordon Papers, vol. 3, file: Cabinet Resignation, A–F, Gordon to Stephen Clarkson, 2 Dec. 1965.

35 Toronto *Star*, 12 Nov. 1965.

36 NAC, Department of Finance Papers, RG 19, vol. 4,854, file 5,508–02 (1), Bryce, "Shared-Cost Programmes," 17 Dec. 1965.

37 Ibid., Johnson to Bryce: "Discussions with R.G. Robertson re Federal-Provincial Relations," 19 Jan. 1966.

38 Kent Papers, vol. 5, file: Correspondence, January–February 1966, memorandum to cabinet, 20 Jan. 1966.

39 NAC, Privy Council Office Papers, Cabinet Minutes, 28 Jan. 1966.

40 Ibid., 19 May 1966.

41 Pearson Papers, MG 26 N5, vol. 45, file: Memoirs, vol. 3, chapter 9, 1959–1970, Mary Macdonald to Davey, 6 June 1966.

42 York University Archives, Winters Papers, vol. 1, file: Government (federal) 1968, Clem Neiman to Winters, 23 March 1966.

43 Privy Council Office Papers, Cabinet Minutes, 9 June 1966. The ministers expressing this sentiment were not identified, but they did not include Finance Minister Mitchell Sharp, who "had been advised by his officials that the participation of private insurance companies would involve serious problems of audit and control which should be taken fully into account in deciding this question." A few days later, Assistant Deputy Finance Minister A.W. Johnson advised Sharp of the dangers of private insurance carriers and "got the clear impression that the Honourable M.W. Sharp will oppose the use of private carriers" (Department of Finance Papers, Acc. 87–88/011, vol. 27, file 5,935–08–1, vol. 1, Johnson to file, 13 June 1966).

44 Bryce Papers, vol. 9, file 7, Johnson to Bryce, 21 June 1966. Senior Quebec civil servant Claude Morin agreed with this opinion of the new Johnson administration. He did not expect that "Mr. Johnson will want to implement an extensive medical insurance scheme as that developed by the Lesage administration" (Department of Finance Papers, Acc. 87–88/011, vol. 27, file 5,935–08–1, vol. 1, E. Gallant to Johnson, 13 June 1966).

45 Ibid., vol. 5,794, file 5,935–08–2, Johnson to file, 13 June 1966.

46 Ibid.

47 Ibid., vol. 27, file 5,935–08–1, vol. 1, Johnson to Bryce, 3 Aug. 1966.

48 Mitchell Sharp, *Which Reminds Me ...: A Memoir*, 149.

49 Department of Finance Papers, Acc. 87–88/011, vol. 27, file 5,935–08–1, vol. 1, Johnson to Bryce, 3 Aug. 1966.

50 Sharp spent most of his time occupied with the details of the tax structure committee, which was designed to determine lasting federal-provincial fiscal arrangements. See Churchill Papers, vol. 87, file: Dominion-Provincial Conference, Sharp, "An Approach to Federal-Provincial Relations in the Fields of Fiscal and Economic Policy," 13 Sept. 1966.

51 Department of Finance Papers, Acc. 87–88/011, vol. 27, file 5,935–08–
1, vol. 1, Pearson to Roblin, 4 Oct. 1966; ibid., vol. 5,794, file 5,935–
08–2, Roblin to Pearson, 13 Oct.; ibid., "Comment Concerning Mr.
Roblin's Letter of October 13," no author, 26 Oct. 1966; Department
of National Health and Welfare Papers, RG 29, vol. 1,408, file 6,425–2–
1, "Draft Statement on Medical Care by the Prime Minister to Federal-
Provincial Conference," 27 Oct. 1966.
52 Interview, Tom Kent, 22 March 1991.
53 Blair Papers, vol. 30, file: President's file, Correspondence, 1965–1967,
Blair to Thompson, 12 Sept. 1966. See also Blair to Pearson and Blair
to Sharp, both 19 Sept. 1966.
54 Gordon Papers, vol. 16, file 11, Lamontagne, "The Federal Liberal
Party," 12 Dec. 1966. As far as Lamontagne's own future was concerned, Pearson was apparently toying with the idea of sending Lamontagne to the Senate, although the latter was worried about his finances
and not eager to take the necessary pay cut. See Private collection,
Gordon Papers, Gordon to Robert M. Fowler, 13 Jan. 1967.
55 Gordon Papers, vol. 16, file 11, Lamontagne, "The Federal Liberal
Party," 12 Dec. 1966.
56 Sharp, A Memoir, 150.
57 Gordon Papers, vol. 16, file 11, Gordon to Pearson, 28 Dec. 1966 (not
sent).
58 Sharp recalls that the three met at the prime minister's residence.
Gordon insisted that Pearson accept his view of economic nationalism
before he would agree to return to cabinet. Sharp "protested that it
was unfair to the Prime Minister and unnecessary to place conditions
on acceptance of membership in the cabinet" (Sharp, A Memoir, 150).
59 Herridge Papers, vol. 49, file 49–3 (#2), "Nation's Business Text by the
Hon. Allan J. MacEachen, CBC-TV, 15 March 1967."
60 Morrison Papers, vol. 38, file: Canadian Welfare Council, Committee
on Principles and Assumption, 1967–68, memo on a project to develop
a comprehensive statement on social welfare for Canada, 12 April 1967.
61 Department of National Health and Welfare Papers, vol. 1,060, file
500–1–20, Pearson to MacEachen, 21 April 1967.
62 Ibid.
63 Globe and Mail, 31 Aug. 1967.
64 Department of Finance Papers, Acc. 87–88/011, vol. 27, file 5,935–08–
1, vol. 1, Johnson to Bryce, 22 Aug. 1967, re: question raised by Sharp
concerning the financing of medicare.
65 Ibid.
66 Gordon Papers, vol. 16, file 13, Gordon, "The Position of the Government at the Present Time," 3 Oct. 1967.
67 Ibid.
68 Ibid.

69 Privy Council Office Papers, Cabinet Minutes, 10 Oct. 1967. When the letter was finally drafted, Gordon took issue with some of its ambiguity. The closing paragraph of the reply "could be interpreted as an invitation to the provinces either to ask for more money or to suggest modifications or deferment of the program because of the difficulties which the provinces, as well as the federal government, will have to face in financing it" (Gordon Papers, vol. 16, file 13, Gordon to Pearson, re: matters to come up in a cabinet meeting Gordon was unable to attend, 1 Nov. 1967). Ultimately, the whole cabinet accepted the deletion of the final paragraph (Privy Council Office Papers, Cabinet Minutes, 2 Nov. 1967).

70 Pearson Papers, MG 26 N5, vol. 45, file: Memoirs, vol. 3, chapter 13, 1963–67, O.G. S[toner] to the prime minister, 18 Oct. 1967.

71 Ibid.

72 Private collection, Gordon Papers, "Notes for Discussion at Cabinet Tuesday, October 24, on the Financial and Economic Situation."

73 Ibid.

74 *Globe and Mail*, 25 Oct. 1967.

75 Private collection, Gordon Papers, Gordon, memo to file, 25 Oct. 1967.

76 Ibid., Memorandum for discussion (with Benson, Trudeau, and Marchand on 7 Nov. 1967), 31 Oct. 1967.

77 Privy Council Office Papers, Cabinet Minutes, 2 Nov. 1967.

78 Department of Finance Papers, Acc. 87–88/011, vol. 27, file 5,935–08–1, vol. 1, Bryce, "Summary of Views Expressed by Provincial Ministers of Finance on the Subject of Medicare at the November 16–17 Meeting of Finance Ministers," 20 Nov. 1967.

79 Ibid.

80 Ibid.

81 Ibid.

82 Douglas Papers, vol. 8, file: Health and Welfare, Medicare, Douglas to Anthony Bilecki (president of Workers' Benevolent Association of Canada), 23 Nov. 1967.

83 Roth, "Health," in Saywell, ed., *Canadian Annual Review for 1967*, 385–6.

84 *Globe and Mail*, 15 Dec. 1967. Walter Gordon had been raising the question of the leadership of the party at cabinet meetings throughout the autumn, often suggesting that the informal campaigning being done by ministers was colouring their approach to governing. See, for example, Private collection, Gordon Papers, Gordon, memo to file, 24 Oct. 1967.

85 Roth, "Health," in Saywell, ed., *Canadian Annual Review for 1968*, 380.

86 Herridge Papers, vol. 50, file 50–13, Normand Belliveau (president of Canadian Medical Association) to Pearson, 17 Jan. 1968; Gordon Papers, vol. 15, file 10, Belliveau to Gordon, 18 Jan. 1968.

87 Privy Council Office Papers, Cabinet Minutes, 18 Jan. 1968.

88 Ibid. The cabinet ministers were not identified but at least seventeen different views were expressed.

89 Ibid.

90 Robarts Papers, Series A–13–1, box 138, file: Medical Insurance, Ontario Participation, 1968, "Transcript of References to Medicare, LBP Press Conference, Jan 19/68."

91 Privy Council Office Papers, Cabinet Minutes, 23 Jan. 1968. Walter Gordon was certainly one of the people who believed the prime minister had been "convinced that Medicare should be deferred." See Private collection, Gordon Papers, Gordon, "Re the Book – Sharp's Troubles," 8 March 1968.

92 Privy Council Office Papers, Cabinet Minutes, 30 Jan. 1968.

93 Ibid.

94 Robarts Papers, Series A–13–1, box 138, file: Medical Insurance, Ontario Participation, 1968, "A Statement re: Medicare," 23 Jan. 1968.

95 Roth, "Health," in Saywell, ed., *Canadian Annual Review for 1968*, 380. Although Roth claims that Robarts made this statement on 24 February, primary sources and other accounts of the event place the date on 24 January. See Peter Oliver, "Ontario," in Saywell, ed., *Canadian Annual Review for 1968*, 124–5.

96 Robarts Papers, Series A–13–1, box 138, file: Medical Insurance, Ontario Participation, 1968, "A Statement re: Medicare," 23 Jan. 1968.

97 Privy Council Office Papers, Cabinet Minutes, 1 Feb. 1968.

98 Among those voting to defeat the proposed delay of medicare were MacEachen, Marchand, Gordon, and Benson. Private collection, Gordon Papers, Gordon, "Re the Book – Sharp's Troubles," 8 March 1968.

EPILOGUE

1 Privy Council Office Papers, Cabinet Minutes, 8 Feb. 1968.

2 Morrison Papers, vol. 32, file: Notes, Drafts and Memoranda, Dec. 1967–March 1968, "Policy Workshop No. 2: Our Life," no date.

3 Winters Papers, vol. 34, file: Leadership Convention – Ontario (D–F), 1968, Winters to M.C. Deans (chairman, Bankers Bond Corporation), 15 March 1968.

4 On the leadership convention, see Saywell, ed., *Canadian Annual Review for 1968*, 25–9; Sullivan, *Mandate '68*, 273–325.

5 Stanfield Papers, vol. 3, file: Speech to PC Association of New Brunswick, 11 May 1968.

6 Department of Finance Papers, vol. 5,794, file 5,935–08–2, "Status of Medicare – August 1968."

7 Ibid.
8 Saywell, ed., *Canadian Annual Review for 1968*, 107.
9 Oliver, "Ontario," in Saywell, ed., *Canadian Annual Review for 1968*, 125.
10 Quoted in Taylor, *Health Insurance and Canadian Public Policy*, 375.
11 Robarts Papers, Series A–13–1, box 394, file: Federal-Provincial Tax Sharing Agreements, Treasury, Jan.–Dec. 1968, speech by E.J. Benson to Liberal Businessmen's Club of Toronto, 10 Dec. 1968.
12 Reid and Burns, *Canada and the World*; *Maclean's*, 1 July 1994, 10–15.
13 House of Commons, *Debates*, 27 Feb. 1996, 3, 21.

Bibliography

PRIMARY SOURCES

Archival Collections

ARCHIVES OF ONTARIO
Fisher, John
Gathercole, George
Latimer, Hugh
Robarts, John P.

NATIONAL ARCHIVES OF CANADA
Government Records
  Department of Finance (RG 19)
  Department of National Health and Welfare (RG 29)
  Privy Council Office (RG 2)
  Royal Commissions/Health Services (RG 33/78)
Manuscript Collections
  Balcer, Leon (MG 32 B18)
  Blair, Gordon (MG 32 C11)
  Canadian Institute of Public Affairs (MG 28 I 121)
  Canadian Labour Congress (MG 28 I 103)
  Canadian Union of Students (MG 28 I 61)
  Canadian Welfare Council (MG 28 I 10)
  CCF/NDP (MG 28 IV 1)
  Chevrier, Lionel (MG 32 B16)
  Churchill, Gordon (MG 32 B9)

Claxton, Brooke (MG 32 B5)
Coldwell, M.J. (MG 27 III C12)
Croll, David (MG 32 C49)
DePoe, Norman (MG 31 D112)
Diefenbaker, John (MG 26 M)
Douglas, T.C. (MG 32 C28)
Forsey, Eugene (MG 30 A25)
Gordon, Walter (MG 32 B44)
Grosart, Allister (MG 32 C65)
Hall, Emmett (MG 31 E11)
Herridge, H.W. (MG 32 C13)
Howe, C.D. (MG 27 III C13)
Kidd, H.E. (MG 32 G9)
LaMarsh, Judy (MG 32 B8)
Marler, George (MG 32 B21)
Martin, Paul (MG 32 B12)
Monteith, J. Waldo (MG 32 B29)
Morrison, Neil (MG 30 E273)
Mott, F.D. (MG 31 J15)
National Council of Women (MG 28 I 25)
National Liberal Federation (MG 28 IV 3)
O'Leary, Gratton (MG 32 C37)
Pearson, L.B. (MG 26 N)
Pickersgill, J.W. (MG 32 B34)
Progressive Conservative Party of Canada (MG 28 IV 2)
Richardson, Burton (MG 30 D289)
Rynard, P.B. (MG 32 C7)
St Laurent, Louis (MG 26 L)
Sauvé, Maurice (MG 32 B4)
Social Credit Party of Canada (MG 28 IV 7)
Stanfield, Robert (MG 32 C21)
Stursberg, Peter (MG 31 D78)
Watson, Ian (MG 32 C69)
Winters, Robert (MG 32 B24)

PRIVATE COLLECTIONS
Gordon, Walter (courtesy of J.L. Granatstein)
Kent, Tom (courtesy of Tom Kent)
Hutchison, Bruce (courtesy of J.L. Granatstein)

QUEEN'S UNIVERSITY ARCHIVES
Crerar, T.A.
Dexter, Grant

Kent, Tom

UNIVERSITY OF WATERLOO ARCHIVES
Hagey, J. Gerald

YORK UNIVERSITY ARCHIVES
Canadian Annual Review – clipping files
Winters, Robert

Interviews

Bryce, R.B. (15 Aug. 1991)
Coutts, James (16 Dec. 1994)
Creery, Tim (5 Nov. 1994)
Davey, Keith (12 March 1992; 16 Dec. 1994)
Hellyer, Paul (26 March 1993)
Johnson, A.W. (23 Aug. 1991; 21 Nov. 1991)
Kent, Tom (22 March 1991; 6 June 1994; 22 Nov. 1994; 2 Aug. 1995)
MacEachen, Allan (6 March 1995)
MacIntosh, A.J. (9 Feb. 1993)
MacIntosh, Robert (29 April 1992)
Martin, Paul (20 Nov. 1990)
McDougall, A.K. (18 Oct. 1991)
O'Hagan, Richard (13 Dec. 1994)
Pickersgill, J.W. (10 April 1991)
Reynolds, J. Keith (11 June 1993)
Robertson, Gordon (21 Dec. 1994)
Sharp, Mitchell (14 Aug. 1991)
Simeon, Richard (13 Sept. 1991)
Smith, Denis (1 Nov. 1991)
Taylor, Malcolm (5 Feb. 1991)

Magazines and Newspapers

(the clippings files of the *Canadian Annual Review* were used for all newspaper
citations for the years 1960 to 1968)

Calgary Herald
Canada's Young Conservatives
Canadian Forum
Canadian Liberal
Canadian Life Insurance Current Topics
Canadian Medical Association Journal

The Economist
Globe Magazine
Globe and Mail
Halifax Chronicle-Herald
Le Devoir
Maclean's
Montreal Gazette
Ottawa Citizen
Saturday Night
Toronto Star
Toronto Telegram
Vancouver Sun
Winnipeg Free Press

SECONDARY SOURCES

Abramovitz, Mimi. *Regulating the Lives of Women: Social Welfare Policy from Colonial Times to the Present*. Boston: South End Press 1988.
Aucoin, Peter. "Federal Health Care Policy," in *Issues in Canadian Public Policy*, G. Bruce Doern and V. Seymour Wilson, eds. Toronto: Macmillan 1974.
– "Public Policy Analysis and the Canadian Health Care System," *Canadian Public Administration*, vol. 23, no. 1 (spring 1980).
– "Regionalism, Party and National Government," in *Party Government and Regional Representation*, Peter Aucoin, research coordinator. Toronto: University of Toronto Press 1985.
Aucoin, Peter and Herman Bakvis. *The Centralization-Decentralization Conundrum: Organization and Management in the Canadian Government*. Halifax: Institute for Research on Public Policy 1988.
Badgley, Robin F. and Samuel Wolfe. *Doctor's Strike: Medical Care and Conflict in Saskatchewan*. Toronto: Macmillan 1967.
Bakvis, Herman. *Regional Ministers: Power and Influence in the Canadian Cabinet*. Kingston and Montreal: McGill-Queen's University Press 1991.
Banting, Keith. "Institutional Conservatism: Federalism and Pension Reform," in *Canadian Social Welfare Policy: Federal and Provincial Dimensions*, Jacqueline S. Ismael, ed. Kingston and Montreal: McGill-Queen's University Press 1985.
– "The State and Economic Interests: An Introduction," in *The State and Economic Interests*, Keith Banting, research coordinator. Toronto: University of Toronto Press 1986.
– *The Welfare State and Canadian Federalism*, 2nd ed. Kingston and Montreal: McGill-Queen's University Press 1987.

Beck, J.M. "Quebec and the Canadian Election of 1958," *Parliamentary Affairs*, vol. 12 (winter 1958–59).

– *Pendulum of Power: Canada's Federal Elections.* Scarborough, Ont.: Prentice-Hall of Canada 1968.

Beck, R.G. "An Analysis of the Demand for Physicians' Services in Saskatchewan," PhD thesis, University of Alberta 1971.

Bella, Leslie. "The Canada Assistance Plan," *The Social Worker/ Le Travailleur Social*, vol. 45, no. 2 (summer 1977).

– "The Provincial Role in the Canadian Welfare State: The Influence of Provincial Social Policy Initiatives on the Design of the Canada Pension Plan," *Canadian Public Administration*, vol. 22, no. 4 (1979).

Berkovitz, Edward and Kim McQuaid. *Creating the Welfare State*, 2nd ed. New York: Praeger 1988.

Bothwell, R.S. "The Health of the Common People," in *Mackenzie King: Widening the Debate*, John English and J.O. Stubbs, eds. Toronto: Macmillan 1977.

Bothwell, Robert and John English. "Pragmatic Physicians: Canadian Medicine and Health Care Insurance, 1910–1945," in *Medicine in Canadian Society*, S.E.D. Shortt, ed. Kingston and Montreal: McGill-Queen's University Press 1981.

Bothwell, Robert and William Kilbourn. *C.D. Howe: A Biography.* Toronto: McClelland and Stewart 1979.

Brennan, Patrick H. *Reporting the Nation's Business: Press-Government Relations during the Liberal Years, 1935–1957.* Toronto: University of Toronto Press 1994.

Bryden, Kenneth. *Old Age Pensions and Policy Making in Canada.* Kingston and Montreal: McGill-Queen's University Press 1974.

– "How Public Medicare Came to Ontario," in *Government and Politics of Ontario*, Donald C. MacDonald, ed. Toronto: Macmillan 1975.

Bryden, P.E. *Liberal Politics and Social Policy in the Pearson Era.* PhD thesis, York University 1994.

Campbell, Robert M. *Grand Illusions: The Politics of the Keynesian Experience in Canada, 1945–1975.* Peterborough, Ont.: Broadview Press 1987.

Canada, *Federal-Provincial Conference, 1955: Preliminary Meeting.* Ottawa: 1955.

Canada, House of Commons, *Debates*, 1957–68.

Canada, *Proceedings of the Federal-Provincial Conference, 1955.* Ottawa: 1955.

Canadian Medical Association, *A Submission by the Canadian Medical Association to the Royal Commission on Dominion-Provincial Relations.* Canada: 1937.

Caplan, Neil. "Some Factors Affecting the Resolution of Federal-Provincial Conflict," *Canadian Journal of Political Science*, vol. 2, no. 2 (June 1969).

Carrigan, D. Owen, *Canadian Party Platforms, 1867–1968*. Scarborough, Ont.: Copp Clark Publishing 1968.

Chandler, Marsha A. and William M. Chandler, *Public Policy and Provincial Politics*. Toronto: McGraw-Hill Ryerson 1979.

Chandler, William M. "Canadian Socialism and Party Impact: Contagion from the Left?" *Canadian Journal of Political Science*, vol. 10, no. 4 (December 1977).

Chandler, William M. "Federalism and Political Parties," in *Federalism and the Role of the State*, Herman Bakvis and William M. Chandler, eds. Toronto: University of Toronto Press 1987.

Comacchio, Cynthia. *Nations Are Built of Babies: Saving Ontario's Mothers and Children, 1900–1940*. Kingston and Montreal: McGill-Queen's University Press 1993.

Comanor, William. *National Health Insurance in Ontario: The Effects of Policy Cost Control*. Washington, D.C.: American Enterprise Institute for Public Policy Research 1980.

Courtney, John C. "Leadership Conventions and the Development of the National Political Community in Canada," in *National Politics and Community in Canada*, R. Kenneth Carty and W. Peter Ward, eds. Vancouver: University of British Columbia Press 1986.

Coward, Laurence, ed. *Pensions in Canada: A Compendium of Fact and Opinion*. Don Mills, Ont.: CCH Canadian Ltd. 1964.

Craven, Paul and Tom Traves. "The Class Politics of the National Policy, 1872–1933," *Journal of Canadian Studies*, vol. 14, no. 3 (fall 1979).

Cuneo, Carl. "Comment: Restoring Class to State Unemployment Insurance," *Canadian Journal of Political Science*, vol. 19, no. 1 (March 1986).

Davey, Keith. *The Rainmaker: A Passion for Politics*. Toronto: Stoddart 1986.

Davidson, George F. "Improving the Social Services," *Public Affairs*, vol. 6, no. 2 (no date).

Deutsch, J.J. "Canada's Economic Problems," *Queen's Quarterly*, vol. 68, no. 4 (winter 1961–62).

Diefenbaker, John G. *One Canada: Memoirs of the Right Honourable John G. Diefenbaker*, vol. 1, *The Crusading Years, 1896–1956*. Toronto: Macmillan of Canada 1975.

– *One Canada: Memoirs of the Right Honourable John G. Diefenbaker*, vol. 2, *The Years of Achievement, 1957–1962*. Toronto: Macmillan of Canada 1976.

– *One Canada: Memoirs of the Right Honourable John G. Diefenbaker*, vol. 3, *The Tumultuous Years, 1962–1967*. Toronto: Macmillan of Canada 1977.

Doern, G. Bruce. "The Role of Royal Commissions in the General Policy Process and in Federal-Provincial Relations," *Canadian Public Administration*, vol. 10, no. 4 (December 1967).

Duverger, Maurice. *Political Parties*, trans. Barbara and Robert North. New York: John Wiley and Sons 1963.

Dyck, Rand. "Poverty and Policy-Making in the 1960s: The Canada Assistance Plan," PhD thesis, Queen's University 1973.

– "The Canada Assistance Plan: The Ultimate in Cooperative Federalism," *Canadian Public Administration*, vol. 19 (1976).

Eden, Lorraine and Maureen Appel Molot. "Canada's National Policies: Reflections on 125 Years," *Canadian Public Policy*, vol. 19, no. 3 (September 1993).

Englemann, Frederick C. and Mildred Schwartz. *Canadian Political Parties: Origins, Character, Impact*. Scarborough, Ont.: Prentice-Hall 1975.

English, John. *The Worldly Years: The Life of Lester Pearson, 1949–1972*. Toronto: Knopf 1992.

Esping-Anderson, Gösta. *Politics against Markets: The Social Democratic Road to Power*, Princeton, N.J.: Princeton University Press 1985.

Evans, Peter B., Dietrich Rueschemeyer and Theda Skocpol, eds. *Bringing the State Back in*. Cambridge, U.K.: Cambridge University Press 1985.

The Federal Program of the New Democratic Party. Ottawa: Mutual Press Ltd 1961

Finkel, Alvin. "Origins of the Welfare State in Canada," in *The Canadian State: Political Economy and Political Power*, Leo Panitch, ed. Toronto: University of Toronto Press 1977.

– "Paradise Postponed: A Re-examination of the Green Book Proposals of 1945," Canadian Historical Association *Journal*, 1993.

Fowke, Vernon. "The National Policy – Old and New," *Canadian Journal of Economics and Political Science*, vol. 18, no. 3 (August 1952).

Gelber, Sylva. "Hospital Insurance in Canada," *International Labour Review*, vol. 79 (January–June 1959).

Glaser, William A. "Doctors and Politics," *American Journal of Sociology*, vol. 66, no. 3 (November 1960).

Goffman, Irving J. "The Political History of National Hospital Insurance in Canada," *Journal of Commonwealth Political Studies*, vol. 3 (1965).

Gordon, Linda. "The New Feminist Scholarship on the Welfare State," in *Women, the State, and Welfare*, Linda Gordon, ed. Madison, Wis.: University of Wisconsin Press 1990.

– *Pitied but Not Entitled: Single Mothers and the History of Welfare, 1890–1935*. New York: Free Press 1994.

– "What Does Welfare Regulate? A Review Essay on the Writing of Frances Fox Piven and Richard A. Cloward," *Social Research*, vol. 55, no. 4 (1988).

Gordon, Walter. *A Political Memoir*. Toronto: McClelland and Stewart 1977.

Granatstein, J.L. *The Ottawa Men: The Civil Service Mandarins, 1935–1957*. Toronto: Oxford University Press 1982.

222 Bibliography

- *Canada, 1957–1967: Years of Uncertainty and Innovation.* Toronto: McClelland and Stewart 1985.
Gray, Gwen and Rodney F. White. "Federalism and the Evolution of Public Hospital and Medical Care Coverage," in *Federalism in Canada and Australia: Historical Perspectives, 1920–1988*, Bruce Hodgins, John J. Eddy, Shelagh Grant, and James Struthers, eds. Peterborough, Ont.: Frost Centre for Canadian Heritage and Development Studies 1989.
Gray, Gwendolyn. *Federalism and Health Policy: The Development of Health Systems in Canada and Australia.* Toronto: University of Toronto Press 1991.
Gruending, Dennis. *Emmett Hall: Establishment Radical.* Toronto: Macmillan 1985.
Guest, Dennis. "The Development of Income Maintenance Programmes in Canada, 1945–1967," PhD thesis, University of London 1968.
- *The Emergence of Social Security in Canada.* Vancouver: University of British Columbia Press 1993.
Haddow, Rodney S. *Poverty Reform in Canada, 1958–1978: State and Class Influences on Policy Making.* Kingston and Montreal: McGill-Queen's University Press 1993.
Harbron, John D. "The Conservative Party and National Unity," *Queen's Quarterly*, vol. 69, no. 3 (autumn 1962).
Hastings, J.E.F. "Federal-Provincial Insurance for Hospital and Physician's Care in Canada," *International Journal of Health Services*, vol. 1, no. 4 (1971).
Hellyer, Paul. *Damn the Torpedoes: My Fight to Unify Canada's Armed Forces.* Toronto: McClelland and Stewart 1990.
Hodgetts, J.E. "The Liberal and the Bureaucrat," *Queen's Quarterly*, vol. 62 (summer 1955).
Horowitz, Gad. *Canadian Labour in Politics.* Toronto: University of Toronto Press 1968.
Hum, Derek P.J. *Federalism and the Poor: A Review of the Canada Assistance Plan.* Toronto: Ontario Economic Council 1983.
- "The Working Poor, the Canada Assistance Plan and Provincial Responses to Income Supplementation," in *Canadian Social Welfare Policy: The Federal and Provincial Aspects*, Jacqueline S. Ismael, ed. Kingston and Montreal: McGill-Queen's University Press 1985.
Hunt, Wayne Austin. "The Federal-Provincial Conference of First Ministers, 1960–1976," PhD thesis, University of Toronto 1982.
Johnson, A.W. "The Dynamics of Federalism in Canada," *Canadian Journal of Political Science*, vol. 1, no. 1 (1968).
- *Social Policy in Canada: The Past as It Conditions the Present* (1986).
Kent, Tom. *A Public Purpose: An Experience of Liberal Opposition and Canadian Government.* Kingston and Montreal: McGill-Queen's University Press 1988.

Kitchen, Brigitte. "Canada," in *International Handbook on Old-Age Insurance*, Martin B. Tracey and Fred C. Pampel, eds. New York: Greenwood Press 1991.

Knowles, Stanley. *The New Party*. Toronto: McClelland and Stewart 1961.

Korpi, Walter. *The Democratic Class Struggle*. Boston: Routeledge and Kegan Paul 1983.

Kunitz, Stephen J. "Socialism and Social Insurance in the United States and Canada," in *Canadian Health Care and the State: A Century of Evolution*, David C. Naylor, ed. Kingston and Montreal: McGill-Queen's University Press 1992.

LaMarsh, Judy. *Memoirs of a Bird in a Gilded Cage*. Toronto: McClelland and Stewart 1968.

Lightman, Ernie and Allan Irving. "Restructuring Canada's Welfare State," *International Social Policy*, vol. 20, no 1 (1993).

Lindenfield, Rita. "The Hospital Insurance and Diagnostic Services Act: Its Federal-Provincial Aspects," PhD thesis, University of Chicago 1963.

MacIntosh, Robert. *Different Drummers: Banking and Politics in Canada*. Toronto: Macmillan 1991.

Mahler, Gregory S. *New Dimensions in Canadian Federalism: Canada in a Comparative Perspective*. London: Associated University Presses 1987.

Mallory, J.R. "Canadian Election in Retrospect I: The Election and the Constitution," *Queen's Quarterly*, vol. 64, no. 4 (winter 1958).

Manhertz, H.E.D. "Social Security in the Maritimes, 1939–1958," MA thesis, University of New Brunswick 1959.

Manzer, Ronald. *Public Policies and Political Development in Canada*. Toronto: University of Toronto Press 1985.

Martin, Paul. *A Very Public Life, Volume II: So Many Worlds*. Toronto: Deneau 1985.

McDougall, A.K. *John P. Robarts: His Life and Government*. Toronto: University of Toronto Press 1986.

McLeod, Thomas H. "Federal-Provincial Relations, 1958," *Canadian Public Administration*, vol. 1, no. 3 (September 1958).

Meisel, John. "The Formation of Liberal and Conservative Programmes in the 1957 Canadian General Election," *Canadian Journal of Economics and Political Science*, vol. 26, no. 4 (November 1960).

– *The Canadian General Election of 1957*. Toronto: University of Toronto Press 1962.

Mendelson, Ronald. "Canadian Light on Australian Retirement Income Security," in *Finance and Old Age*, Ronald Mendelson, ed. Canberra, Australia: Centre for Research on Federal Financial Institutions 1986.

Mishler, William and David B. Campbell. "The Health State: Legislative Responsiveness to Public Health Care Needs in Canada, 1920–1970," *Comparative Politics*, vol. 10, no. 4 (July 1978).

Moon, Robert. *Pearson: Confrontation Years against Diefenbaker.* Hull, Que.: High Hill Publishing House 1963.

Morgan, John S. "Old Age Pensions in Canada: A Review and a Result," *Social Science Review,* vol. 26, no. 2 (June 1952).

Morin, Claude. *Quebec versus Ottawa: The Struggle for Self-Government, 1960–1972.* Toronto: University of Toronto Press 1976.

Morton, Desmond. *The New Democrats, 1961–1986.* Toronto: Copp Clark Pitman 1986.

Moscovitch, Allan and Glenn Drover. "Social Expenditures and the Welfare State," in *Inequality; Essays on the Political Economy of Social Welfare,* Allan Moscovitch and Glenn Drover, eds. Toronto: Garamond 1981.

Munro, John A. and Alex I. Inglis, eds. *Mike: The Memoirs of the Rt. Hon, Lester B. Pearson,* vol. 3. Toronto: University of Toronto Press 1975.

Naylor, David C. *Public Practice, Private Payment: Canadian Medicine and the Politics of Health Insurance, 1911–1966.* Kingston and Montreal: McGill-Queen's University Press 1986.

Newman, Peter C. *Renegade in Power: The Diefenbaker Years.* Toronto: McClelland and Stewart 1963.

– *The Distemper of Our Times: Canadian Politics in Transition, 1962–1968.* Toronto: McClelland and Stewart 1968.

Norrie, Kenneth and Douglas Owram. *A History of the Canadian Economy.* Toronto: Harcourt Brace Jovanovich 1991.

Pal, Leslie. "Relative Autonomy Revisited: The Origins of Canadian Unemployment Insurance," *Canadian Journal of Political Science,* vol. 19, no. 1 (March 1986).

Peon, Monte M. *Harry S. Truman versus the Medical Lobby: The Genesis of Medicare.* Columbia, Mo.: University of Missouri Press 1979.

Pickersgill, J.W. *My Years with Louis St Laurent: A Political Memoir.* Toronto: University of Toronto Press 1975.

– *The Road Back by a Liberal in Opposition.* Toronto: University of Toronto Press 1986.

Piven, Frances Fox and Richard A. Cloward. *Regulating the Poor: The Functions of Public Welfare.* New York: Pantheon 1971.

– *Poor People's Movements: Why They Succeed, How They Fail.* New York: Pantheon 1979.

Pollard, Bruce G. *Managing the Interface: Intergovernmental Affairs Agencies in Canada.* Kingston: Institute of Intergovernmental Affairs 1986.

Purvis, Douglas D. and Constance Smith. "Fiscal Policy in Canada," in *Fiscal and Monetary Policy in Canada,* John Purvis, research coordinator. Toronto: University of Toronto Press 1986.

Quagagno, Jill S. "Welfare Capitalism and the Social Security Act of 1935," *American Sociological Review,* vol. 49 (1984).

Redekop, John. "Social Policy: The Role of the Government Party," in *Canadian Social Policy*, rev. ed., Shankar A. Yelaja, ed. Waterloo, Ont.: Wilfrid Laurier University Press 1987.

Regenstreif, S. Peter. "The Canadian General Election of 1958," *Western Political Quarterly*, vol. 13, no. 2 (1960).

Rimlinger, Gaston. *Welfare Policy and the Industrialization of Europe and America*. New York: Wiley 1971.

Roth, F.B. "Hospital Care Insurance in Canada: Background to Developments," paper presented at the Medical Care Section, American Public Health Association, 14 Nov. 1961.

Royal Commission on Dominion-Provincial Relations. *Final Report*. Ottawa: 1940.

Russell, Peter H. *Constitutional Odyssey: Can Canadians Be a Sovereign People?* Toronto: University of Toronto Press 1992.

Saywell, John T., ed. *The Canadian Annual Review*, 1960–1968. Toronto: University of Toronto Press 1961–69.

Sharp, Mitchell. *Which Reminds Me ...: A Memoir*. Toronto: University of Toronto Press 1994.

Shillington, C. Howard. *The Road to Medicare in Canada*. Toronto: Del Graphics 1972.

Simeon, Richard. *Federal-Provincial Diplomacy: The Making of Recent Policy in Canada*. Toronto: University of Toronto Press 1972.

– and Robert Miller. "Regional Variation in Public Policy," in *Small Worlds: Provinces and Parties in Canadian Political Life*, David J. Elkin and Richard Simeon, eds. Toronto: Methuen 1980.

Skocpol, Theda. *Protecting Soldiers and Mothers: The Political Origins of Social Policy in the United States*. Cambridge, Mass.: Belknap Press of Harvard University Press 1992.

Smiley, Donald. "The National Party Leadership Convention in Canada: A Preliminary Analysis," *Canadian Journal of Political Science*, vol. 1, no. 4 (December 1968).

Smith, David E. *The Regional Decline of a National Party: Liberals on the Prairies*. Toronto: University of Toronto Press 1981.

– "Cabinet and Commons in the Era of James G. Gardiner," in *The Canadian House of Commons: Essays in Honour of Norman Ward*, John C. Courtney, ed. Calgary: The University of Calgary Press 1985.

Smith, Denis. *Gentle Patriot: A Political Biography of Walter Gordon*. Edmonton: Hurtig Publishers 1973.

– *Rogue Tory: The Life and Legend of John G. Diefenbaker*. Toronto: Macfarlane Walter and Ross 1995.

Special Committee on Social Security. *Health Insurance: Report of the Advisory Committee on Health Insurance Appointed by Order in Council P.C. 836 Dated February 5, 1942*. Ottawa: 1943.

Stevenson, Michael and A. Paul Williams. "Physicians and Medicare: Professional Ideology and Canadian Health Care Policy," in *Sociology of Health Care in Canada*, B. Sigh Bolaria and Harley D. Dickinson, eds. Toronto: Harcourt, Brace, Jovanivich 1988.

Stursberg, Peter. *Diefenbaker*, vol. 1, *Leadership Gained, 1956–1962*. Toronto: University of Toronto Press 1975.

– *Diefenbaker*, vol. 2, *Leadership Lost, 1962–1967*. Toronto: University of Toronto Press 1976.

– *Lester Pearson and the Dream of Unity*. Toronto: Doubleday Canada 1978.

Swartz, Donald. "The Politics of Reform: Conflict and Accommodation in Canadian Health Policy," in *The Canadian State: Political Economy and Political Power*, Leo Panitch, ed. Toronto: University of Toronto Press 1977.

Taylor, Malcolm G. "The Saskatchewan Hospital Services Plan," PhD thesis, University of California at Berkeley 1949.

– *Health Insurance and Canadian Public Policy: The Seven Decisions That Created the Canadian Health Insurance System and Their Outcomes*, 2nd ed. Kingston and Montreal: McGill-Queen's University Press 1987.

– "Health Insurance: The Roller-Coaster in Federal-Provincial Relations," in *Federalism and Political Community: Essays in Honour of Donald Smiley*, David P. Shugarman and Reg Whitaker, eds. Peterborough, Ont.: Broadview Press 1989.

Thomas, Paul G. "The Role of the National Party Caucus," in *Party Government and Regional Representation in Canada*, Peter Aucoin, research coordinator. Toronto: University of Toronto Press 1985.

Thompson, Walter P. *Medical Care: Programs and Issues*. Toronto: Clarke-Irwin 1964.

Thomson, Dale C. *Louis St. Laurent: Canadian*. Toronto: Macmillan 1967.

– "The Political Ideas of Louis St. Laurent," in *The Political Ideas of the Prime Ministers of Canada*, Marcel Hamelin, ed. Ottawa: Les Éditions de l'Université d'Ottawa 1969.

– *Jean Lesage and the Quiet Revolution*. Toronto: Macmillan 1984.

Tollefson, Edwin A. *Bitter Medicine: The Saskatchewan Medicare Feud*. Saskatoon: Modern Press 1963.

Tuohy, Carolyn Joy. "The Political Attitudes of Ontario Physicians: A Skill Group Perspective," PhD thesis, Yale University 1974.

– *Policy and Politics in Canada: Institutionalized Ambivalence*. Philadelphia: Temple University Press 1992.

Ursel, Jane. "The State and the Maintenance of Patriarchy: A Case Study of Family, Labour and Welfare Legislation in Canada," in *Family, Economy and State: The Social Reproduction Process Under Capitalism*, J. Dickinson and B. Russell, eds. Toronto: Women's Press 1986.

Walters, Vivienne. "State, Capital and Labour: The Introduction of Federal-Provincial Insurance for Physician Care in Canada," *Canadian Review of Sociology and Anthropology*, vol. 19, no. 2 (1982).

Ward, Norman. "The Liberals in Convention: Revised and Unrepentant," *Queen's Quarterly*, vol. 65, no. 1 (spring 1958).

- ed. *A Party Politician: The Memoirs of Chubby Power*. Toronto: Macmillan 1966.

- and David Smith. *Jimmy Gardiner: Relentless Liberal*. Toronto: University of Toronto Press 1990.

Wearing, Joseph. *The L-Shaped Party: The Liberal Party of Canada, 1958–1980*. Toronto: McGraw-Hill Ryerson 1981.

Weir, Margaret, Ann Shola Orloff, and Theda Skocpol, eds. *The Politics of Social Policy in the United States*. Princeton, N.J.: Princeton University Press 1988.

Weir, Richard A. "Federalism, Interest Groups and Parliamentary Government: The Canadian Medical Association," *Journal of Commonwealth Political Studies*, vol. 9, no. 2 (July 1973).

Weller, G. R. "Health Care and Medicare Policy in Ontario," in *Issues in Canadian Public Policy*, G. Bruce Doern and V. Seymour Wilson, eds. Toronto: Macmillan 1974.

- "From 'Pressure Group Politics' to 'Medical Industrial Complex': The Development of Approaches to the Politics of Health," *Journal of Health Politics*, vol. 1, no. 4 (winter 1977).

Wilensky, Harold. *The Welfare State and Equality*. Berkeley and Los Angeles: University of California Press 1975.

- and Charles N. Lebeaux. *Industrial Society and Social Welfare*. New York: Russell Sage Foundation 1958.

Whitaker, Reginald. *The Government Party: Organizing and Financing the Liberal Party of Canada, 1930–1958*. Toronto: University of Toronto Press 1977.

Willms, A.M. "The Administration of Research on Administration in the Government of Canada," *Canadian Public Administration*, vol. 10 no. 4 (December 1967).

Wilson, V. Seymour. "The Role of the Royal Commissions and Task Forces," in *The Structure of Policy-Making in Canada*, G. Bruce Doern and Peter Aucoin, eds. Toronto: Macmillan 1971.

Wolfe, David. "The Rise and Demise of the Keynesian Era in Canada: Economic Policy, 1930–1980," in *Modern Canada, 1930–1980s*, M.C. Cross and G.S. Kealey, eds. Toronto: McClelland and Stewart 1984.

Wrong, Dennis H. "Parties and Voting in Canada: A Backward and Forward Glance in the Light of the Last Election," *Political Science Quarterly*, vol. 73, no. 3 (1958).

Young, Walter D. *The Anatomy of a Party: The National CCF, 1932–1961*. Toronto: University of Toronto Press 1969.

Index

Alberta, 126, 128, 132, 143, 148, 175n.39, 206n.53
Allan, James, 97
Argue, Hazen, 67

Bakvis, Herman, 109
Balcer, Leon, 134
Bennett, R.B., 29
Bennett, W.A.C., 7, 159
Benson, Edgar, 166, 213n.98
Blakeney, Allan, 128
British Columbia, 7, 9, 22, 126, 143, 159, 165, 206n.53
Brown, Colin, 148
Bryce, Robert, 11, 17, 19, 99, 115, 138, 140–2, 150, 152
budgets: 1963, 70, 84–7, 106, 114, 145; 1968, 166
Byrne, James, 37

Cameron, Donald, 82
Camp, Dalton, 48, 134
Campbell, Douglas, 7
Canada Assistance Plan, 139–40

Canada Pension Plan, xi, xiii, xv–xvi, 167–9, 80–4, 87–107, 110–23, 124–5, 132–4, 136, 140, 143. *See also* old age pensions.
Canadian Bankers Association, 89
Canadian Chamber of Commerce, 75, 103, 131
Canadian Labour Congress, 56, 131, 136
Canadian Life Insurance Officers Association, 11–13, 82, 88–9, 93, 103, 111–12. *See also* insurance industry.
Canadian Manufacturers' Association, 88
Canadian Medical Association, 4–5, 10–11, 61, 66, 74, 126, 130–1, 133, 148, 160
Canadian Pension Conference, 91, 102
Canadian Tax Foundation, 58
Canadian Welfare Council, 53, 155, 164

Castonguay, Claude, 90, 119
Chevrier, Lionel, 80, 92, 108, 190n.15
Clark, Robert, 89
Claxton, Brooke, 30, 35, 52, 150
Coldwell, M.J., 24, 67
Confédération des syndicats nationaux, 56
Connolly, J.J., 30, 39, 45, 55, 72, 147, 192n.52
Conway, G.R., 70, 85
Co-operative Commonwealth Federation (CCF), 5, 22, 47, 53, 56; on pension increases, 1957, 18; in 1957 election, 24–5; Winnipeg Declaration of, 24, 66; as New Party, 62; in Saskatchewan, 62, 87, 126–8; reorganization as NDP, 66–8. *See also* New Democratic Party.
Coward, Laurence, 102, 121
Crerar, T.A., 37, 86, 89, 149, 151

Croll, David, 37–9, 44–5

Dalgleish, Dr. H.D., 127
Davey, Keith, 51, 70, 73, 79–80, 82, 94–5, 107, 119, 135, 146–7, 149–50, 185n.41
Davidson, George, 4, 7, 12, 14
Deutsch, John, 111
Dexter, Grant, 81, 179n.32
Diefenbaker, John G., 3, 18, 20, 23, 30, 44–5, 47, 92, 130; in 1958 election, 46, 49; as prime minister, 53, 59, 66, 69, 187n.67; in 1962 election, 72–3; in 1963 election, 76–7; in opposition, 85, 89, 134, 147, 156
Douglas, Monteith, 58
Douglas, Tommy, 7, 67, 87, 107, 126, 128, 136, 140, 159
Drew, George, 47
Dunning, Charles, 30

Economic Council of Canada, 111
elections, federal: 10 June 1957, 3–4, 18, 20–5, 54; 31 March 1958, 45–6, 49, 51, 54; 18 June 1962, 72, 146; 8 April 1963, 76–7, 146; 8 November 1965, 133–4, 138, 146–9; 25 June 1968, 165

family allowances, 5, 24, 45–6, 117
Favreau, Guy, 90, 108, 116, 118, 148–9
federal-provincial confer-ences: 1945, 5; 1950, 5; 1955, 6–10; Septem-ber 1963, 92–100; November 1963, 102–5, 111; April 1964, 113–16; May 1965,

136–8; July 1965, 138, 140–4; of finance min-isters, November 1966, 158–9. See also federal-provincial relations.
federal-provincial rela-tions, 31, 44, 62–3, 67, 69, 71, 99, 107, 167; on pensions, 80, 84, 89–95, 101–3, 110–11, 113, 117–22, 125; on medicare, 80, 124–5, 132–3, 136–48. See also federal-provincial conferences.
Finlayson, Deanne, 24
Fisher, Douglas, 85
Forsey, Eugene, 45
Fowler, Robert, 60, 64
Fraser, Blair, 45
Frost, Leslie, 7–9, 13–14, 87, 188n.75

Gardiner, James, 22, 28, 42, 49
Garson, Stuart, 22, 28, 31–2
Gathercole, George, 7, 88–9, 110, 120, 174n.14
Gérin-Lajoie, Paul, 90, 114
Gordon, Walter, 34–5, 37, 41, 49, 52–3, 57; at Liberal Rally, 60–4; designing policies, 65, 69–71; as minister of finance, 80, 82, 85–7, 95–6, 99, 108, 112, 116, 118–20, 122, 134–5, 138, 140, 146–7, 149–51; post-1965, 154–68, 162, 168, 212n.84, 213n.91
Green Book on Recon-struction, 5–6
Grosart, Allister, 47–8

Hagey, Gerald, 129
Hall, Emmett, 66
Hall, Frank, 56
Hannah, J.A., 10

Harkness, Douglas, 134
Harris, Joseph, 39
Harris, Walter, 8, 16–20, 22, 40, 48
Hays, Harry, 116
Heagerty, J.J., 4
health insurance: and 1942 Heagerty commis-sion, 4–5, 11, 30; in 1955–56 intergovern-mental discussion, 7–9; in 1957 election, 24, 33; in 1958 leadership, 38–9, 42–5; in 1958 election, 46; in Liberal platform, 52–3, 55, 58–9; at Liberal Rally, 61–5, 124; designing of, 65, 69–71, 74–5, 78–9; NDP and, 67; in 1962 election, 72–3; in 1963 election, 76–7; in Saskatchewan, 126–8, 130; in Alberta, 128; in British Colum-bia, 128; in Ontario, 128–9. See also medicare, hospital insurance.
Hees, George, 23
Hellyer, Paul, 112, 164, 190n.15
Henderson, Lloyd, 41
Hodgetts, J.E., 28
Hogan, George, 107, 113
hospital insurance, xv, 6–15, 20–1, 25, 30, 39, 42, 53, 58, 137; in Saskatchewan, 126
Howe, C.D., 17, 22, 34, 47–9, 52
Hutchison, Bruce, 32, 34, 49

insurance industry: response to hospital insurance, 11–13, 39; response to health insurance, 75, 130; response to Canada Pension Plan, 82, 97, 102–4, 111–12; in

Ontario, 88–9, 92, 102–3

Jewett, Pauline, 81, 138
Jodoin, Claude, 56
Johnson, Al, 87, 99–100, 140–3, 152–3, 156–7
Johnson, Daniel, 152, 159

Kennedy, John F., 109
Kent, Tom, 19, 49, 76, 134, 168; at 1958 leadership, 37–40; in 1958 election, 46–7; in designing policy, 50, 53, 65, 68–72, 78; at Kingston conference, 55–9; at Liberal Rally, 60–1, 64; in 1962 election, 72–3; in 1963 election, 79; as coordinator of programs, 81–5, 87, 90, 92–3, 95–6, 100–11, 104, 108, 113–22, 125, 135–7, 141, 146, 148–50; as deputy minister of manpower and immigration, 150
Kidd, H.E. "Bob," 33, 52
Kilgour, David, 39–40, 75–6, 112, 129
King, W.L.M., 3–4, 6, 22, 29–30, 37, 43, 49, 62, 173n.7
Kingston Conference, 53–60, 62, 64, 83, 108, 134, 154
Knowles, Stanley, 18, 67, 106

LaMarsh, Judy, 80–4, 86, 81, 91, 93–9, 106, 108, 111–12, 116, 118, 122, 125, 133, 136–7, 150–1
Lamontagne, Maurice, 37, 40, 50, 58–60, 69, 82, 90, 92, 98, 116, 118, 154, 168, 191n.28
Laporte, Pierre, 90
Laurier, Wilfrid, 3, 36

Leiff, Mrs A.H., 37
Lesage, Jean, 53, 89, 92–6, 111, 113–19, 141, 152, 187n.67
Lévesque, René, 90, 114, 117
Lewis, David, 67
Liberal Party: organization, 20–3, 27, 35–7, 45, 49–51, 167–8; in 1957 election, 20–6, 27–34; leadership convention, 1958, 36–46, 51, 53; in 1958 election, 45–6; restructuring in opposition, 47–9, 52, 65, 68–72; at Kingston conference, 54–60; at Liberal Rally, 60–4; in 1962 election, 72–3; in 1963 election, 76–7; in office, 86–8, 95–6, 107–9, 122–3, 125, 132–3, 139, 145, 151, 153–4, 156–8, 160, 163; in 1965 election, 146–9; in Ontario, 130, 154; in Saskatchewan, 130
Liberal Rally, 54–5, 60–4, 68, 71, 83, 124, 154
Life Underwriters Association of Canada, 89
Lloyd, Woodrow S., 110, 127
Lynch, Charles, 116

Macdonald, W.A., 108–9
MacEachen, Allan, 116, 118, 150–1, 155, 158, 162, 164, 213n.98
MacIntosh, Robert, 56, 61, 85–6
Mackay, Don, 41
Mackenzie, Ian, 4
Mackenzie, Michael, 56
Mackintosh, W.A., 31
MacLeod, J. Wendell, 58
McLeod, John T., 80
MacNaughton, Charles, 159

MacTavish, Duncan, 32–3, 52
Mahoney, William, 56
Manitoba, 7, 22, 29, 49, 111, 179n.32; Young Liberals, 34; Liberal Association, 65
Manning, Ernest, 128, 143, 148
Marchand, Jean, 56, 59, 162
Marier, André, 90
Marler, George, 36
Martin, Paul, 5, 19–22, 37, 40–1, 43, 57, 59, 71, 80, 118, 158, 164, 176n.48, 180n.56
Matthews, General Bruce, 51, 95
Medical Society of Nova Scotia, 133
medicare, xii, 80, 83–4, 87, 105, 125–6, 132–44, 146–8, 150–62, 164–9. See also health insurance.
Menzies, Merril, 23–4, 46
Monteith, J.Waldo, 66, 187n.67
Morin, Claude, 117, 119, 142, 210n.44
Morrison, Neil, 164

National Liberal Federation, 32–3, 35–6, 49–51, 53. See also Liberal Party.
Naylor, C.A., 148
New Brunswick, 153, 157, 159
New Democratic Party: in 1962 election, 73; in 1963 election, 77; in Parliament, 85, 93–4, 106–8. See also Co-operative Commonwealth Federation.
Newfoundland, 22, 29, 34, 59, 115, 153, 158
Newman, Peter, 152
Nova Scotia, 110

O'Connell, M.P., 70, 85
O'Hagan, Richard, 72
old age pensions, xi, 15,
187n.67; in 1927, 4,
14; in 1951, 5–6;
increases, 1957, 17–21,
23, 66; American style,
23, 88; in 1957 elec-
tion, 24–5, 31–3; in
1958 leadership, 38,
43, 45; in 1958 elec-
tion, 46; in platform
development, 55, 58,
60, 65, 69–71, 78–9;
at Liberal Rally, 63–5;
in Conservative plat-
form, 66; in NDP
platform, 67; in 1962
election, 72–3; in 1963
election, 76–7;
increases tied to
Canada Pension Plan,
91, 95–6, 105–6, 122;
Quebec and, 97. See
also Canada Pension
Plan.
Oliphant, P.F., 70
Ontario, 155; and hospi-
tal insurance, 7–15,
20; and 1957 election,
22–3; and pensions,
73, 76, 87–90, 92–3,
95, 102–3, 105, 110–
13, 117, 119–21; and
1963 election, 80; and
health insurance, 83,
126, 128–30, 132,
143, 148, 159, 166,
206n.53; at 1963
federal-provincial con-
ference, 94, 95–101;
and 1963 provincial
election, 94–6, 99
Ontario Federation of
Labour, 88
organized labour, 12, 47,
53, 56, 67, 103, 130,
158

Payne, John, 108
Pearson, Lester B., xv; at
leadership convention,

1958, 40–5, 51; in elec-
tion, 1958, 45–7; as
opposition leader, 45–
52, 68–70, 89; at King-
ston conference, 55–6;
at Liberal Rally, 60–2,
64–5; in 1962 election,
73; in 1963 election,
77; as prime minister,
79–81, 85–7, 90–2, 94–
6, 101–4, 108–11,
114, 116, 117–18, 120–
1, 123, 134–5, 137,
142–4, 146–52, 154–5,
157–8, 160–4
Pickersgill, J.W., 22, 34,
45, 48, 59, 107,
173n.7, 190n.15
Power, Charles
"Chubby," 3, 36, 45
Prince Edward Island, 29
Progressive Conservative
Party, 18–19, 29, 31–
2, 42–3, 47–8; in 1957
election, 23–5, 30;
in 1958 election, 46; in
power, 53, 66, 71; in
1962 election, 72–3;
in 1963 election, 76; in
opposition, 106–8,
134, 147

Quebec, 108, 134, 162;
and 1957 election, 22–
23, 28; and 1958 elec-
tion, 46; and Liberal
Party, 50; and health
insurance, 65, 138,
141–3, 150, 152, 159–
62, 165–7; and 1963
election, 80; and pen-
sions, 89–90, 92, 94–
106, 110–21; and
1965 election, 149;
and 1968 election, 165

Rasminsky, Louis, 111
Robarts, John, 88–9, 92,
94–7, 99, 101, 106,
110–11, 113–14, 116,
119–21, 129, 143, 161–
2, 166

Robertson, Gordon, 92,
115–17
Robichaud, Louis, 157
Roblin, Duff, 111, 153,
155
Rowell-Sirois commis-
sion, 4, 23
Royal Commission on
Economic Prospects,
34–5
Royal Commission on
Health Services, 66,
75, 126, 128–33, 136–
9, 147

St Laurent, Louis, xv, 3–
4, 6–8, 13–14, 21–2,
29, 37, 49, 57, 150
Saskatchewan, 7, 9, 22,
62, 80, 87, 110, 140,
153, 159, 165; and
health insurance, 73,
75, 83, 125–8, 130,
133, 153, 159
Saskatchewan College of
Physicians and Sur-
geons, 126–7
Sauvé, Jeanne, 59
Sauvé, Maurice, 59–60,
65, 90, 117–18, 152,
158, 191n.28
Sharp, Mitchell, 55–6,
59, 85, 118, 150, 152–
60, 162, 164, 190n.15
Sinclair, James, 22
Smallwood, Joey, 115
Smith, David E., 28
Social Credit Party, 73,
76–7, 128
social security, 37–9, 43–
4, 46, 53, 58, 60. See
also Canada Assistance
Plan, Canada Pension
Plan, health insurance,
hospital insurance,
medicare, old age
pensions.
Spencer, George, 149
Stanfield, Robert, 111,
156–7, 165
Stanley, David, 70, 85
Strachan, Robert, 128

tax structure committee, 115, 117, 119, 141
Taylor, Lord, 127–8
Taylor, Malcolm, 9
Thatcher, Ross, 151, 159, 179n.33
Thompson, Andrew, 70, 154
Thompson, W.P., 126–7

Trudeau, Pierre Elliott, 164–5
Turner, John, 59, 191n.28

unemployment policy, 6–7, 59, 63, 66
United Steelworkers of America, 56
Upper, Boyd, 62, 65

Ward, Norman, 44
Willard, J.W., 82, 111
Wintermeyer, John, 95–7, 99
Winters, Robert, 164–5